FOR DUMMIES

COMPUTER
BOOK SERIES
FROM IDG

Internet Explorer 3 For W...
For Dummies®

C000156435

Internet Mail Buttons

Internet Mail Button	What It Does
New Message	Creates a new e-mail message
Reply to Author	Sends a message back to the author of an incoming message
Reply to All	Sends a message to everyone to whom the original message was addressed
Forward	Forwards a message to another user
Send and Receive	Delivers any pending mail and checks for new mail

Internet...

Internet News Button	What It Does
New Message	Creates a new newsgroup article
Reply to Group	Posts a reply to a newsgroup article
Reply to Author	Sends e-mail to the author of the article
Forward	Forwards an article message to another user
Newsgrou...	Allows you to select newsgroups to connect to
Connect	Connects you to the news server if you have been working offline
Disconnect	Disconnects you from the news server so you can work offline

Web Addresses to Remember

URL	What It Is
www.microsoft.com/iesupport	Internet Explorer Technical Support Site
www.microsoft.com/ie	Internet Explorer download site (where you can get cool add-ons)
198.105.232.5/ie/most/howto/vrml.htm	The Microsoft VRML page
microsoft.com/imedia	The Microsoft interactive media technologies Web site (ActiveMovie)
home.microsoft.com/access/allinone.asp	The Microsoft all-in-one search page
metacrawler.cs.washington.edu:8080/index.html	A consolidated all-in-on search page
guaraldi.cs.colostate.edu:2000	Another consolidated all-in-one search page

Add Your Own Favorite Sites:

_____

_____

_____

_____

_____

_____

Internet Explorer 3 For Windows® For Dummies®

Essential Connection Information

If you don't know what to put in the following blanks, call your online service provider for help.

My user ID:
_____

My password: (*No! Don't write it here!*)

Phone number I dial to access the Internet:
_____

My e-mail address:
_____

Customer service phone number:
_____

DNS Server IP Address: _____ . _____ . _____ . _____

SMTP Server Address:
_____

POP3 Server Address:
_____

News Server Name:
_____

Internet Explorer Toolbar Buttons

Toolbar Button	What It Does
⇦ Back	Goes back to the previously displayed page
⇨ Forward	Returns to the page where you were before you went back
⊗ Stop	Stops downloading the current page
Refresh	Downloads a fresh copy of the current page
Home	Goes to your designated start page
Search	Goes to your designated search page
Favorites	Accesses your favorite Web sites
Print	Prints the current page
Font	Increases or decreases the size of the text displayed on the page

Internet Explorer Keyboard Shortcuts

Keyboard Shortcut	What It Does
Backspace	Back (previous page)
Shift+Backspace	Forward (next page)
Shift+F10	Display the pop-up menu for a link
Ctrl+Shift+Tab	Move to the next frame
F5	Refresh the current page
Esc	Stop downloading
Ctrl+O	Go to a new location
Ctrl+N	Open a new window
Ctrl+S	Save the current page
Ctrl+P	Print the current page

...For Dummies: #1 Computer Book Series for Beginners

INTERNET EXPLORER 3
FOR
WINDOWS®
FOR
DUMMIES®

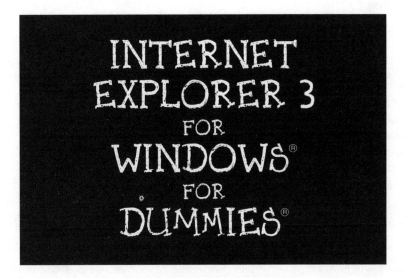

INTERNET EXPLORER 3
FOR
WINDOWS®
FOR
DUMMIES®

by Doug Lowe

IDG
BOOKS
WORLDWIDE

IDG Books Worldwide, Inc.
An International Data Group Company

Foster City, CA ♦ Chicago, IL ♦ Indianapolis, IN ♦ Southlake, TX

Internet Explorer 3 For Windows® 95 For Dummies®

Published by
IDG Books Worldwide, Inc.
An International Data Group Company
919 E. Hillsdale Blvd.
Suite 400
Foster City, CA 94404
www.idgbooks.com (IDG Books Worldwide Web Site)
http://www.dummies.com (Dummies Press Web Site)

Library of Congress Catalog Card No.: 96-77076

ISBN: 0-7645-0031-7

Printed in the United States of America

10 9 8 7 6 5 4 3 2 1

1C/TQ/QZ/ZW/IN

Distributed in the United States by IDG Books Worldwide, Inc.

Distributed by Macmillan Canada for Canada; by Contemporanea de Ediciones for Venezuela; by Distribuidora Cuspide for Argentina; by CITEC for Brazil; by Ediciones ZETA S.C.R. Ltda. for Peru; by Editorial Limusa SA for Mexico; by Transworld Publishers Limited in the United Kingdom and Europe; by Academic Bookshop for Egypt; by Levant Distributors S.A.R.L. for Lebanon; by Al Jassim for Saudi Arabia; by Simron Pty. Ltd. for South Africa; by Pustak Mahal for India; by The Computer Bookshop for India; by Toppan Company Ltd. for Japan; by Addison Wesley Publishing Company for Korea; by Longman Singapore Publishers Ltd. for Singapore, Malaysia, Thailand, and Indonesia; by Unalis Corporation for Taiwan; by WS Computer Publishing Company, Inc. for the Philippines; by WoodsLane Pty. Ltd. for Australia; by WoodsLane Enterprises Ltd. for New Zealand. Authorized Sales Agent: Anthony Rudkin Associates for the Middle East and North Africa.

For general information on IDG Books Worldwide's books in the U.S., please call our Consumer Customer Service department at 800-762-2974. For reseller information, including discounts and premium sales, please call our Reseller Customer Service department at 800-434-3422.

For information on where to purchase IDG Books Worldwide's books outside the U.S., please contact our International Sales department at 415-655-3172 or fax 415-655-3295.

For information on foreign language translations, please contact our Foreign & Subsidiary Rights department at 415-655-3021 or fax 415-655-3281.

For sales inquiries and special prices for bulk quantities, please contact our Sales department at 415-655-3200 or write to the address above.

For information on using IDG Books Worldwide's books in the classroom or for ordering examination copies, please contact our Educational Sales department at 800-434-2086 or fax 817-251-8174.

For authorization to photocopy items for corporate, personal, or educational use, please contact Copyright Clearance Center, 222 Rosewood Drive, Danvers, MA 01923, or fax 508-750-4470.

is a trademark under exclusive license to IDG Books Worldwide, Inc., from International Data Group, Inc.

About the Author

Doug Lowe

Doug Lowe lives in sunny Fresno, California (where the motto is "At least it's a *dry* heat") with his wife Debbie, daughters Rebecca, Sarah, and Bethany, and female Golden Retrievers Nutmeg and Ginger. He works full-time creating outstanding literary works such as *Internet Explorer 3 For Windows For Dummies* and wonders why he hasn't yet won a Pulitzer Prize or had one of his books made into a movie starring Harrison Ford so he can retire. Doug really thinks that Harrison Ford would be excellent as the Dummies Guy and thinks that John Kilcullen's people should call Harrison's people real soon before someone else steals the idea.

In between writing computer books, which leaves about three free hours per month, Doug enjoys golfing and makes it a point to play at least once each decade. Hiking is also a favorite hobby, so much so that Doug would really like to write *Backpacking For Dummies* but hasn't had the time to write a proposal yet because these computer books just keep coming up. Maybe someday.

Welcome to the world of IDG Books Worldwide.

IDG Books Worldwide, Inc., is a subsidiary of International Data Group, the world's largest publisher of computer-related information and the leading global provider of information services on information technology. IDG was founded more than 25 years ago and now employs more than 8,500 people worldwide. IDG publishes more than 270 computer publications in over 75 countries (see listing below). More than 90 million people read one or more IDG publications each month.

Launched in 1990, IDG Books Worldwide is today the #1 publisher of best-selling computer books in the United States. We are proud to have received eight awards from the Computer Press Association in recognition of editorial excellence and three from *Computer Currents'* First Annual Readers' Choice Awards. Our best-selling ...*For Dummies*® series has more than 25 million copies in print with translations in 30 languages. IDG Books Worldwide, through a joint venture with IDG's Hi-Tech Beijing, became the first U.S. publisher to publish a computer book in the People's Republic of China. In record time, IDG Books Worldwide has become the first choice for millions of readers around the world who want to learn how to better manage their businesses.

Our mission is simple: Every one of our books is designed to bring extra value and skill-building instructions to the reader. Our books are written by experts who understand and care about our readers. The knowledge base of our editorial staff comes from years of experience in publishing, education, and journalism — experience which we use to produce books for the '90s. In short, we care about books, so we attract the best people. We devote special attention to details such as audience, interior design, use of icons, and illustrations. And because we use an efficient process of authoring, editing, and desktop publishing our books electronically, we can spend more time ensuring superior content and spend less time on the technicalities of making books.

You can count on our commitment to deliver high-quality books at competitive prices on topics you want to read about. At IDG Books Worldwide, we continue in the IDG tradition of delivering quality for more than 25 years. You'll find no better book on a subject than one from IDG Books Worldwide.

John J. Kilcullen

John Kilcullen
President and CEO
IDG Books Worldwide, Inc.

Dedication

This book is dedicated to Bethany. May all your explorations be fruitful.

Author's Acknowledgments

I'd like to thank project editors Shannon Ross and Colleen Rainsberger, who showed great patience as deadlines came and went, and manuscript didn't, until Microsoft finally made beta versions of the software available. Thanks also to Joe Salmeri for his excellent technical review, and to copy editors Joe Jansen and Christa Carroll for correcting all my embarrassing spelling errors and other silly mistakes.

Publisher's Acknowledgments

We're proud of this book; please send us your comments about it by using the Reader Response Card at the back of the book or by e-mailing us at feedback/dummies@idgbooks.com. Some of the people who helped bring this book to market include the following:

Acquisitions, Development, and Editorial

Project Editor: Shannon Ross

Acquisitions Editor: Tammy Goldfeld

Assistant Acquisitions Editor: Gareth Hancock

Product Development Manager: Mary Bednarek

Permissions Editor: Joyce Pepple

Copy Editors: Joe Jansen, Christa Carroll

Technical Editor: Joe Salmeri

Editorial Manager: Kristin A. Cocks

Editorial Assistant: Chris H. Collins

Production

Project Coordinator: Sherry Gomoll

Layout and Graphics: J. Tyler Connor, Dominique DeFelice, Angie Hunckler, Brent Savage

Proofreaders: Melissa Buddendeck, Rachel Garvey, Nancy Price, Rob Springer, Karen York

Indexer: Steve Rath

Special Help

Colleen Rainsberger, Project Editor

General & Administrative

IDG Books Worldwide, Inc.: John Kilcullen, President and CEO; Steven Berkowitz, COO and Publisher

Dummies, Inc.: Milissa Koloski, Executive Vice President and Publisher

Dummies Technology Press and Dummies Editorial: Diane Graves Steele, Associate Publisher; Judith A. Taylor, Brand Manager

Dummies Trade Press: Kathleen A. Welton, Vice President and Publisher; Stacy S. Collins, Brand Manager

IDG Books Production for Dummies Press: Beth Jenkins, Production Director; Cindy L. Phipps, Supervisor of Project Coordination; Kathie S. Schutte, Supervisor of Page Layout; Shelley Lea, Supervisor of Graphics and Design; Debbie J. Gates, Production Systems Specialist

Dummies Packaging and Book Design: Patti Sandez, Packaging Assistant; Kavish+Kavish, Cover Design

◆

The publisher would like to give special thanks to Patrick J. McGovern, without whom this book would not have been possible.

◆

Contents at a Glance

Cartoons at a Glance

By Rich Tennant • Fax: 508-546-7747 • E-mail: the5wave@tiac.net

page 37

page 201

page 295

page 229

page 7

page 137

page 95

Table of Contents

Introduction

• •

*T*he Internet has taken the computer world by storm. Everybody seems to
be online these days. According to the recent hit movie *Independence Day,*
even the alien invaders from outer space are on the Internet. Good thing, too, or
Jeff Goldblum wouldn't have been able to hack into their system to plant that
planet-saving virus. It is indeed fortunate for humanity that aliens from 60
million light years away use TCP/IP. But I digress.

The point is that the Internet is the fastest growing segment of the computer
business, and Microsoft has felt left out of the game for long enough. A relatively late entrant in the online arena, Microsoft has become an instant con-
tender for the Internet crown with the introduction of its latest and greatest
software, Internet Explorer 3.0.

Internet Explorer 3.0 is what's technically known as a *Web browser* because it
lets you browse the most popular area of the Internet — the World Wide Web.
Prior to Internet Explorer 3.0, the Web browser market was dominated by a
company called Netscape, with its Web browser called Navigator. Internet
Explorer 3.0 is out to change all that. Netscape is no longer the only kid on the
block. In fact, Netscape now has to play catch-up. Simply put, Internet Explorer
3.0 is the best software you can use to access the Internet. Whether you're new
to the Internet or a seasoned surfer, Internet Explorer is the Web browser of
choice.

Why Another Internet Book?

Unfortunately, when it comes right down to it, Internet Explorer — like the
Internet itself — isn't as easy to use as *they* would have you believe. Alas,
Internet Explorer is nothing more than a computer program, and like any
computer program, it has its own commands to learn, menus to traverse, icons
to decipher, nuances to discover, and quirks to work around. Bother.

Oh, and then take the Internet itself. Frankly, the Internet is a sprawling mess.
It's filled with klutzy interfaces, programs that don't work the way they should,
and systems that were designed decades ago. Finding the information you need
on the Internet can be like the proverbial search for a needle in a haystack. The
Internet is everything they say it is except easy to use.

That's why you need this book to take you by the hand and walk you step-by-step through all the details of using Internet Explorer 3.0. This book doesn't bog you down with a bunch of puffed-up techno-jargon that makes you feel like your head is about to explode. Instead, this book spells out what you need to know in plain, everyday English.

Sure, plenty of books about the Internet already crowd the computer section of your local bookstore. IDG Books Worldwide, Inc. even has several excellent books available: *The Internet For Dummies,* 2nd Edition is an especially good general introduction to the Internet. But if you are using — or are planning to use — Internet Explorer, you need to know more than generic Internet stuff. You need to know specifically how to use the features of Internet Explorer 3.0. Many of these features are unique to Internet Explorer 3.0, and not found in any other Web browser.

How to Use This Book

The beauty of this book is that you don't have to read it through from start to finish. You wouldn't dare pick up the latest Clancy or Grisham novel and skip straight to page 173. But with this book, you can. That's because this book works like a reference. You can read as much or as little of it as you need. You can turn to any part of the book and start reading, and then put the book down after finding the information you needed and get on with your life.

On occasion, this book directs you to use specific keyboard shortcuts to get things done. I indicate such key combinations like this:

Ctrl+Z

which means to hold down the Ctrl key while pressing the Z key, and then release both together. Don't type the plus sign.

Sometimes, I tell you to use a menu command. For example, you may see something like this:

File⇨Open

which means to use the keyboard or mouse to open the File menu and then choose the Open command. (The underlined letters are the keyboard hot keys for the command. To use them, first press the Alt key. In the preceding example, you press and release the Alt key, press and release the F key, and then press and release the O key.) Whenever I describe a message or information you see on-screen, it looks like this:

```
Are we having fun yet?
```

Anything you are instructed to type appears in bold, like so: Type **puns** in the field. You type exactly what you see, with or without spaces.

Internet links are shown <u>underlined</u>, the way they appear on-screen in Internet Explorer. Internet addresses (technically known as *URLs*) appear like this: www.whatever.com.

Another little nicety about this book is that when I tell you to click one of those little toolbar buttons on Internet Explorer's screen, a picture of the button appears in the margin. Seeing what the button looks like helps you find it on-screen.

This book rarely directs you elsewhere for information — just about everything you need to know about using Internet Explorer is in here. However, two other books may come in handy from time to time. The first is *Windows 95 For Dummies* by Andy Rathbone, which is helpful if you're not sure how to perform a Windows 95 task such as copying a file or creating a new folder. The second book is *The Internet For Dummies* by John R. Levine and Carol Baroudi, which is helpful if you decide to venture into the dark recesses of Internet.

Foolish Assumptions

I'm making only three assumptions about you:

- ✔ You use a computer.
- ✔ You use Windows 95.
- ✔ You access (or are thinking about accessing) the Internet with Internet Explorer 3.0.

Nothing else. I don't assume that you're a computer guru who knows how to change a controller card or configure memory for optimal usage. Such technical chores are best handled by people who like computers. Hopefully, you are on speaking terms with such a person. Do your best to keep it that way.

How This Book Is Organized

Inside this book are ample chapters arranged into seven parts. Each chapter is broken down into sections that cover various aspects of the chapter's main subject. The chapters have a logical sequence, so reading them in order makes sense (if you're crazy enough to read this entire book). But you don't have to read them that way. You can flip open the book to any page and start reading.

Here's the lowdown on what's in each of the seven parts:

Part I: Preparing for an Internet Expedition

The two chapters in this part deal with really introductory stuff: what the Internet is and how to get connected to it. Part I is the place to start if you haven't visited the Internet before and you're not sure what the World Wide Web is, what `www.microsoft.com` means, or how to connect your computer to the Internet.

Part II: Embarking on a World Wide Web Adventure

This part is the heart and soul of the book. Its chapters show you how to use the basic features of Internet Explorer to untangle the World Wide Web — the graphical arm of the Internet.

Part III: Customizing Your Explorations

The four chapters in this part show you how to configure Internet Explorer by tweaking its options so that it suits your working style. This stuff is best read by people who like to show their computers who's the boss.

Part IV: Ports of Call

The chapters in this part show you how to use four Microsoft programs that work alongside Internet Explorer to access those parts of the Internet that fall outside the World Wide Web. You can discover how to use Internet Mail to send and receive e-mail, Internet News to participate in Internet newsgroups, Comic Chat to access online chat areas, and NetMeeting to use voice communications on the Internet and work collaboratively with other Internet users.

Part V: Multimedia and Interactivity on the Web

These chapters cover some of the hottest new features of the World Wide Web: online sound and video, three-dimensional worlds you can explore, and interactive Web pages. You also discover how to get in on the Java and ActiveX craze safely and responsibly.

Part VI: Adding New Internet Explorer Features to Your Own Web Page

If you're someone who enjoys creating your own Web pages, check out the four chapters in this part. Here, I show you the new features of Internet Explorer 3.0 that are designed specifically for Web authors and developers. Find out about new HTML features you can incorporate into your Web pages, how to format your pages with Internet Explorer's new style sheets, and how to use ActiveX controls.

Even if you are not a Web author or developer, these chapters can serve as an overview of what you can expect to see on Web pages that sport the "Best Experienced with Internet Explorer 3.0" logo.

Part VII: The Part of Tens

This wouldn't be a ...*For Dummies* book if it didn't include a collection of chapters with lists of interesting snippets: Ten Hot New Features of Internet Explorer 3.0, My Ten Favorite Web Sites, and so on.

Glossary

People use so much techno-babble when they discuss the Internet that I decided to include an extensive glossary of online terms, free of charge. With this glossary in hand, you can beat the silicon-heads at their own game.

Icons Used in This Book

As you read all this wonderful prose, you occasionally encounter the following icons. They appear in the margins to draw your attention to important information.

Oh-oh, some technical drivel is about to come your way. Cover your eyes if you find technical information offensive.

This icon points out traps you may fall into if you're not careful. Heed these warnings and all shall go well with you, with your children, and with your children's children.

Pay special attention to this icon — it points to some particularly useful tidbit, perhaps a shortcut or a way of using a command that you may not have considered.

This icon points out information you should definitely remember as you use the Internet Explorer features being discussed. The information may not be totally new to you; it may just remind you of something you've temporarily forgotten.

Where to Go from Here

The Internet is an exciting new computer frontier, and Internet Explorer is hands-down the best way to experience the Internet. So where do you go from here? Online, of course. With this book at your side, you can visit the world from your desktop. Happy exploring!

Part I

Preparing for an Internet Expedition

The 5th Wave   By Rich Tennant

"HONEY! OUR WEB BROWSER GOT OUT LAST NIGHT AND DUMPED THE TRASH ALL OVER MR. BELCHER'S HOME PAGE!"

In this part . . .

The Internet is one of the best things to happen to computers since the invention of the On button. Everyone and his uncle is going online these days. Even television commercials are in on the act — it's amazing how many ads flash Internet addresses right at the end. The Internet promises to revolutionize the way we do business, the way we buy cars, the way kids learn at school, even the way we shop for groceries.

The two chapters in this Part give you a gentle introduction to the Internet. In Chapter 1, you get a crash course on what the Internet is and why everyone is so excited about it. Then, in Chapter 2, you find out how to get yourself connected so that you don't miss out on all the excitement.

Chapter 1

Welcome to the Internet

In This Chapter

▶ A mercifully brief description of the Internet

▶ A rational explanation of why you should give a hoot about the Internet

▶ An overview of the different faces of the Internet

▶ How the Internet differs from online services

*L*ast I heard, the only people on the entire planet who haven't heard about the Internet are those seven stranded castaways still trying to get off Gilligan's Island. And sooner or later, the Professor will figure out a way to access the Internet using that old radio. Heck, they'll probably have their own home page sooner or later (www.rescue.com?). Of course, Gilligan will figure out some way to screw it up, so their home page will go down just as a Coast Guard sailor is about to access it. But I digress.

If you feel about as informed about the Internet as Gilligan, this chapter is for you. It provides a brief introduction to what the Internet is and why you would want to use it. So grab your pith helmet, and let's start exploring!

Just What Is the Internet?

The Internet is an enormous computer network that links tens of millions of computers all across the planet. The Internet allows you, sitting at your own private computer in a small town in Iowa, to access computers in Moscow or Geneva or Tokyo or Washington, D.C. The Internet is the most exciting thing to happen to computers since the invention of the mouse.

Most people are actually referring to the Internet when they talk about the *Information Superhighway.* The Information Superhighway is supposed to allow every man, woman, and child in the United States — indeed, on the entire planet — to access every conceivable bit of information that has ever been discovered, instantly and without error.

Come on, 9 million?

The plain fact is, no one really knows just how big the Internet really is. That's because no one really owns the Internet. But several organizations make it their business to periodically try to find out how big the Internet is. The science is far from exact, but these organizations are able to come up with pretty reasonable estimates.

The best known of these Internet bean-counters is *Network Wizards,* which does a survey every year. In January of 1996, Network Wizards found that the Internet connected 240,000 separate computer networks and that more than 9.4 million separate computers existed on the Internet. When compared with 1995's numbers, the 1996 survey shows that the Internet has more than doubled in size in the past year. Or to put it another way, three new computers were added to the Internet *every second.*

Truth is, estimates such as Network Wizards are probably *low.* Consider that three of the largest online services — America Online, CompuServe, and The Microsoft Network — together support more than 10 million users. No one knows exactly how many of these users actually use the Internet. Still, the indisputable point is that the Internet is big — and getting bigger every day.

If you find these figures interesting, you can check up on the latest Internet statistics from Network Wizards by accessing its Web site, www.nw.com.

Unfortunately, the Information Superhighway is, at best, a promise of what the future holds. Currently, the Internet still requires a fairly major investment in computer equipment (a decent computer for accessing the Internet still costs around $2,000). And although an enormous amount of information is available on the Internet, the entire contents of the Internet amounts to only a tiny fraction of human knowledge, and what information *is* there is haphazardly organized and difficult to sift through.

Still, even a tiny fraction of all human knowledge is worth having, even if it is poorly organized. And that's why the Internet has become so popular. People love to "surf the Web" (I explain what the *Web* is later in this chapter), hoping to glean some useful bit of information that will make their investment of online time and money worthwhile.

The Network of Networks

The Internet is actually a network of networks. The world is filled with computer networks. Large and small businesses have networks that connect the computers in their offices. Universities have networks that students and faculty can access. Government organizations have networks. And many people belong to online services such as CompuServe, America Online, or The Microsoft Network; these online services are themselves large computer networks.

The Internet's job is to connect all these networks together to form one gigantic mega-network. In fact, the very name *Internet* comes from the fact that the Internet allows connections among distinct computer networks.

The Internet consists of several hundreds of thousands of separate computer networks. These networks in turn connect a whopping 9 million computers to one another.

Where Did the Internet Come From?

Some people are fascinated by history. They love to watch Ken Burns specials about the Civil war and subscribe to cable TV just to get the History Channel. If you're one of those history buffs, you may be interested in the following history of the Internet's humble origins.

In the summer of 1969, the four mop-topped singers from Liverpool were breaking up. The war in Vietnam was escalating. Astronauts Neil Armstrong and Buzz Aldrin walked on the moon. And the Department of Defense built a computer network called ARPANET to link its defense installations with several major universities throughout the United States.

In the early 1970s, ARPANET was getting difficult to manage, so it was split into two networks: one for military use, called MILNET, and the other for nonmilitary use. The nonmilitary network retained the name ARPANET. To link MILNET with ARPANET, a new network link, called *Internet Protocol,* or IP, was invented.

The whole purpose of IP was to allow these two networks to communicate with one another. Fortunately, the designers of IP realized that it wouldn't be long before other networks wanted to join in the fun, so they designed IP to allow for more than two networks. In fact, their ingenious design allowed for tens of thousands of networks to communicate via IP.

The decision was a fortuitous one, as the Internet quickly began to grow. By the mid-1980s, the original ARPANET reached its limits. Just in time, the National Science Foundation (NSF) decided to get into the game. NSF had built a network called NSFNET to link its huge supercomputers. (*Supercomputers* are those behemoth computers — the kind of computers that, even today, fill entire rooms and are used to calculate the orbits of distant galaxies, discover new prime numbers, and play chess masters like Kasparov to a draw.)

NSFNET replaced ARPANET as the new background for the Internet. Around that time, magazines like *Time* and *Newsweek* began writing articles about this new phenomenon called the Internet, and the *Net* (as it became nicknamed) began to grow like a wildfire. Soon NSFNET couldn't keep up with the growth, so several private commercial networks took over management of the Internet backbone. The Internet has doubled in size every year for quite a few years now, and who knows how long this dizzying rate of growth will continue.

If the story of the Internet has a moral, it is that the Internet has probably been so successful precisely because it is not strictly a commercial or government venture. No one is really in charge of the Internet. Instead, the Internet sprang up pretty much on its own. No rules dictate who can and who cannot join the Internet, and no one can kick you or anyone else off the Internet. Kinda warms your cockles, doesn't it?

The Many Faces of the Internet

The Internet is not a single, monolithic entity that has a consistent look and feel for all of its services. Quite the contrary. Over the years, many different services have sprung up on the Internet, each with its own style and appearance. Microsoft Internet Explorer has features that let you access most, but not all, of these services.

World Wide Web

The most popular Internet venue is the World Wide Web, usually called "the Web" for short. The Web is to the Internet what Windows is to DOS: a graphical interface to what otherwise would be a bland and boring place. The Web enables you to view the information that is available on the Internet using fancy graphics and formatted text, and even incorporates trendy multimedia such as sounds and video.

Information on the World Wide Web is organized into documents called *pages*. A single Web page can be as short as one word, or it can contain hundreds of lines of text. Most pages contain no more information than you can comfortably squeeze onto an 8.5-x-11-inch printed page.

Each page on the Web can contain text, graphics, sounds, videos, and — most important — links to other Web pages with related information. For example, a page that contains information about frogs may contain links to other pages with information about princes, muppets, or hallucinogenic substances.

Every Web site has a *home page,* which is the starting point for exploring information available at the Web site. The home page may have links to additional pages at the same site, as well as to pages on different Web sites. Thus, clicking a link may take you to an entirely different Web site that's located halfway around the world from the one you were accessing, without jet lag, airsickness, or even a noticeable hesitation!

That's the neat thing about surfing the Web. It allows you to travel the world without leaving your home — and without long-distance charges! Your Internet service provider charges you a flat monthly or hourly rate, whether you're retrieving data from a Web site 4 miles or 4 *thousand* miles from your computer.

To access the Web, you need a special program called a Web browser. A *Web browser* knows how to display the special formats and codes used to send information over the World Wide Web. The Web browser reads these special codes over the Internet and translates them into fancy displays and beautiful pictures for your screen. The browser also lets you follow the links from one Web page to another, simply by clicking the link.

Just as you can choose among many different word processing or spreadsheet programs, you have your choice of many different Web browsers to use. Internet Explorer is the latest and greatest Web browser program from Microsoft. Figure 1-1 shows Internet Explorer in action, displaying a page from the World Wide Web.

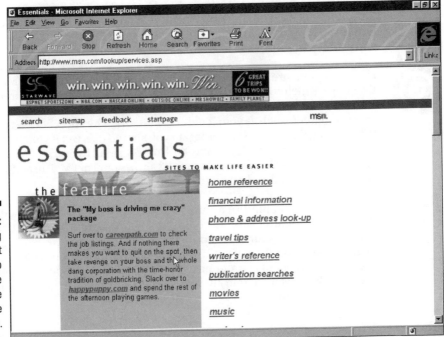

Figure 1-1:
Using
Internet
Explorer to
view a page
from the
World Wide
Web.

Internet Explorer isn't the only Web browser on the block, of course. Another popular Web browser is Netscape Navigator. Netscape and Microsoft are in a neck-and-neck race to see who can create the best browser software — kind of like the way Microsoft and WordPerfect were in a race to see who could create the best word processing software a few years ago. Obviously, this book is about exploring the Internet using Internet Explorer. If you use Netscape, you should probably be reading *Netscape For Dummies* instead.

Web browsers such as Internet Explorer aren't limited to accessing just the World Wide Web. In fact, you can access most of the other parts of the Internet directly from Internet Explorer or from programs that come with Internet Explorer.

Electronic mail

Electronic mail (sometimes called *e-mail*) lets you exchange private messages with any other user on the Internet, no matter where in the country or world that user lives. Unlike the postal service, Internet e-mail is delivered almost instantly. And unlike Federal Express, you don't have to pay $13 for fast delivery. In fact, Internet e-mail is probably the least expensive yet most efficient forms of communication available.

E-mail is not just for sending short notes to your friends, either. You can use e-mail to send entire files of information to coworkers. For example, I used Internet e-mail to send the document files for this book to my editor at IDG Books Worldwide, Inc. and she in turn used e-mail to send me back corrections and technical questions.

Many programs are available for reading Internet e-mail, including Microsoft Exchange, which comes with Windows 95. However, Internet Explorer comes with its own e-mail program called Microsoft Internet Mail. If you get e-mail from several sources, such as your local area network, The Microsoft Network, and the Internet, Exchange is the program you should use. But if your e-mail comes strictly from the Internet, you may find Internet Mail to be a much easier and more efficient e-mail program. Figure 1-2 shows Internet Mail in action. I describe Internet Mail in shocking detail in Chapter 11.

The world is still waiting for a universal e-mail program that can handle all of your e-mail, no matter where it comes from. As it stands today, Exchange can handle e-mail from your local area network, The Microsoft Network, and the Internet. But if you also get mail from America Online or CompuServe, you must use those services' mail programs to get their mail. Sigh. Soon, a single program may be able to get mail from all of these sources, but until then, you must use separate programs.

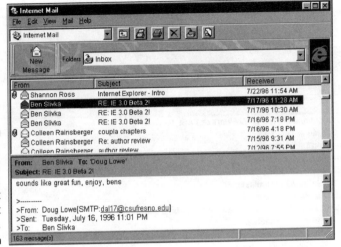

Figure 1-2:
Reading
e-mail with
Microsoft
Internet
Mail.

Newsgroups

Newsgroups are online discussion groups — places where users with common interests gather to share ideas. Thousands of newsgroups exist, covering just about every topic imaginable. You can find newsgroups that discuss obscure computer topics, fan clubs for various celebrities, online support groups, and who knows what else.

Most Internet newsgroups are distributed over *Usenet,* a network of special server computers that contain the special software needed to handle newsgroups. As a result, you sometimes see the terms *Usenet* and *newsgroups* used together. However, you can access some newsgroups that aren't a part of Usenet.

Internet Explorer does not itself handle newsgroups. However, a companion program from Microsoft, called Microsoft Internet News, does let you access newsgroups. With Internet News, you can read messages posted by other newsgroup users and you can post messages yourself. I give you the ins and outs of Internet News in Chapter 12.

Don't be confused by the term *news* in newsgroups. Newsgroups are *not* a news service designed to give you accurate, up-to-date, and unbiased information about current events. Newsgroups are places where people with common interests can share opinions. In this sense, newsgroups are more like talk radio than a news program. Figure 1-3 shows an example of a sports newsgroup accessed through Microsoft Internet News.

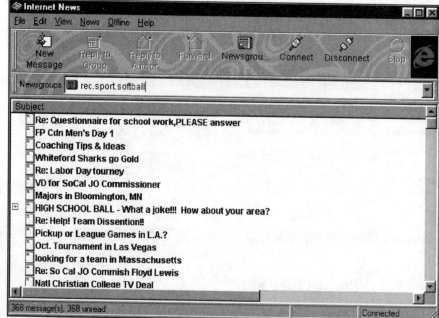

Figure 1-3:
Accessing
newsgroups
with
Microsoft
Internet
News.

File Transfer Protocol (FTP)

File Transfer Protocol, or FTP as it is usually called, is the Internet equivalent of a network file server. FTP is the Internet's primary method of moving files around. Thousands of FTP sites make their files available for downloading. All you have to do is sign in to the FTP site, find the file you want to download, and click.

Internet Explorer has built-in support for FTP, so you can easily log in to an FTP site and download files to your computer. In fact, you don't have to do anything special to access FTP from Internet Explorer; you may not even be aware that you're using FTP, unless you happen to notice the little status message at the bottom of the screen mentioning that you have entered an FTP site.

Telnet

Telnet is a way of connecting to another computer on the Internet and actually running programs on that computer, as if your computer were a terminal attached to the other computer. Telnet is one of the many Internet services that is rapidly losing popularity as the World Wide Web becomes more popular. However, some Internet sites are still available only via Telnet. Most of these seem to be public libraries, so if you want to be able to search the card catalog of your local public library, you may need to learn how to use Telnet.

Although Telnet may be a bit archaic for Internet Explorer's taste, if you're using Windows 95, you already have a built-in program that lets you Telnet to other computer sites.

Internet Relay Chat (IRC)

Internet Relay Chat, or IRC, is an online feature that enables you to talk with other Internet users live. IRC is kind of like a huge online party line; it's the Internet feature that keeps many users connected into the wee hours of the morning, chatting with other cyberjunkies around the planet.

Although Internet Explorer doesn't directly support IRC, Microsoft does offer a companion program called *Microsoft Comic Chat* that does. Comic Chat, which I cover in Chapter 13, is one of the most unusual programs you'll ever encounter. As you chat on the Internet, it actually draws a comic strip on-screen, using comic-book style characters to represent the different people you are conversing with.

Gopher

Gopher was an early attempt to make the Internet easy to use. Before gopher, people had to use cryptic commands to access the Internet. Gopher presented Internet information using a series of text-based menus.

Gopher has been largely replaced by the World Wide Web, which is easier to use because of its graphic nature. The good news is that Internet Explorer can handle what few gopher sites still exist. In fact, Internet Explorer presents gopher as if it were a part of the World Wide Web. So you probably won't even notice when you display a gopher page.

Be Warned: The Internet Is Not Censored

No censorship exists on the Internet. If you look hard enough, you can find just about anything on the Internet — not all of it wholesome. In addition to information about fly fishing, knitting, and the solar system, you can find photographs of men and women in various states of dress and undress, and often engaged in unmentionable acts that would make Hugh Hefner blush.

Unfortunately, you can't do much about the content on the Internet. Congress has tried legislation that would ban indecent content from the Internet, but the Supreme Court has ruled such legislation unconstitutional. After all, indecency is a pretty ambiguous concept, and the First Amendment pretty much prohibits Congress from banning any but the most obscene materials from publication on any medium.

However, just because Congress can't prevent people from publishing offensive material on the Internet doesn't mean that you have to view it. One of the newest developments on the Internet is a voluntary system of ratings that lets you know whether an Internet site contains offensive material. Internet Explorer lets *you* control whether you (or anyone in your household) can view such material. The solution's not perfect, but it does go a long way toward controlling the amount of offensive material kids are exposed to. In Chapter 9, I describe Internet Explorer's controls for blocking offensive material.

Chapter 2

Connecting to the Net with Internet Explorer

*T*he hardest part about using the Internet is figuring out how to get connected to it the first time. After you figure that out, the rest is easy. (Well, *relatively* easy. Nothing about computers is easy!)

This chapter explores the various options for connecting your computer to the Internet using Internet Explorer. With luck, you'll discover that you already *are* connected to the Internet, and Internet Explorer has already been set up on your computer, so you can skip this chapter and get on with the fun. If not, read on.

You May Already Be on the Internet . . .

It's true. You may have been on the Internet for years now and not realized it. And you may have already won $10,000,000 from Publisher's Clearinghouse, and maybe tomorrow you'll get struck by lightning, and your IQ will double.

Actually, the possibility that you already have access to the Internet isn't that outlandish. Here are some reasonable scenarios:

✔ If you subscribe to one of the major online services such as America Online, CompuServe, or The Microsoft Network, you already have access to the Internet. Each of these online services provides a link to the Internet, but online services are usually the most expensive way to hook up to the Net. Moreover, some online services don't provide all the

Internet features that a direct connection offers. I explain why later in this chapter, when I compare different Internet rate plans and discuss different methods of connecting to the Internet.

✔ If you use a computer at work, and that computer is a part of a local area network (LAN), you may be able to access the Internet via the LAN. Talk to your resident network guru to find out.

✔ The computers at many schools are connected to the Internet. If you're a student, you may be able to bribe your teachers into letting you access the Internet. You may even get extra credit for using the Internet — especially if you use it to do your homework.

✔ Some public libraries have computers that are connected to the Net. With access at a public library, you probably won't be able to set up your own account to send and receive private e-mail. But you may be able to access newsgroups and the World Wide Web.

What about the Unlucky Rest of Us?

If you don't have access to the Internet through one of the sources listed in the preceding section, you have no alternative but to set up your own Internet access at home. Unfortunately, you can't do so without having to contend with at least some of the boring technical details.

Following are a few general tips I want to offer before I get into the details of setting up your Internet access:

✔ Upgrade to one of the latest and greatest versions of Windows: Windows 95 or Windows NT 4.0. One of the best things about these new versions of Windows is that they have built-in support for the Internet. Setting up Internet access for Windows 3.1 is much more difficult; besides, you need one of the newer versions of Windows to experience all the new features of Internet Explorer 3.0. This book assumes that you are running Windows 95 or Windows NT 4.0.

✔ Make sure that your computer is located near a telephone outlet.

✔ If you have a friend who already has access to the Internet, treat him to lunch and pick his brain (well, not literally). Find out what kind of modem he has, who his service provider is, how much he is paying for it, what he likes best about it, what he hates about it, what he would do differently, whom he thinks is going to win the World Series, and whether he prefers Leno or Letterman.

✔ If you have a friend who happens to be a computer expert, see if you can't bribe her into helping you set up your Internet access. Don't offer cash; barter is better. Offer to mow her lawn or wash her car.

First, You Need a Modem

The first thing you need to connect your computer to the Internet is a modem. If your computer is brand new, you're lucky: It probably already has a modem in it. In that case, all you have to do is plug the modem into the telephone jack using a phone cord, and you're ready to go.

If your computer doesn't have a modem already, you have to purchase and install one yourself. The basic rule of modem buying is this:

Buy the fastest modem you can afford.

Modems come in two speeds: 14,400 bps and 28,800 bps. bps stands for *bits per second* and is simply a measure of how fast the modem can pump data through the phone lines. (The term *baud* is sometimes used as a substitute for bps. Both have pretty much the same meaning.)

✔ The slower but less expensive modems are the 14,400 bps variety. You often see these modems referred to as 14.4 or V.32 (pronounced *vee-dot-thirty-two*). You can buy 14.4 modems for as little as $50.

✔ The faster modems are the 28,800 bps modems, also known as 28.8 or V.34 (you guessed it — *vee-dot-thirty-four*). If you shop around, you can probably find a 28.8 modem for about $125.

✔ If your computer has an older modem in it, watch out. Older modems may not be fast enough to efficiently access the World Wide Web. The slowest acceptable speed for Web access is 14.4. If your computer has a 2400 bps modem, you need to replace it with a faster model.

Before you purchase a 28.8 modem, find out whether the Internet provider you plan on using can support 28.8 modems. Most can, but some provide only 14.4 access. In that case, half the speed capacity of your modem will go unused. Most modems also allow you to send and receive faxes. Because this feature is handy and doesn't increase the cost of the modem, make sure that the modem you buy includes fax support.

Your modem must be connected to a phone line so your computer can access the outside world. Unfortunately, whenever you use the Internet, the modem ties up your phone line. Anyone calling your number gets a busy signal, and you can't use the phone to call out for pizza. If being deprived of telephone privileges while you're online proves to be a problem, you can always have the phone company install a separate phone line for your modem.

If the thought of installing a modem nauseates you, pack up your computer and take it to your friendly local computer shop. The folks there can sell you a modem and install it for you for a small charge.

What about ISDN?

ISDN, which stands for *Integrated Services Digital Network,* is a digital rather than analog phone line. ISDN allows data to be sent much faster than a conventional phone line — up to 128 Kbps rather than 28.8 Kbps. As an added plus, a single ISDN line can be logically split into two separate channels, so you can carry on a voice conversation while your computer is connected to the Internet.

Sounds great. The only catch is that it's expensive. An ISDN connection doesn't require a modem. Instead, a special ISDN adapter is used, and that will set you back at least $250. In addition, you'll have to pay the phone company anywhere from $50 to $200 to install the ISDN line, and you'll have to pay a monthly fee ranging from $25 to $50 depending on your area. On top of that, you may be billed by the minute for usage. For example, in my area, an ISDN line costs $24.95 per month, plus usage fees of about a penny a minute.

Over the next few years, the cost of ISDN will probably come down. Until then, ISDN will be used mostly by die-hard computer geeks.

(If you're not a die-hard computer geek, but you still want to learn more about ISDN, check out *ISDN For Dummies.*)

Next, You Need a Service Provider

An Internet service provider, or ISP, is a company that charges you, usually on a monthly basis, for access to the Internet. The ISP has a bunch of modems connected to phone lines that you can dial into. These modems are connected to a computer system, which is in turn connected to the Internet via a high-speed data link. The ISP's computer acts as a liaison between your computer and the Internet.

Typically, an ISP provides you with the following services in exchange for your hard-earned money:

- **Access to the World Wide Web via one of two types of connections — a PPP connection or a SLIP connection:** You don't have to worry about the technical differences between these two types of connections; you just have to know which type you have so you can configure your software properly.

- **Electronic mail:** You will be assigned an e-mail address that anyone anywhere on the Internet can use to send you mail. You can use Microsoft's Internet Mail to access your e-mail, as described in Chapter 11.

- **Access to Internet newsgroups:** In the newsgroups, you can follow ongoing discussions about your favorite topics. Read all about newsgroups in Chapter 12.

✔ **Software to access the Internet:** In many cases, this software includes Microsoft Internet Explorer. Or it may include a different Web browser, such as Netscape Navigator. (If Internet Explorer isn't provided by your ISP, you can obtain it free from Microsoft after you set up your Internet connection. Find out how later in this chapter, under "Finally, You Need Internet Explorer.")

✔ **Technical support, the quality of which varies greatly:** If you have trouble with your Internet connection, try calling your ISP's technical support line. If you're lucky, an actual human being who knows something about computers will pick up the phone and help you solve your problem. Next best: You'll be put on hold, but someone will eventually answer and help you. Not so good: The technical support line will always be busy. Worse: You'll get a recording that says, "All our support engineers are busy. Please leave a message and we'll get back to you." Yeah, right.

Basically two types of companies provide access to the Internet: commercial online services such as America Online, CompuServe, and The Microsoft Network, and independent Internet service providers. The following sections describe the pros and cons of both types of providers and the Internet access they provide.

Online services

All of the major online services allow you to connect to the Internet. On the plus side, you get access to unique content that's available only to members of the online service. On the minus side, you pay for this extra service. The following paragraphs describe the pricing plans of the three major online services.

✔ **America Online (AOL):** The most popular online service, with something like 5 million users, America Online offers a basic rate of $9.95 per month. This basic rate includes five free hours of usage per month, with each additional hour costing $2.95. The America Online Value Plan gives you 20 hours a month for $19.95, with each additional hour costing $2.75.

Unfortunately, at the time I write this, America Online still does not provide a way of connecting to the Internet with Internet Explorer 3.0. A new version of America Online that will let you use Internet Explorer 3.0 is being readied and may even be available by the time you read this. In fact, this newest version of America Online will even include a *built-in* version of Internet Explorer 3.0, so you won't have to download and install Internet Explorer yourself.

✔ **CompuServe:** The second most popular online service, CompuServe claims about 4 million users. CompuServe has two pricing plans. The Standard Plan gives you five free hours per month for $9.95, with each additional hour costing $2.95 (it's the same as America Online's basic rate). The Super Value plan gives you 20 hours per month for $24.95, with each additional hour costing $1.95. With CompuServe, you can use Internet Explorer 3.0 via a PPP connection.

✔ **The Microsoft Network (MSN):** MSN is Microsoft's attempt to challenge America Online and CompuServe. The Microsoft Network offers two price plans: Standard, which gives you three hours of connect time each month for $4.95, with each additional hour costing $2.50; and Frequent User, which gives you 20 hours per month for $19.95, with each additional hour costing $2.00. The Microsoft Network provides full Internet Access with Internet Explorer 3.0.

If you opt to use an online service as your Internet service provider, you need to carefully select the correct pricing plan for the number of hours you intend to use the service. To make the point, Table 2-1 shows the monthly cost for each of the preceding plans for monthly usage of 10, 20, 40, and 60 hours. As you can see, the actual monthly cost varies tremendously depending on which plan you select.

I've heard too many horror stories about families that have signed up for America Online or CompuServe, expecting the monthly bill to be only $9.95, only to discover a $200 bill the first month. The problem is that the kids discover the Internet some evening and end up spending three or four hours online every night for two weeks before the parents catch on.

Are the online services worth it?

Because you can access the Internet in less expensive ways, the question naturally comes up, are the extra features you get with an online service worth the extra cost? This may sound like a cop out, but there's no right or wrong answer to that question. It all depends on whether you use and benefit from the additional features provided by online services.

One of the biggest benefits online services have over the Internet is that online services are organized. The Internet is a sprawling mess, and sometimes it's hard to find what you want. In contrast, online services are well organized. Information in online services is neatly arranged according to topic. Not so on the Internet.

Another benefit of online services is that you can probably expect better support from your online service's customer service staff. CompuServe and America Online both have large support staffs that can help make sure that you get on and stay on the Internet without a lot of technical headaches. The quality of technical support you get with an ISP varies a great deal from one ISP to the next.

Still, if you subscribe to an online service and then discover that you use it only to access the Internet, you may be better off canceling your online service subscription and signing up with a simple Internet Service Provider instead.

My advice is that if you sign up for an online service, always start off with the frequent user plan. Such a plan may cost you $10 or $15 more if you end up not using it as much as you expect, but that's a lot better than paying $50 to $100 more if you end up using it more than you expect. And make sure you explain how the pricing plan works to all members of the family, including the kids.

Table 2-1	Pricing Plans Compared			
Price Plan	*10 hours*	*20 hours*	*40 hours*	*60 hours*
America Online	$24.70	$54.20	$113.20	$172.20
America Online Value Plan	$19.95	$19.95	$74.95	$99.95
CompuServe Standard	$24.70	$54.20	$113.20	$172.20
CompuServe Super Value	$24.95	$24.95	$63.95	$102.95
Microsoft Network Standard	$22.45	$47.45	$97.45	$147.45
Microsoft Network Frequent User	$19.95	$19.95	$59.95	$99.95

The changing role of online services

The sudden growth of the Internet has had a profound impact on established online services such as CompuServe and America Online, and even on newer online services, such as The Microsoft Network. In the past, online services required that you use software provided by the online service to access the information available at the service. For example, to access America Online, you must use special software provided by America Online. CompuServe and The Microsoft Network are the same.

All that is changing, however. Online services are discovering that users prefer to have their choice in access software, and so they are slowly but surely moving their services over to a format that allows users to access them with standard Internet Web browsers such as Netscape Navigator and Internet Explorer.

Now these developments don't mean that online services are becoming simply a part of the World Wide Web, or that you will be able to access CompuServe or America Online for free. The online services will continue to have their distinct features that are available only to subscribers, such as discussion forums, file libraries, stock quote services, and reference databases.

What it does mean is that you will be able to move from the World Wide Web to your online service without switching software programs, and you will be able to choose which browser program you want to use to access your online service.

These changes are coming slowly. You can't change the software used by 4 or 5 million subscribers all at once. But the change is certain, and within a few years, all of the major online services will allow you to use Internet Explorer or any other Web browser to access their content.

Internet service providers

The alternative to using a commercial online service is to sign up with an Internet service provider, or ISP. ISPs provide the same Internet access that online services do, but they don't provide their own additional content. ISPs are invariably less expensive than commercial online services because they don't have the added expense that results from providing their own proprietary services.

Technically, any company that provides you with Internet access is an ISP, including commercial online services. However, I prefer to use the term ISP to refer to a company that specializes in providing only Internet access, without providing a separate online service of its own.

You can choose from nationally known service providers such as NETCOM or AT&T WorldNet Service, or you can choose a local ISP. To find the ISPs in your area, check the Yellow Pages under *Computers — Online Services and Internet.*

Most ISPs offer unlimited access for about $20 per month. Some offer a limited hour plan for slightly less (for example, 40 hours for $15). Either way, the cost of using an ISP is likely to be less than using a commercial online service, unless you end up using the Internet for only a few hours each month.

Finally, You Need Internet Explorer

Naturally, before you can begin to use Internet Explorer, you must get Internet Explorer and install it on your computer. The section explains how.

As you may know, Internet Explorer is free. You can freely download it from any of several sites on the Internet, and you can use it without charge. There are no restrictions on how you can use it: At home or at the office, Internet Explorer is completely free.

How can the good people at Microsoft afford to distribute Internet Explorer for free? Because they're hoping that the browser will catch on like wildfire. Microsoft plans to make plenty of money from Internet Explorer, but not by selling Internet Explorer itself. Instead, Microsoft hopes that so many people will use its browser that Internet Explorer will become a standard. Microsoft will then make its money by selling the development tools that Web authors and software developers need to create interesting content viewable only with Internet Explorer. The business strategy is an interesting one, but one that could potentially be good not only for Microsoft but also for the whole Internet community.

Here are some of the ways you can obtain Internet Explorer:

- ✔ If you already have Internet access using another program (such as Netscape Navigator), you can download Internet Explorer from the Microsoft Internet Explorer download page at www.microsoft.com/ie. Note that the download for Internet Explorer can take a couple of hours. Better go to the local video store and rent a movie before proceeding.

- ✔ If you purchased a new computer with Windows 95 preinstalled, you already have Internet Explorer. However, you may have an older version. Fortunately, you can use the older version initially to connect to the Internet and then download the latest version from www.microsoft.com/ie.

- ✔ You can download Internet Explorer from America Online, CompuServe, or The Microsoft Network.

- ✔ You can buy an earlier version of Internet Explorer as a part of Microsoft Plus!, an add-on utility package for Windows 95. Then, you can connect to www.microsoft.com/ie to download Internet Explorer 3.0.

- ✔ You can purchase the Microsoft Internet Add-on for Windows 95. The Internet Add-on includes a special version of Internet Explorer that is actually integrated with the Windows 95 Explorer.

- ✔ You can subscribe to an Internet provider that uses Internet Explorer as its default browser. But make sure that the service uses the latest version of Internet Explorer; some services (like the CompuServe offshoot called WOW!) offer only older, customized versions of Internet Explorer.

Internet Explorer has been through several major revisions. The current version, Internet Explorer 3.0, is among the most powerful Web browsers available. If you have an earlier version (2.0 or 1.0), be sure to upgrade to version 3.0 as soon as possible. You can find Internet Explorer 3.0 available for download at www.microsoft.com/ie.

After you have downloaded the Internet Explorer file, exit from your Web browser and run the file you downloaded by opening the folder you downloaded the file into and double-clicking the file's icon. The Internet Explorer setup program then begins and installs Internet Explorer for you. (Depending on the browser you use, Internet Explorer may automatically install itself after the download is finished. If so, just sit back and enjoy the ride.)

Now You Can Set Up Your Internet Connection

In the old, pre-Windows 95 days, setting up a connection to the Internet was a complicated affair best handled by computer experts with pocket protectors and tape on their glasses. Now, with Windows 95 and Internet Explorer 3.0, configuring your computer to connect to the Internet is a simple, straightforward process. All you have to do is run a special program called the *Internet Connection Wizard.* The Wizard handles all of the configuration details for you.

To run the Internet Connection Wizard, follow these steps:

1. **Gather the information you need to configure your Internet connection.**

   You need the following information, which your Internet service provider should be able to supply:

   - The name of your Internet service provider

   - The telephone number you dial to connect to the Internet

   - The name and password you must use to access the system

   - Your IP address, unless an IP address is assigned automatically each time you log on

   - The DNS server address, which looks like a bunch of numbers with periods where they don't belong, as in 123.4.56.789.

   - Your e-mail address and the address of your e-mail server

2. **Fetch your Windows 95 installation diskettes or CD-ROM.**

   You may not need these, but the Setup Connection Wizard sometimes asks for them. Better keep them handy just in case.

3. **Start the Internet Connection Wizard.**

   Click the Start button and choose Programs⇨Accessories⇨Internet Tools\Get on the Internet. When you start the Internet Connection Wizard, the dialog box shown in Figure 2-1 greets you.

4. **Click Next>.**

   The Internet Connection Wizard displays the dialog box shown in Figure 2-2, which gives you three choices for configuring your computer for the Internet.

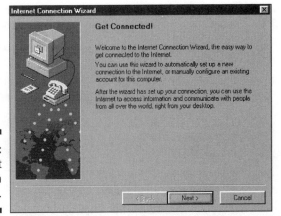

Figure 2-1:
The Internet
Connection
Wizard.

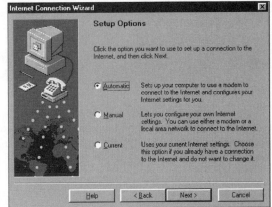

Figure 2-2:
You have
three
choices.

You have three options for configuring the Internet:

- **Automatic:** Automatically configures your computer for the Internet. Use this option if you don't already have an Internet account. The Internet Connection Wizard uses your modem to dial into a Microsoft computer that maintains a list of Internet service providers. A list of ISPs in your area appears, and you are granted the privilege of signing up with one of these providers and having your connection configured automatically.

- **Manual:** This is the option to use if you already have an account with an Internet service provider. The Internet Connection Wizard asks you to enter information about your account so that it can configure your Internet connection.

- **Current:** Use this option if your computer has already been configured for the Internet and you want to retain your current settings.

5. Select Manual (assuming that you already have an Internet account) and then click Next>.

The Internet Connection Wizard now hands off to another wizard, called the Internet Setup Wizard. The Internet Setup Wizard is shown in Figure 2-3.

Figure 2-3:
Enter the Internet Setup Wizard.

6. Click Next>.

The Internet Setup Wizard displays the dialog box shown in Figure 2-4, asking whether you plan to connect to the Internet via a modem and phone line or through a local area network.

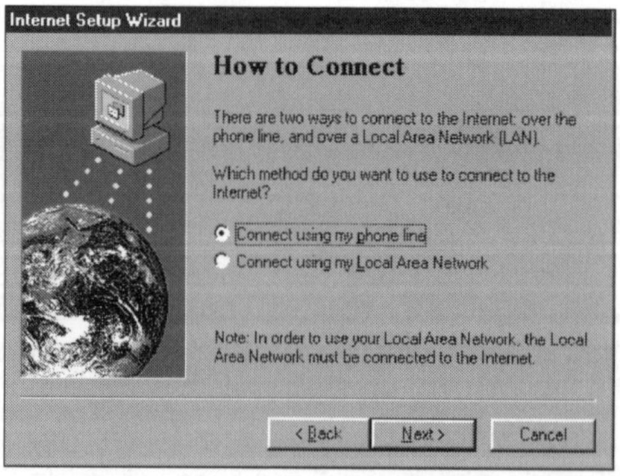

Figure 2-4:
The Internet Setup Wizard asks how you will connect to the Internet.

7. Check the appropriate connection option and then click Next>.

If you are connecting via a phone line, the Wizard displays the dialog box shown in Figure 2-5. If you are connecting to the Internet via a local area network, skip ahead to Step 14 (Figure 2-11).

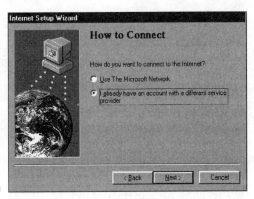

Figure 2-5:
The Internet
Setup
Wizard asks
if you want
to connect
via The
Microsoft
Network.

8. **Select whether you want to connect to the Internet via The Microsoft Network or a private Internet service provider and then click Next>.**

If you opt for The Microsoft Network, you can skip ahead to Step 15. Otherwise, the Wizard displays the dialog box shown in Figure 2-6.

Figure 2-6:
The Internet
Setup
Wizard asks
for the name
of your ISP.

9. **Type the name of your ISP into the text box and then click Next>.**

If your ISP is already listed in the drop-down list, you can just select it rather than typing it in. Either way, the dialog box shown in Figure 2-7 appears next.

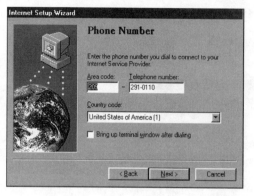

Figure 2-7:
The Internet
Setup
Wizard asks
for your
ISP's phone
number.

10. Type in the phone number for your service provider and then click Next>.

The dialog box shown in Figure 2-8 is displayed next.

Figure 2-8:
Now the
Internet
Setup
Wizard
wants to
know your
name and
password.

11. Type your name and password and then click Next>.

Your password is not displayed when you type it, so you don't need to worry about anyone watching over your shoulder. When you click Next>, the Internet Setup Wizard displays the dialog box shown in Figure 2-9.

12. Type in your IP address if necessary and then click Next>.

Most ISPs are set up to assign your IP address automatically whenever you log on, so you probably don't have to type in an address here. When you click Next>, the Internet Setup Wizard displays the dialog box shown in Figure 2-10.

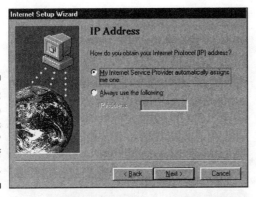

Figure 2-9:
The Setup
Wizard asks
for your IP
address, if
required.

Figure 2-10:
The Setup
Wizard
demands to
know your
DNS
address.

13. **Type in your DNS server address and click Next>.**

    You may need to call up your Internet service provider to find out what
    DNS server address it uses — that's not the type of information most of us
    carry around in our wallets. Type the address and click Next>. If your ISP
    gives you two addresses, type the second one as an alternate DNS server
    address.

    The dialog box shown in Figure 2-11 appears when you click Next>.

14. **Type your e-mail address and the address of your e-mail server; then
    click Next>.**

    Your ISP should provide you with this information. When you click Next>,
    yet another dialog box appears, as shown in Figure 2-12, with one final
    question.

Figure 2-11:
Will it ever
end?

Figure 2-12:
Almost
there!

15. Click Next> to finish the Wizard.

You don't need to change the setting for the messaging profile, so just click Next>. The Wizard displays one more dialog box (Figure 2-13) asking for your final permission to configure your Internet access.

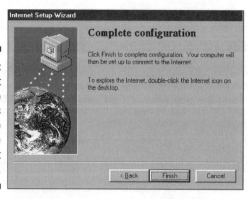

Figure 2-13:
The Internet
Setup
Wizard is
ready to
configure
your Internet
access.

16. Click Finish.

Your computer grinds and whirls for a moment, and then the Internet Setup Wizard disappears — finally!

Now, you can access the Internet by double-clicking on the Internet Explorer icon which appears on your desktop. When a Connect To dialog box appears, click Connect and start exploring!

Part II

Embarking on a World Wide Web Adventure

The 5th Wave   By Rich Tennant

"IT HAPPENED AROUND THE TIME WE SUBSCRIBED TO AN ON-LINE SERVICE."

In this part . . .

This is the part of the book where you discover the basics of using Internet Explorer: how to start Internet Explorer, how to use Internet Explorer to browse the World Wide Web, how to look for and find the information you're interested in, how to keep track of your favorite places, and how to get help when you don't know what you're doing.

This part is for your early Internet explorations. When you have these basics under your belt, you're ready to take on the more advanced topics covered in the rest of this book. But as a great king once advised, it is best to begin at the beginning, and go on 'til you come to the end; then stop. So grab your pith helmet and your mouse, and get ready to go exploring!

Chapter 3

Pushing Off

● ●

In This Chapter

▶ Starting Internet Explorer

▶ Understanding World Wide Web addresses

▶ Displaying pages on the World Wide Web

▶ Going back to pages you've already seen

▶ Saving and printing Web pages

▶ Exiting Internet Explorer and disconnecting from the Internet

● ●

*W*hen you have your Internet connection in place and Internet Explorer installed, you're ready to begin your Internet explorations. This chapter shows you how to use the basic features of Internet Explorer to surf the Web. You won't become intimate with all the subtle nuances of using Internet Explorer — I save some of the more exotic features for later chapters. In this chapter, I focus on the basics: how to start Internet Explorer, how to explore the Web, and so on.

Starting Internet Explorer

The first step in surfing the Web using Internet Explorer is starting the program. To start up Internet Explorer, just follow these steps:

The Internet

1. Double-click the Internet Explorer icon that appears on your desktop.

(If you don't have this icon on your desktop, you probably need to install Internet Explorer — read Chapter 2.)

Internet Explorer grinds and churns for a moment and then displays the Connect To dialog box, as shown in Figure 3-1.

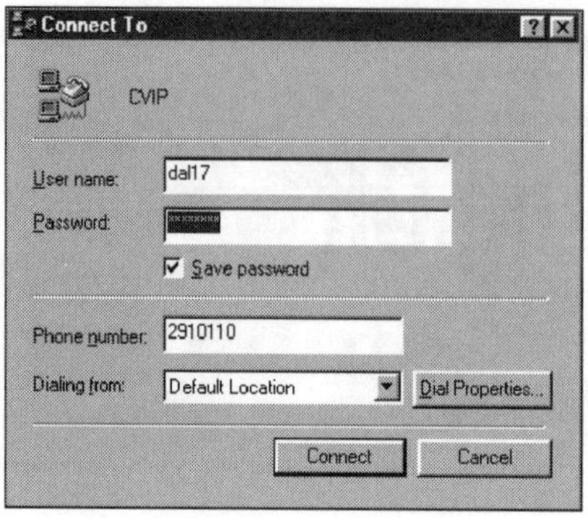

Figure 3-1:
The Connect
To dialog
box.

2. **Type your User name and Password in the Connect To dialog box.**

   Internet Explorer is asking for the name and password you use to sign on to whatever online service you use. To avoid having to type your name and password every time you want explore the Net, check the Save password check box — but remember that anyone with access to your computer will be able to use your connection.

3. **Click the Connect button to connect to your Internet service provider (ISP).**

   Your computer uses the modem to dial the phone number of your ISP. If the modem volume is turned up, you hear a dial tone, the familiar tones as the number is dialed, two or three rings, and then a few moments of rather obnoxious squealing as the modems establish their connection.

   After a connection is established, the Internet Explorer window appears and goes directly to your start page, as shown Figure 3-2.

You can resize the Internet Explorer window just like any other window. I usually like to work with Internet Explorer maximized so that it fills the entire screen and displays as much of each Web page as possible. To maximize a window, click the Maximize button.

After Internet Explorer dials into your ISP, you may be faced with a blank window, in which you must type log-in information. For example, my ISP requires me to type in my user ID and password, even though the Connect To dialog box knows my user ID and password. Then it displays a menu from which I must choose option 4 to connect to the World Wide Web (see Figure 3-3). Next, I must type the word **Default** and press Enter. If your ISP tells you to type similar information, you have to follow its instructions.

Maximize button

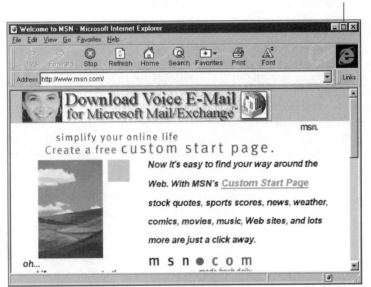

Figure 3-2:
The Internet
Explorer
window.

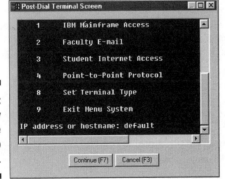

Figure 3-3:
The crazy
stuff I have
to type to
log on.

Typing all this log-in information every time you access the Internet is a big-time
hassle. Fortunately, Windows 95 lets you create a special file, called a *dial-up
script,* which supplies the information automatically whenever you dial up your
ISP. Creating a dial-up script isn't rocket science, but it's a little more advanced
than this chapter can handle. When you grow weary of typing this log-in
information every time you call up your ISP, skip ahead to Chapter 10, which
explains in detail how to create a dial-up script.

Making Sense of the Internet Explorer Screen

Before telling you how to actually explore the Internet, let me pause for a moment to examine all the bells and whistles that Microsoft has loaded on the Internet Explorer window. Figure 3-4 shows the Internet Explorer window, maximized for your viewing pleasure, with some of the more important parts labeled for easy identification.

The following items on the Internet Explorer screen are worthy of note:

✔ **Title bar:** At the very top of the window, the title bar always displays the name of the Internet page you are currently viewing. For example, in Figure 3-4, MSN welcomes you to the Internet.

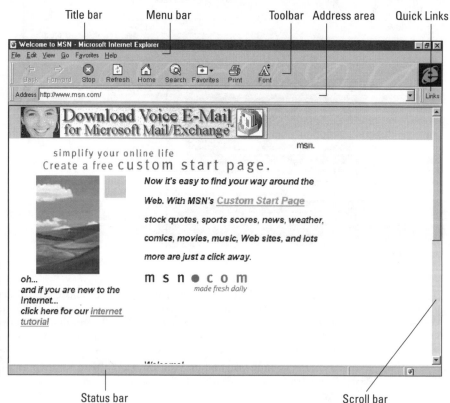

Figure 3-4: The different parts of the Internet Explorer screen.

✔ **Menu bar:** Just below the title bar lives the menu bar, as in any Windows program. Internet Explorer's deepest secrets are hidden within the menus located on the menu bar. Several of these menus are familiar: File, Edit, View, and Help. Two of the menus — Go and Favorites — provide features that are unique to Internet Explorer.

✔ **Toolbar:** Beneath the menu bar is the toolbar, which contains buttons you can click to perform common tasks. The purpose of each of these buttons is summarized in Table 3-1, but don't feel as though you need to understand these buttons at first. As you gain experience with Internet Explorer, the function of each of these buttons becomes apparent.

✔ **Address area:** Beneath the toolbar is an address area that displays the Internet address (called a URL) of the page currently being displayed. The drop-down list also reveals addresses of pages you've recently visited. (If you don't understand Internet addresses, don't worry. I explain them later in this chapter under the heading "Understanding Web addresses.")

✔ **Quick Links:** To the right of the address area, you find the word *Links*. Clicking this word reveals Internet Explorer's Quick Links: a collection of five of your favorite Internet locations that you can access with just a click of the mouse. To save space, the links themselves are temporarily hidden from view until you click *Links*. When activated, the Quick Links overlay the space occupied by the address area. You can restore the address area by clicking the word *Address*.

✔ **Status bar:** The status bar, located at the bottom of the window, periodically displays useful information, such as what Internet Explorer is trying to do or how much progress it has made downloading a large file.

✔ **Scroll bars:** Located at the right and bottom of the window, the scroll bars appear and disappear as needed. Whenever Internet Explorer can't display all the information on an Internet page on a single screen, a scroll bar appears so that you can scroll to the hidden information.

Table 3-1	Internet Explorer Toolbar Buttons
Button	**What It Does**
⇦	Moves back to the most recently displayed page
⇨	Moves forward to the page you most recently moved back from
⊗	Cancels a time-consuming download
🗋	Forces Internet Explorer to obtain a fresh copy of the current page
🏠	Takes you to your start page

(continued)

Table 3-1 *(continued)*	
Button	**What It Does**
Q	Takes you to your search page
⊡▾	Displays a list of your favorite Internet locations
🖨	Prints the current page
A	Changes the font size

Oh, the Places You'll Go!

As its name implies, the chief function of Internet Explorer is to let you explore the Internet. To do so, you need to know how to get around — that is, how to *navigate* from one Internet location to another. The following sections explain Internet Explorer's navigation features.

Understanding Web addresses

Just as every house in a neighborhood has a street address, every page of the World Wide Web has an Internet address. Because the Web has so many pages, simply assigning a name to each page on the Web would quickly become unmanageable. As a result, Web addresses are constructed using a method called the *Uniform Resource Locator (URL)*.

URLs are becoming commonplace in our society. Just think about how many times you've seen addresses such as `www.whatever.com` appear at the end of a television advertisement. These days, every company that advertises seems to have a Web page.

In order to use Internet Explorer effectively, you need to know how to compose URL Web addresses. Entering URLs isn't too hard, but it takes some practice.

An URL consists of three parts, written as follows:

```
protocol://host-address/resource-name
```

✔ For World Wide Web pages, the *protocol* portion of the URL is always `http` (http stands for *Hypertext Transfer Protocol,* but you don't need to know that to use URLs).

✔ The *host-address* is the Internet address of the computer on which the Web page resides (for example, `www.dummies.com`).

✔ The final part, the *resource-name*, is a name assigned by the host computer to a specific Web page or other file. In many cases, this name contains additional slashes that represent directories on the host system. Most of the time, you can omit the resource-name altogether if you simply want to display the home page for a company's Web site.

Here are some examples of complete URLs:

```
http://www.yahoo.com

http://www.cbs.com/lateshow/lateshow.html

http://asylum.cid.com/hhgttg/hhgttg.html
```

 Notice that all Internet addresses must also be prefixed by `http://`. However, Internet Explorer cleverly adds the `http://` automatically, so you don't have to type it yourself. Throughout this book, I leave off the `http://` from any World Wide Web address.

Because Internet Explorer always allows you to omit the protocol part (`http://`), and because you can often omit the resource name, the only URL component you really need to worry about is the Internet address. Internet addresses themselves consist of three components, separated from one another by periods, usually called *dots*.

✔ The first part of the Internet address is almost always `www`, to indicate that the address is for a page on the World Wide Web.

✔ The second part of the Internet address is usually a company or organization name, sometimes abbreviated if the full name is too long.

✔ The third and final part of an Internet address is a category that indicates the type of organization the name belongs to. The most common categories are

- **gov:** Government agencies

- **com:** Private companies

- **edu:** Educational institutions

- **org:** Organizations

- **net:** Networks

Putting these three address parts together, you get addresses such as `www.microsoft.com`, `www.nasa.gov`, and `www.ucla.edu`.

Following the links

The most popular method of navigating through the Internet is by following links. A *link* is a bit of text on one Web page that leads you to another Web page. A link may lead to another page at the same Web site, or it may lead to a page at a different Web site altogether.

Yes, it's true that Internet Explorer refers to links as *shortcuts.* But most Web users (including me) prefer the term *link,* so that's the term I use in this book.

You can easily identify the text links on a Web page because they are underlined and displayed in a different color than the rest of the text. (The default colors for links are blue for links you haven't yet viewed and purple for links you have already visited; however, you can change the color of your links if you wish.) For example, back in Figure 3-4, <u>internet tutorial</u> and <u>Custom Start Page</u> are links to other Web pages.

In addition to text links, many Web pages contain graphical links — graphics that you can click to jump to another Web page. Unlike text links, graphical links are not identified with a special color or underlining. But you can spot them by watching the mouse pointer as you glide it over the graphic. If the mouse pointer changes from an arrow to a pointing finger, you know that you've found a link.

For technical reasons you don't want to know, graphical links are often called *image maps.*

In most cases, Web-page designers try to make their graphical links obvious by including text next to them. For example, Figure 3-5 shows the Web page for the National Park Service, which sports the following graphical links:

- Links to the Past
- Park Smart
- Info Zone
- Nature Net
- Parks for Tomorrow
- Visit Your Parks
- Park Store
- E-Mail
- Search

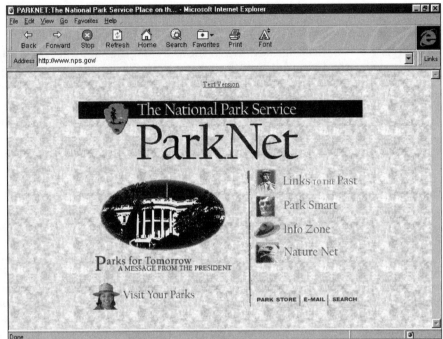

Figure 3-5:
The
National
Park
Service
page, which
uses a
lovely image
map.

You can tell where a link leads by moving the mouse pointer over it. After a few moments, a message appears in the status bar indicating the address of the page that will be displayed if you click the link. For example, if you point the mouse at one of the links on the National Park Service page, the status bar displays the following message:

```
Shortcut to http://www.nps.gov/cgi-bin/imagemap/index.map
```

If the status bar displays a shorter message, such as Shortcut to index.map, the Show Friendly Addresses option has been set. You can tell Internet Explorer to display *complete* Internet addresses for links by choosing View⇨Options, clicking the Advanced tab, unchecking the Show friendly URLs check box, and then clicking OK.

Yes, you can go back

Exploring links on the Web can be kind of like exploring paths in the woods. You see a link that looks promising, so you take it. The page the link leads to has other links that look promising, so you pick one and take it. And so on, until pretty soon you're lost. You should have marked your path with bread crumbs.

Fortunately, Internet Explorer allows you to retrace your steps easily. Two buttons on the toolbar exist for just this purpose:

 ✔ The Back button moves backward along the path you've taken. Clicking this button retraces the links you've followed, only backward. You can click the Back button several times in a row if necessary to retrace your steps through several links.

 ✔ The Forward button moves you forward along your path. As long as you keep plowing ahead, this button is grayed out — meaning you can't use it. However, after you begin to retrace your steps with the Back button, the Forward button becomes active. Clicking the Forward button takes you to the page where you were when you clicked the Back button.

It's all history now

Internet Explorer automatically keeps track of the pages you've visited during the current session. To quickly return to one of these pages, click <u>G</u>o on the menu bar to open the Go menu. Near the bottom of the menu, you find the five Web sites you have most recently visited. You can quickly return to one of these sites simply by selecting the site from the Go menu.

Internet Explorer also keeps track of all the Web pages you have visited for the past 14 days. To access this two-week history, choose <u>G</u>o⊏>Open <u>H</u>istory Folder. A list of Web addresses appears, as in Figure 3-6. You can display any page in this list by double-clicking on its name.

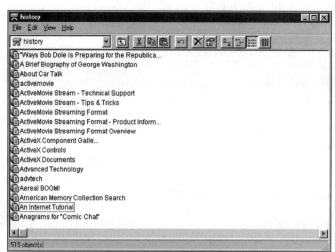

Figure 3-6: The history folder.

Don't forget that every place you visit is recorded in the history folder. Thus, the history folder provides a record of where you've been and what you've seen . . . and that can be incriminating! However, you can delete individual items from the history folder by clicking them and then pressing the Delete key. Poof!

If your kid denies that he's been sneaking peaks at www.playboy.com, pop up the history folder and find out. (Pretty tricky, eh?) Hmm. You're pretty sure he's been lurking at www.playboy.com, but you don't see a record of it in the history folder? Try checking the Recycle Bin. Any item deleted from the history folder remains in the Recycle Bin until you (or someone else) empties the Recycle Bin. Of course, if the kids read this book, they'll know all your tricks. Better tear out this page before anyone else sees it.

Going home

Exploring the Web can be fun, but sometimes the exploration turns out to be a wild goose chase. Fortunately, Internet Explorer can bail you out if you find yourself hopelessly lost. Just click the Home button, and you're instantly transported to your start page. Then you can start over with a clean slate.

If you want to change your start page, may I recommend Chapter 7?

Going to a specific page

What if a friend gives you the address of a Web page you want to check out? No problem. To visit a specific Web page for which you know the address, all you have to do is follow these simple steps:

1. **Click the mouse anywhere in the address area.**

   Refer to Figure 3-4.

2. **Type the address of the Web page you want to retrieve.**

3. **Press Enter.**

Many Web addresses are complicated — complicated enough that typing them without making a mistake is difficult. Fortunately, if you already have the Web address in another document, such as a word processing document or e-mail message, you can always copy and paste it into Internet Explorer's Address list box. Here's how:

1. **From Internet Explorer, press Alt+Tab and then open the document or e-mail message that contains the address you want to copy.**

2. Highlight the entire address and then press Ctrl+C to copy the address to the clipboard.

If you're a mouse fan, you can select Edit⇨Copy.

3. Press Alt+Tab again to return to Internet Explorer.

You may have to press Alt+Tab several times to bring up Internet Explorer, depending on what other programs are currently running.

4. Click in the Address list box in the toolbar.

5. Press Ctrl+V to paste the address.

Pressing Ctrl+V is the only way to accomplish this paste; for some unknown reason, the Edit⇨Paste command doesn't work with the Address field.

6. Press Enter.

Printing a Web Page

If you find a page with really interesting information that you want to print a copy of, all you have to do is print the page. Make sure that your printer's turned on and ready to go; then follow these steps:

1. Choose File⇨Print.

The Print dialog box appears, as shown in Figure 3-7.

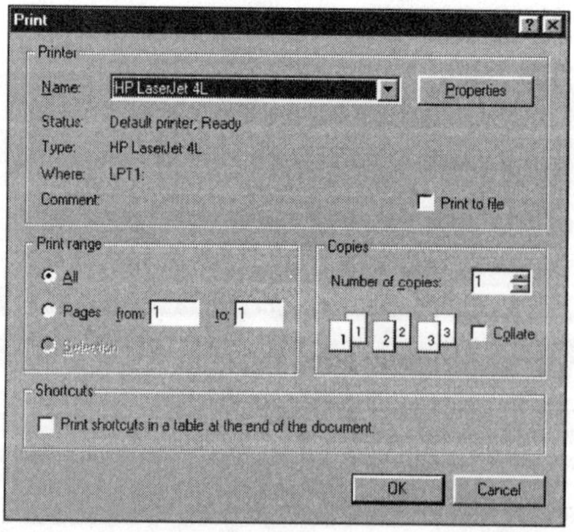

Figure 3-7: The Print dialog box.

2. **Stare at the Print dialog box for a moment.**

   If you have more than one printer at your disposal, make sure that the correct printer is selected in the Name drop-down list. If you want to print more than one copy of the page, change the Number of copies setting.

3. **Click OK.**

4. **Wait a moment while your printer grinds and whirls.**

 A faster way to print a Web page — assuming that you want only one copy and you know that the correct printer has already been selected as your default printer — is to simply click the Print button.

Saving a Page

You can save the contents of any Web page to a file on your computer by following these steps:

1. **Choose File⇨Save As File.**

   The Save As dialog box appears, as shown in Figure 3-8.

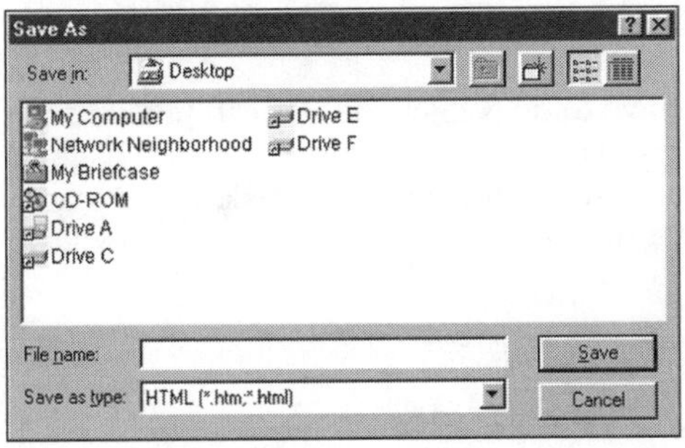

Figure 3-8:
The Save As
dialog box.

2. **Select a suitable location for the file.**

   By default, Internet Explorer saves the file on your desktop. If this is not an appropriate location, you can browse your way to a better locale.

3. **Type a name for the file you want to save in the File name field.**

4. **Choose the file type in the Save as type field.**

   You have two choices: HTML (which saves the page complete with formatting) and Plain Text (which saves the text without the formatting information).

5. **Click the Save button.**

If you don't want to save the entire page as a text file, you can select the text you want to save and then press Ctrl+C to copy it. Next, switch to a word processing program, such as Microsoft Word, open an existing document or create a new document, and then press Ctrl+V to paste the copied text into the document.

Refreshing a Page

The first time you access a Web page, Internet Explorer copies the entire page over the network from the Web site to your computer. Depending on the size and complexity of the page and the speed of your connection, this process can take a few seconds or a few minutes.

To avoid repeating this download, Internet Explorer saves the information for the page in a special area of your hard disk known as the *cache* (rhymes with *sashay*). The next time you retrieve the same page from the Web, your computer will get the page directly from your hard disk rather than download it again from the Web site. Thus, you get to see the page much faster.

What happens if the page has changed since the last time you downloaded it? Most Web pages don't change very often, but some do. In fact, some pages change daily or even more often. For such pages, you can force Internet Explorer to refresh its view of the page.

To refresh a page, all you have to do is click the Refresh button and then twiddle your thumbs while Internet Explorer downloads the page. Refreshing a page takes longer than grabbing it from your hard disk, but at least you know that the information is current.

Stopping a Long Download

Every once in a while, you wander into a Web page you wish you hadn't. The link that led you to the page may have looked interesting, but after you get there, the page isn't what you expected. According to Murphy's Law, that page will also be the page that has a 200K graphic that takes forever to download.

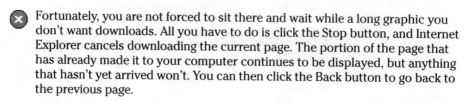

Fortunately, you are not forced to sit there and wait while a long graphic you don't want downloads. All you have to do is click the Stop button, and Internet Explorer cancels downloading the current page. The portion of the page that has already made it to your computer continues to be displayed, but anything that hasn't yet arrived won't. You can then click the Back button to go back to the previous page.

Sometimes, you go to a page that appears to remain blank while a large graphic is downloading. In many cases, simply scrolling the page a bit reveals text that has already been downloaded to your computer, but which (for some reason) Internet Explorer hasn't yet displayed. Any time you find yourself staring at a blank page that appears to be in the midst of downloading a large graphic, try clicking in one of the scroll bars just to see whether any text is hiding.

Exiting Internet Explorer

After you're finished browsing the Web, you can exit Internet Explorer using any of the following techniques:

- Choose File➪Exit.
- Click the Close button, which is located at the top right corner of the Internet Explorer window. (It's the one with an X in it.)
- Press Alt+F4.

After closing Internet Explorer, you should disconnect from your Internet Service Provider. To do so, press Alt+Tab (several times if necessary) to bring up the Connected to dialog box that you see in Figure 3-9. Then click the Disconnect button.

Figure 3-9: The Connected to dialog box.

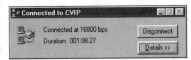

Be aware that connect time charges continue to accumulate if you close Internet Explorer but forget to disconnect from your ISP. The extra time probably won't hurt if you pay a flat monthly rate with unlimited access, but if you're paying $2.00 or $2.50 per hour, you don't want to remain accidentally connected overnight!

Chapter 4

Searching the Web

*M*any people think of the Internet as a vast library of online information, but the Internet hardly resembles a library. Libraries are run by compulsive neat freaks known as *librarians,* whose mission in life is to make sure that, at least within their library, there is a place for everything and everything is in its place. In the old days, librarians devoted much of their energy to maintaining the ever-useful card catalog, which served as a crude but effective index to every book in the library. Nowadays, most libraries have replaced their card catalogs with more-sophisticated online card catalogs. So now, not only is every book in the library indexed in the catalog, but you can find any book by searching for it according to author, title, or subject.

Contrary to popular belief, the Internet is nothing like a library; no one person or organization is officially in charge of the Internet. Anyone can put anything on the Internet, and no one is responsible for making sure that new entries are cataloged in any way, shape, or form.

Fortunately, all is not lost. Several excellent search services are available to help you locate information on the Internet. Although none of these services is truly comprehensive, several of them come pretty close. No matter what you're looking for, these services are likely to turn up a few Internet sites that pertain to that topic.

Finding Stuff Fast

The easiest way to locate information on the Internet is to click the Search button in Internet Explorer's toolbar. Doing so takes you to the Microsoft all-in-one search page, as shown in Figure 4-1.

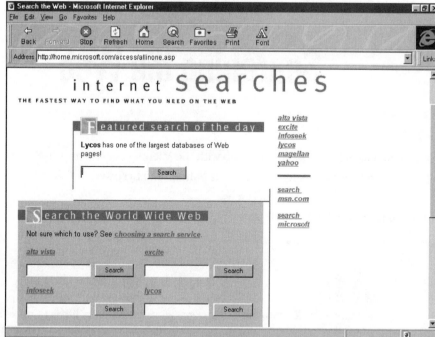

Figure 4-1:
The
Microsoft
all-in-one
search
page.

The Microsoft all-in-one search page enables you to search the Internet using any of several popular search services. All you have to do is type in the word or phrase you want to search for in the appropriate box and then click the Search button for the service you want to search.

If you obtained your copy of Internet Explorer from someone other than Microsoft, you may discover that the Search button leads you to a different search page. For example, your local ISP might distribute its own customized version of Internet Explorer that uses a different search page. If so, go ahead and try the search page you get. If you want to try out the Microsoft search page, just go to the following address:

```
home.microsoft.com/access/allinone.asp
```

You can reconfigure Internet Explorer to use any Web page you wish as your default search page. See the section "Changing Your Default Search Page," later in this chapter, to find out how.

About the search services

The following search services are accessible from the Microsoft all-in-one search page:

- ✔ **AltaVista:** AltaVista is a large and fast catalog of individual Web pages found throughout the Internet. It includes Usenet discussion groups.

- ✔ **Excite:** The Excite search service indexes millions of Web pages, plus Usenet classified ads and newsgroup articles.

- ✔ **Infoseek:** Infoseek is a large database that indexes millions of Web pages. It also allows you to browse through its catalog by subject.

- ✔ **Lycos:** Lycos is a very large database of Internet information that is compiled by the computer nerds at Carnegie Mellon University. It's my personal favorite when I'm looking for obscure information.

- ✔ **Magellan:** Magellan is not just an index of Web sites, but also includes reviews of many sites.

- ✔ **Yahoo!:** Yahoo! is one of the most popular search services on the Internet. It allows you to search by keyword or to browse by category. Yahoo! is usually where I begin my search efforts.

You can find out more information about each of these search services by clicking the link above the service's text box.

Using the all-in-one search page

To use the all-in-one search page to search for information on the Internet, just follow these easy steps:

 1. **Click the Search button on the toolbar.**

   The all-in-one search page appears (refer back to Figure 4-1).

2. **Pick a search service.**

   If you're new to Internet searching, just start with the first one: AltaVista. As you gain experience with the Internet, try each of the search services and decide for yourself which one you like best.

3. **Type the word or phrase you're looking for in the text box for the search service you want to use.**

   For example, type the word **potato** in the Excite text box. (Note that most search services are not sensitive to case, so you can use lower- or upper-case letters interchangeably.)

4. **Click the Search button next to the search service you want to use.**

   Your search request is submitted to the search service you selected.

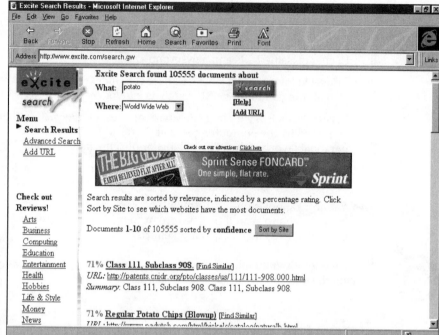

Figure 4-2:
Excite finds
several
entries for
potato.

5. Whistle "Dixie."

You'll probably be able to make it through the song at least once before the results of the search appear. The format in which the search results are displayed depends on which search service you chose. Figure 4-2 shows how Excite displays the results of a search for the word *potato.* The results for other search services are similar.

6. If you find something that looks promising, click it.

Internet Explorer follows the link to the page you select.

7. If nothing looks promising, click the link for the next set of entries.

Each search service displays only a certain number of *hits* at a time, typically 10 or 15. If none of the hits on the first page look promising, scroll to the bottom of the page and look for a link that says something along the lines of <u>Next 10 Entries</u>. Clicking this link displays additional results for the search.

Here are some thoughts to keep in mind when searching:

✔ If the search comes up empty, try again using a different search word or phrase. For example, try **spuds** instead of **potato**. Or try using one of the other search services. Or check your spelling: Maybe you'll have better luck if you search for **potatoe.**

✔ When picking search words, try to think of words that are specific enough that you don't end up with thousands of hits, but general enough to encompass the topic you're trying to find.

✔ Most of the search services list their results in sorted order, with the pages that most closely match your search criteria listed first. In particular, if you search on two words, those pages that contain both words are listed before pages in which just one of the words appears.

✔ Don't forget that you can always use the Back button in the toolbar to return to the all-in-one search page. Depending on how far you've traveled in your quest, you may have to click several times.

More thorough searches

Did you notice the menu of search services that appears at the top of the all-in-one search page? If you click the name of one of the search services in this menu, you see a page devoted to that search service. For example, Figure 4-3 shows the page that appears when you click the excite link. As you can see, this search service enables you to search by concept or keyword, and you can restrict the search to Web pages, classifieds, or Usenet newsgroups.

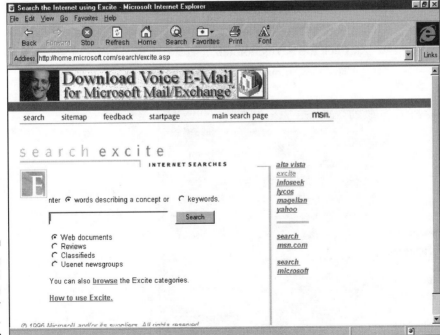

Figure 4-3: Additional search options for Excite.

Each of the search services has its own special options for performing different types of searches. For example, some services allow you to search only for pages that include all of the words you list. Unfortunately, the rules for indicating such advanced searches are different for each search service. You can find out what types of searches a given service allows by following the <u>How to choose search terms</u> link that appears on each search page accessible from the Microsoft all-in-one search page.

Changing Your Default Search Page

Although the Microsoft all-in-one search page is interesting and useful, it's not the only search service available. In fact, you have dozens of search services to choose from. Fortunately, Internet Explorer enables you to easily change the search page that it displays when you click the Search button. Just follow these steps to display your favorite search page when you click the Search button:

1. **Navigate to the search page you want to use.**

   The remaining sections of this chapter contain information about several excellent search pages. Find the one you want to use, type its address in the Address field, and then press Enter.

2. **Choose View⇨Options.**

   The Options dialog box appears.

3. **Click the Navigation tab.**

   The Navigation options appear, as shown in Figure 4-4.

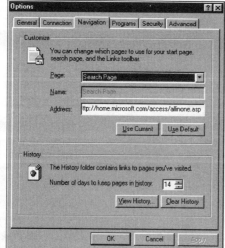

Figure 4-4:
Setting a new search page from the Navigation options.

4. From the **P**age drop-down list, choose Search Page.

5. Click the **U**se Current button.

> The page you are currently viewing becomes your search page.

6. Click OK.

Now when you click the Search button, Internet Explorer takes you to your designated search page rather than Microsoft's.

You can change your default search page back to the Microsoft all-in-one search page at any time by following these steps:

1. Choose **V**iew⇨**O**ptions.

2. Click the Navigation tab.

3. From the **P**age drop-down list, choose Search Page.

4. Click U**s**e Default.

5. Click OK.

Popular Search Services

The following sections describe the most popular search services, all of which appear on the Microsoft all-in-one search page, but which you can also reach directly by entering each service's URL. Each of these services has its own peculiar approach to categorizing information and searching its database in response to your queries. As a result, you should experiment with the various services to determine which one best suits your needs.

AltaVista

```
www.altavista.digital.com
```

AltaVista is a project of Digital Equipment Corporation, one of the largest computer companies in the world. AltaVista uses a special program called a *spider,* which automatically reads and catalogs 3 million Web pages every day. The AltaVista catalog lists more than 30 million Web pages. Figure 4-5 gives you a glimpse of the AltaVista home page.

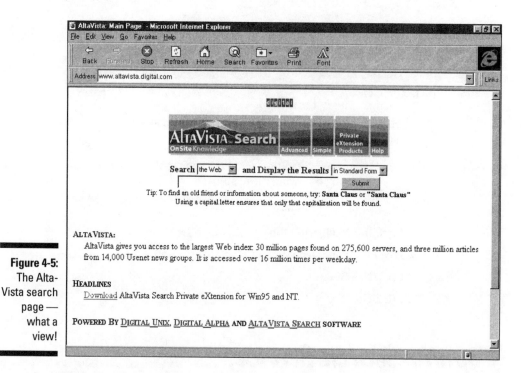

Figure 4-5:
The Alta-
Vista search
page —
what a
view!

Excite

www.excite.com

Excite is a search service that includes not only Web sites but also Usenet newsgroup articles. (Chapter 12 covers Usenet newsgroups.) Excite's opening page appears in Figure 4-6.

In addition to ordinary search capabilities, Excite offers the following additional cool services:

- **Reviews:** Excite includes more than 60,000 reviews of Web sites, which are arranged by category. To access these reviews, click the reviews link in the graphic at the top of the Excite home page.

- **News:** The news link takes you to a list of the day's top news stories, with links to related Web sites.

- **Custom start page:** You can also click the Personal Excite link, located in the left column of the page, to go to a form you can fill out to create your very own, custom start page (see Chapter 7).

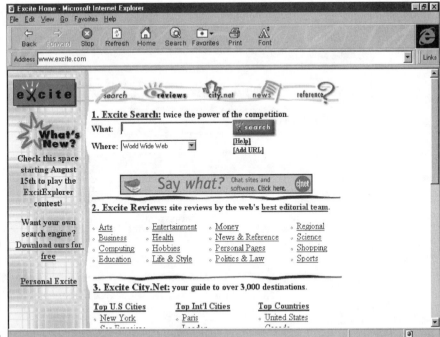

Figure 4-6:
Excite's
exciting
search
service.

Infoseek

`www.infoseek.com`

Infoseek enables you to browse through category listings or search by key-words. Infoseek is not just limited to the Web; it also allows you to search Usenet newsgroups, e-mail addresses, news stories from Reuters News, and a catalog of Frequently Asked Question (FAQ) files from popular newsgroups. Infoseek's main page appears in Figure 4-7.

Infoseek also includes a personalized start page, called *Infoseek Personal,* which allows you to customize the information you want displayed on your start page (see Chapter 7). To create your own Infoseek start page, click the <u>Your News</u> link (the cute button with the little puppy).

Lycos

`www.lycos.com`

Lycos is a huge Web index affiliated with Carnegie Mellon University. Lycos is primarily a keyword search tool, but it also includes categories you can browse. Figure 4-8 shows the Lycos opening page.

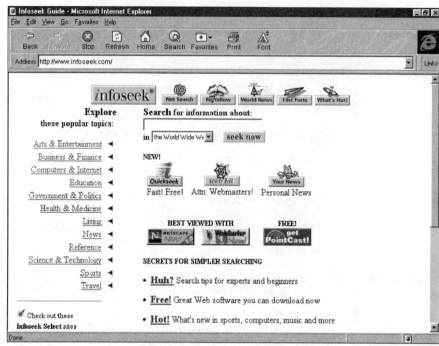

Figure 4-7:
Infoseek
and ye
shall find.

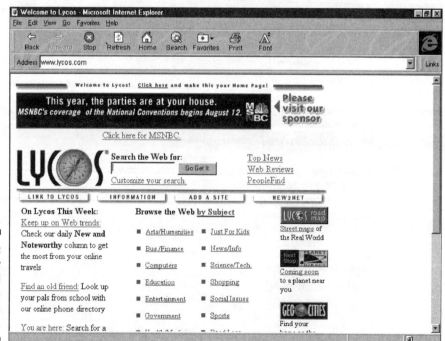

Figure 4-8:
Lycos: My
personal
favorite
search
page.

What's with all the advertisements?

Just when you thought the Internet was kind of like public television, along comes advertising. You may have noticed that most of the pages for the search services described in this chapter include commercials. What's the deal?

The deal is that these advertisements are how the search services are able to offer their services free of charge. The business model for Internet search services is actually very similar to commercial television. The programming is free; the companies make their money by selling advertising space. So the next time you see a McDonald's or J C Penney ad on your favorite search page, don't curse it. Instead, remember that if it weren't for the advertising, you would have to pay some kind of access charge or membership fee to cover the cost of maintaining the service.

You can perform a customized search by clicking the <u>Customize your search</u> link. Doing so brings up the customized search page shown in Figure 4-9.

The Lycos customized search page enables you to change the search options in the following ways:

- ✔ You can indicate how many of the words you type (Lycos calls these keywords *terms*) must occur in the page for the page to be considered a match. The default (match any term) is that only one of the terms you type must be found, but you can change the setting to find only those pages that contain all the words you enter (match all terms). Or you can specify that two, three, or up to seven of the terms must appear in the pages Lycos retrieves.

- ✔ You can indicate how closely the words must match the words you typed. The choices are loose match, fair match, good match, close match, and strong match. If the default option, loose match, results in hundreds of pages that seem unrelated to your search, change to a more selective option and try the search again.

- ✔ You can indicate how many search results to show per page. The default is 10, but you can change it to 20, 30, or 40.

- ✔ You can select the amount of information to be displayed for each result. The default, Standard results, displays the name of the link, the link's title, and an abstract that sometimes (but not always) includes a helpful description of the page. You can change this option to Summary, which displays only the name of the link, or to Detailed, which displays more detailed information than the Standard format.

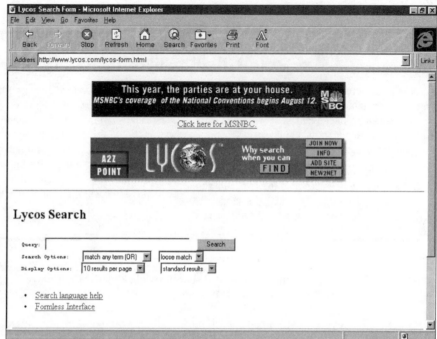

Figure 4-9:
The Lycos
customized
search
page.

Where did the name Lycos come from? It's derived from the Latin word for Wolf Spider. You can read Lycos's own explanation at `www.lycos.com/reference/etymology.html`:

> "Lycos comes from *Lycosidae,* a cosmopolitan family of relatively large active ground spiders that catch their prey by pursuit, rather than in a web. They are noted for their running speed, and are especially active at night."

Magellan

`www.mckinley.com`

Magellan, named after the great explorer, offers an extensive list of sites arranged by categories, plus a searchable keyword index. Many of the Magellan sites have been rated and reviewed; you can choose to search the entire database, or only the rated and reviewed sites. Figure 4-10 shows the Magellan opening page.

Like many of the other search services, Magellan offers additional features such as sports, news and weather, and hot site listings.

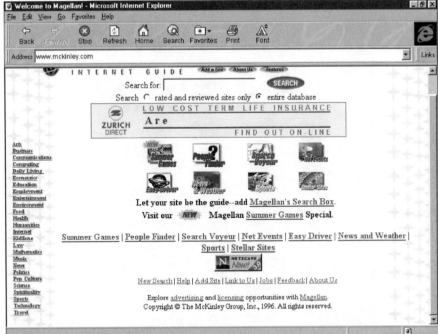

Yahoo!

www.yahoo.com

Yahoo! is one of the most popular search services around. It contains tens of thousands of listings, organized into categories such as Art, Business and Economy, Computers and Internet, Education, and so on. You can browse through Yahoo!'s categories or search for specific pages by keyword. Yahoo!'s opening page appears in Figure 4-11.

To search for a keyword in Yahoo!, type the word or words you want to search for in the text box and then click the Search button. If you want to, you can click the <u>options</u> link to display a page that gives you more selective control over your searches.

At the top of the page, Yahoo! includes a few other services you may find interesting:

✔ **New:** Click <u>New</u> to see a list of new entries in the Yahoo! database. Note that on a typical day, 2,000 or more entries are added to the Yahoo! database.

✔ **Cool:** Click <u>Cool</u> to see a list of sites that the Yahoo! staff thinks is worth checking out.

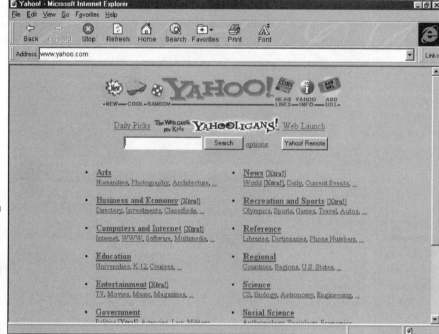

Figure 4-11:
Yahoo! is
one of the
hottest
search
services on
the Net.

✔ **Random:** Click Random to go to a Web page chosen at random — the ultimate way to wander aimlessly about the Web.

✔ **Headlines:** Click Headlines to see a list of newsworthy items, sorted into categories such as Business, Technology, World, Sports, Entertainment, Politics, and Weather.

Yahoo! was founded by two college students at Stanford University. Rumor has it that Yahoo! stands for *Yet Another Hierarchical Officious Oracle,* but the two student founders deny the allegation.

Other All-In-One Search Pages

Microsoft isn't the only company that has created an all-in-one search page. Several others exist. In fact, Yahoo! has an entire category devoted to all-in-one search pages, with more than 70 listings. Savvy Search and MetaCrawler are two all-in-one pages you may want to consider using.

You can access any of these search pages simply by typing the page's URL into Internet Explorer's address area and pressing Enter. If you find that you prefer one of these pages to the Microsoft all-in-one search page, you can always set the preferred page as your default search page for Internet Explorer. Refer back to the section "Changing Your Default Search Page" for more information.

MetaCrawler

```
metacrawler.cs.washington.edu:8080/index.html
```

Unlike the Microsoft all-in-one search page, which forces you to choose from several popular search services, MetaCrawler actually sends your search requests to nine different search services at the same time. MetaCrawler then consolidates the search results into a single listing. Figure 4-12 shows MetaCrawler's search page:

MetaCrawler sends your search requests simultaneously to the following nine search services:

- ✔ AltaVista
- ✔ Excite
- ✔ Galaxy
- ✔ Infoseek
- ✔ Inktomi
- ✔ Lycos
- ✔ Open Text
- ✔ Web Crawler
- ✔ Yahoo!

Savvy Search

```
guaraldi.cs.colostate.edu:2000
```

Savvy Search is similar to MetaCrawler, but it queries even more search services — 19 in all. The results are consolidated and displayed in sorted order. Figure 4-13 shows the Savvy Search search page, which you reach by clicking the Search link from the Savvy Search home page.

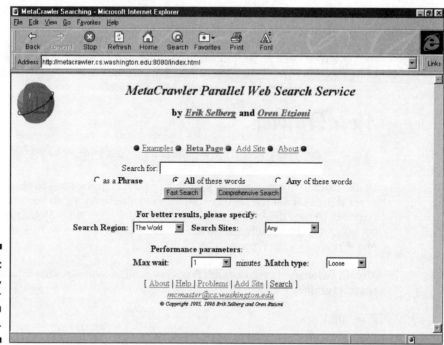

Figure 4-12:
MetaCrawler,
a true all-in-
one search
page.

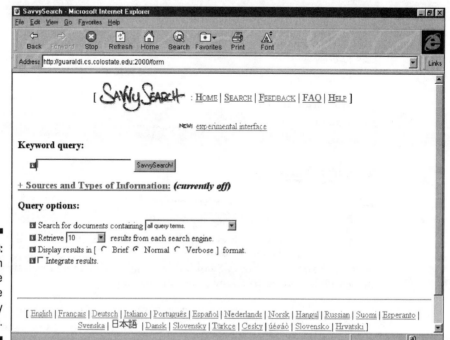

Figure 4-13:
The search
form for the
all-in-one
Savvy
Search.

Chapter 5

Internet Explorer Shortcuts and Timesavers

· ·

In This Chapter

▶ Building a list of your favorite Web pages

▶ Downloading files from the World Wide Web

▶ Locating text on a page

▶ Speeding performance by skipping the glitzy pictures, sounds, and videos

▶ Saving your eyesight by displaying text in a larger size

· ·

*T*hink of this chapter as a bag of useful tricks for surfing the Web with Internet Explorer. Although these tricks are strictly optional, several of them are so helpful that you may find yourself using them every day.

Right-Clicking

Like just about everything else in Windows 95, Internet Explorer puts the right mouse button to good use. When you click the right mouse button, a pop-up menu appears, as shown in Figure 5-1.

The commands that appear on this pop-up menu vary depending on what you were pointing to when you right-clicked. Table 5-1 summarizes the function of each command that may appear on the pop-up menu. Note that not all these commands appear in each pop-up menu; the exact mix of commands that appears depends on what type of object you right-click. For example, if you right-click a picture, a pop-up menu appears that includes commands for manipulating pictures. But if you right-click a text link, the picture commands aren't included.

Throughout this chapter, I describe the little tricks and shortcuts possible by right-clicking the mouse.

Figure 5-1:
Right-click
to call up a
pop-up
menu.

Table 5-1   Commands That Appear in Pop-Up Menus

Command	What It Does
Open	Opens a hyperlink, the same as if you clicked on the link
Open in New Window	Opens the link in a new window while leaving the current page open in the current window, allowing you to toggle between windows by pressing Alt+Tab
Save Target As	Saves (as a file on your hard disk) the content of the Web page you're currently viewing so you can access it later without connecting to the Internet
Save Picture As	Saves a graphic image as a file on your hard disk
Set As Wallpaper	Uses a graphic image as your Windows 95 wallpaper
Copy	Copies the selected item to the clipboard
Copy Shortcut	Copies the address (URL) of a Web link to the clipboard
Add to Favorites	Adds the current page or shortcut to your Favorites folder
View Source	Displays the HTML source file for the current page in a separate window
Properties	Displays a Properties dialog box for the selected item

Playing Favorites

The World Wide Web offers millions of interesting destinations. Exploring them all just to see what's available would be fun, assuming you could live long enough. But after you've seen a few hundred or a few thousand Web pages, you'll probably come to realize that not all Web pages are created equal. You soon settle on a few Web sites that are your personal favorites.

Internet Explorer's Favorites feature is designed to allow you to get to those few favorite Web sites as quickly as possible, without having to remember a bunch of Web addresses or navigate your way through link after link. The following sections describe how to use Internet Explorer's Favorites feature.

Adding a page to Favorites

To designate a Web page as one of your Favorites so that you can later find it quickly, follow these steps:

1. **Browse your way to the page you want to add to your list of favorite pages.**

 2. **Click the Favorites button on the toolbar and then select Add to Favorites (or choose Favorites⇨Add to Favorites).**

   The Add to Favorites dialog box appears, as shown in Figure 5-2. The Name text box displays the name of the Web site you want to add to your Favorites list.

Figure 5-2:
The Add to Favorites dialog box.

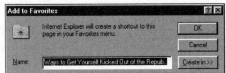

3. **Click the OK button.**

   The Web page is added to the Favorites menu.

 If you're on a Web page that contains a link to another Web page that you want to add to your Favorites menu, you can right-click the link you want to add; then choose Add to Favorites from the pop-up menu that appears. This trick adds the link to your Favorites list without actually taking you to that Web site.

Going to one of your favorite places

After you've added your favorite Web pages to the Favorites menu, you can call up the Favorites menu to quickly go to any of the pages it contains. Here's how:

 1. **Choose Favorites from the menu bar (or click the Favorites button).**

   The Favorites menu reveals your list of favorite places, as shown in Figure 5-3.

2. **Select the Web page you want to view, and off you go.**

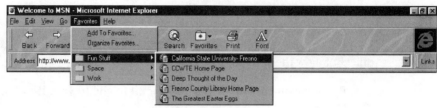

Figure 5-3:
The
Favorites
menu.

Using Favorites folders

If you keep adding pages to it, pretty soon the Favorites menu becomes so full of your favorite links that you won't be able to find anything. To ease crowding on the Favorites menu, and to help you organize your favorite links, Internet Explorer lets you create separate folders in which you can categorize your favorite sites.

To create a Favorites folder in which to place the Web page you're viewing, follow these steps:

1. **Choose Favorites⇨Add to Favorites.**

   The Add to Favorites dialog box appears.

2. **Click Create In>>.**

   The Add to Favorites dialog box expands, as shown in Figure 5-4.

3. **Click the New Folder button.**

4. **Type a name for the new folder.**

5. **Click OK.**

When you click the Favorites button, notice that the folders within the Favorites menu appear as menu items with arrows next to them. If you point the mouse to one of these menu items, a second menu appears, listing the contents of the folder.

Organizing your Favorites

Eventually, your Favorites menu becomes filled with Web links that no longer hold your interest, that are out of date, or that just need to be reorganized. When you reach this point, it's time to roll up your sleeves and reorganize your Favorites. Fortunately, Internet Explorer provides a command just for this purpose.

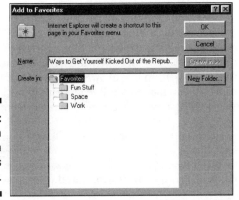

Figure 5-4:
Adding a
page to a
Favorites
folder.

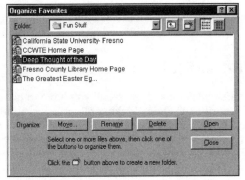

To organize your Favorites, click the Favorites button on the toolbar and select Organize Favorites (or choose Favorites➪Organize Favorites from the menu bar). The Organize Favorites dialog box appears, as shown in Figure 5-5.

Figure 5-5:
The
Organize
Favorites
folder.

The buttons in the Organize Favorites dialog box allow you to delete, rename, or move items around in your Favorites folders.

- To delete a page or folder, select the page or folder and then click the Delete button.

- To rename a page or folder, select the page or folder and click the Rename button. Type a new name for the page or folder and then click OK.

- To move a page or folder, select the page or folder and click the Move button. Then select the folder to which you want move the item and click OK.

Quick Links

Internet Explorer's Favorites are a great way to keep track of all the Web pages you visit periodically. However, Internet Explorer provides an even more convenient method of quickly visiting up to five of your absolute favorite Web sites: Quick Links. Quick Links lets you place your five favorite Web sites on a Quick Links toolbar that you can access with just a few clicks of the mouse.

When you first install Internet Explorer, the Quick Links toolbar is configured with the following five default links:

- ✔ **Today's Links:** A set of links to cool Web sites updated weekly by the Microsoft staff

- ✔ **Services:** A page with links to various services that are available at the Microsoft Network home page

- ✔ **Web Tutorial:** The Microsoft online help for using the World Wide Web

- ✔ **Product Update:** A page that gives you access to the latest version of Internet Explorer and its components

- ✔ **Microsoft:** Takes you directly to the Microsoft home page

Accessing Quick Links

To access Internet Explorer's Quick Links feature, all you have to do is summon the Quick Links menu. Ordinarily, the Quick Links toolbar is obscured by the Address toolbar. To reveal the Quick Links toolbar, click on the word *Links* near the top right of the Internet Explorer window. Doing so reveals the Quick Links menu, as shown in Figure 5-6.

To access one of the Quick Links, just click on its button. To show the Address toolbar again, click the word Address to the left of the QuickLinks toolbar.

⌐Quick Links toolbar

Figure 5-6:
Getting to
your top five
sites fast.

Creating your own Quick Links

Internet Explorer allows you to customize the Quick Links toolbar so that the five Quick Links point to any Web page you wish. To customize any of the five Quick Links, follow these steps:

1. **Find a Web page that you want to display in the Internet Explorer window as a Quick Link.**

2. **Choose View⇨Options and click the Navigation tab.**

   The Navigation options appear, as shown in Figure 5-7.

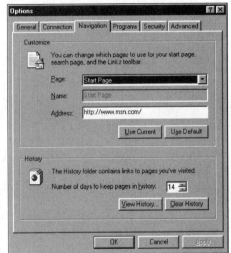

Figure 5-7:
Setting the
Navigation
options.

3. **Click the down arrow next to the Page drop-down list and select the Quick Link you want to use.**

   You have five selections from which to choose: Quick Link 1, Quick Link 2, and so on — up to Quick Link 5.

4. **Click the Use Current button.**

5. **Type a name for your Quick Link in the Name field.**

6. **Click OK.**

The Quick Links toolbar now displays the Quick Link you created.

To restore a Quick Link to its default setting, open the Navigation options, select the Quick Link you want to restore, and click the Use Default button.

Downloading Files

One of the main reasons many people use the Internet is to *download files* — that is, to copy files from other computer systems and place them on their own computers. The Internet offers many types of files for downloading: documents, pictures, sounds, movies, animation, and programs.

Internet Explorer makes downloading files easy. In fact, the only hard part is finding the file you want to download. The best way to find a file to download is to search for the file using one of the search services described in Chapter 4. For example, if you want to download the popular computer game *Doom,* use any of the search services to search for the word Doom. You're sure to find several sites from which you can download the file.

To actually download a file, just follow these steps:

1. **Find a Web site that contains a file that you want to download.**

   You may have to use one of the search services described in Chapter 4. Usually, a search leads you to a page that includes a link that you can click to download the file. This link usually, but not always, gives you some indication of how large the file is. For example, Figure 5-8 shows a page at `www.microsoft.com` from which you can download a program called Internet Assistant for PowerPoint. You can see that clicking the <u>Click to download pptia.exe (253K)</u> link downloads a 253K program file.

2. **Click the link to download the file.**

   Internet Explorer grinds and churns for a moment. Eventually, the dialog box shown in Figure 5-9 appears.

3. **Click OK.**

   A dialog box displays a progress bar that allows you to monitor the download progress, as shown in Figure 5-10.

4. **Wait until the download is finished.**

   After the download finishes, the file opens. If the file is a graphics file, sound clip, or other type of document file, an appropriate program launches to allow you to view (or hear) the file. If the file is a program, the program runs. In many cases, the file is an installation program that sets up an application on your hard disk.

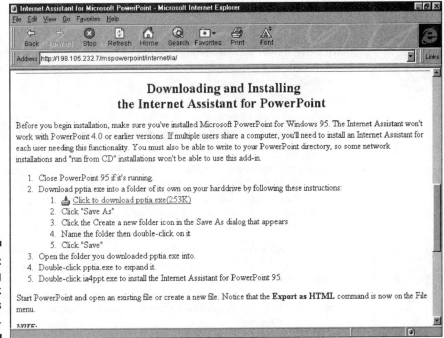

Figure 5-8:
Clicking
this link
downloads
a large file.

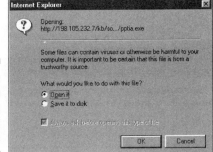

Figure 5-9:
Use caution
when
downloading
files.

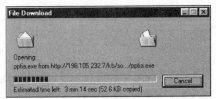

Figure 5-10:
The
progress
bar tracks
download
time.

Here are some pertinent points to ponder when performing a download:

✔ You should always make sure that you have enough disk space on your hard drive before downloading a large file. Nothing is more frustrating than discovering that you have only 3MB of free disk space an hour into a 4MB download.

To check your free disk space, double-click the My Computer icon on your desktop and then click the icon for your C drive. The My Computer window displays the amount of free space on the C drive in the status bar at the bottom of the window.

✔ You don't have to open the file when you download it. If you just want to save a copy of the file on your hard disk, click the Save it to disk option when the dialog box shown in Figure 5-9 appears. You are greeted with a standard Save As dialog box, allowing you to specify the folder in which you want to save the file.

✔ You don't have to twiddle your thumbs while the file is downloading. In fact, as I write this, I am downloading a 4MB file from the Internet. To continue with other work, simply click anywhere outside the progress bar dialog box. The progress bar kindly steps out of the way, allowing you to work with other programs while the download continues. You can even use Internet Explorer to browse other Web sites while the download takes its sweet time.

Saving a Picture

You can save any picture you see in a Web site as a graphic file on your hard disk. To save a picture, all you have to do is follow these steps:

1. **Right-click the picture you want to save.**

   A pop-up menu appears.

2. **Choose the Save Picture As command.**

   A standard Save As dialog box appears, as shown in Figure 5-11.

Figure 5-11:
The Save As
dialog box.

3. **Navigate to the folder in which you want to save the file.**

4. **Type a new filename for the file, if you don't like the one that is supplied.**

5. **Click the Save button.**

Note that you can also choose to use the picture as your desktop wallpaper. Simply right-click the image and then select Set As Wallpaper.

Beware of copyright protections when you save a graphic. Many images, especially artwork, photographs, and company logos, are copyrighted. If you save a graphic that may be protected by copyright law, be sure to get the owner's permission before you use the graphic.

Finding Text

Sometimes, you stumble across a large page of text that you know contains some useful tidbit of information, but you can't seem to locate the information you're trying to find. When this happens, you can use the Find command to locate text on the page. Simply follow these steps:

1. **Choose Edit⇨Find (or press Ctrl+F).**

   The Find dialog box appears, as shown in Figure 5-12.

Figure 5-12:
The Find
dialog box.

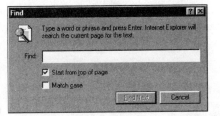

2. **Type in the text that you want to find.**

3. **Click Find Next.**

   Internet Explorer finds the first occurrence of the text on the current page. The Find dialog box remains active, so you can quickly find additional occurrences of the text.

4. **Keep clicking Find Next until you find the text you want.**

5. **Click Cancel to close the Find dialog box.**

Keep in mind that the Find command searches for text only on the current page; it does not search the Internet for other pages that have the text you're trying to find. To do that type of search, you must use one of the search services described in Chapter 4.

Turning Off Pictures, Sound, and Video

Pictures, sound, and video are what make the World Wide Web interesting. Those multimedia elements are also what make the Web so darn slow. If you're stuck browsing the Web with 14,400 bps modem or slower, you may enjoy your Web time more if you strip away the pictures. True, the pages won't look as good. But for most pages, the really important content is in the text — and text loads quickly compared to graphics.

To tell Internet Explorer not to automatically download graphics, sounds, and videos, follow these steps:

1. **Choose View⇨Options.**

   The Options dialog box appears.

2. **Click the General tab.**

   The General options appear, as shown in Figure 5-13.

3. **To disable pictures, sounds, or videos, uncheck the appropriate boxes.**

   Unchecking the box prevents Internet Explorer from automatically opening pictures, sounds, or videos when you enter a Web site. Placeholders appear where the page would normally have pictures, sounds, or videos.

4. **Click OK.**

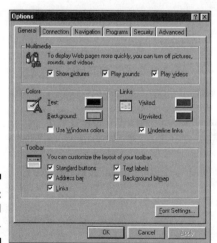

Figure 5-13:
The General
options.

Figure 5-14 shows what a typical page looks like without the fancy graphics. Note that each picture is represented by a placeholder with a bit of descriptive text. You can download or display any of the pictures simply by clicking its placeholder.

Easing Eye Strain

If you consistently find that the text displayed on the Internet is too small, you may want to visit your ophthalmologist. On the other hand, if every once in a while you come across a page you have to squint at to see, the problem may not be with your eyes; it could be that the text is simply displayed too small.

 Fortunately, Internet Explorer provides a simple solution for too-small text. All you have to do is click the Font button, and all of the text on the page jumps to a larger size. To see what a difference the size can make, compare Figures 5-15 and 5-16. Figure 5-15 shows a page displayed with normal text. Figure 5-16 shows the same page after clicking the Font button.

If the text is still too small, click again to make it larger yet. Internet Explorer has five text sizes from which to choose. Repeatedly clicking the Font button cycles through the five sizes, so after you get to the largest size, clicking the Font button once more returns you to the smallest size.

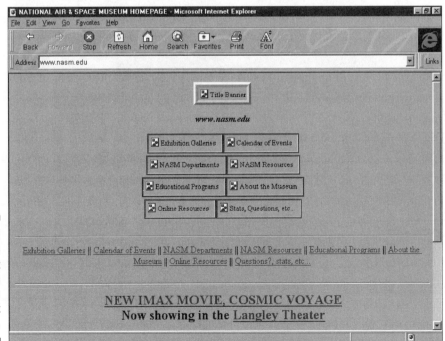

Figure 5-14:
A page
without
pictures is
like a zoo
without
monkeys.

Figure 5-15:
A page with normal-sized text.

Figure 5-16:
Use the Font button to adjust text size.

Chapter 6

Getting Help While You Explore

• •

In This Chapter

▶ Getting assistance with Internet Explorer's Help features

▶ Searching for specific help topics

▶ Using Windows 95 troubleshooters

▶ Finding help on the Internet

• •

*W*ouldn't it be great if you had a pet Internet guru who sat by at your side while you surfed the Web, ready and willing to answer your questions with straightforward answers in plain English, gently but firmly correcting you when you made silly mistakes, never giggling at you behind your back? All you'd have to do would be to keep your guru supplied with pizza and Diet Coke, and let him or her out twice a day.

The next best thing to having your own, personal Internet guide is using the Internet Explorer built-in Help features. No matter how lost you become while exploring the Internet, help is but a few keystrokes or mouse clicks away.

Summoning Help

Internet Explorer comes with an excellent built-in Help system, which can probably answer your most burning questions about the Web and Internet Explorer. You can summon this help in any of the following ways:

✔ **Press F1.** This action catapults you into Internet Explorer's Help system.

✔ **Choose Help⇨Help Topics.** This menu command is the mouse lover's equivalent to pressing F1.

✔ **Click the Question Mark icon.** Dialog boxes often have a question-mark icon near the upper-right corner. Click this icon to transform the mouse pointer into a big question mark. You can then click any field in the dialog box to call up specific help for that field.

Getting to Know the Help Window

When you call up Internet Explorer's Help system, a separate window, like the one shown in Figure 6-1, appears. This Help window has three tabs across the top, providing three different ways to access the various nuggets of help that are hidden within:

✔ **Contents:** Shows you help information arranged by subject

✔ **Index:** Enables you to locate help topics by certain keywords

✔ **Find:** Enables you to search the help text itself for specific words

You can click any of these tabs to access Help. All three tabs access the *same* help information — they just present it to you differently.

Scanning the Contents

Clicking the Contents tab of the Help window displays a window with three specific Help documents, each providing general information about the Web and Internet Explorer:

✔ Windows, the Web, and You

✔ Welcome to Internet Explorer

✔ What's New in Internet Explorer?

In addition, you find the following three categories, which give you different ways to access the contents of Help:

✔ How To...

✔ Tips and Tricks

✔ Accessibility

As Figure 6-1 shows, each category has a closed-book icon next to it. To expand a category, double-click the book icon. The help topics associated with that category appear and the closed book icon changes to an open book. In addition, a category may include subcategories, which may themselves include additional subcategories.

Notice that individual help topics (as opposed to categories that contain several topics) are represented by an icon resembling a page with a big question mark. For example, Figure 6-2 shows the Help Contents after you open the How To... category and then open the Explore the Internet category.

Figure 6-2:
Help
Contents
with some
categories
open.

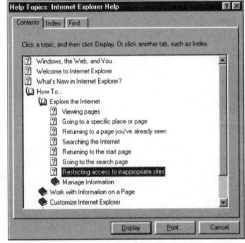

To display help for a particular topic, you can double-click the topic (or click the topic once and then click the Display button). To close a topic, double-click the topic again (or click the topic and then click the Close button).

Many help topics include small buttons that you can click to display additional help information. For example, the help topic shown in Figure 6-3 includes a Related Topics button, which you can select to display a list of other help topics that provide information on related subjects.

Figure 6-3:
Clicking the Related Topics button displays additional information.

Here are some additional tips for using help topics:

✔ Some help topics offer buttons that actually assist you in completing the task at hand. For example, the help topic on restricting access to potentially offensive Web sites includes a button that takes you directly to the Options dialog box, where you can establish such restrictions.

✔ Clicking a word or phrase underlined with a dashed line displays additional information about that term.

✔ You can move and resize the Help windows to meet your needs. As you resize a Help window, the help text automatically adjusts to fit within the margins dictated by the new window size.

Searching the Index

You can search for help topics by keyword: Just click the Index tab in the Help dialog box, as shown in Figure 6-4. To search for a particular help topic, type the word you want to look for in the first text box. Then locate and double-click the appropriate help topic in the list that appears below, in the second text box.

Using the Find feature

For an even more thorough search of help topics, click the Find tab in the Help dialog box to display a dialog box that lets you search for any topic containing a specific word or phrase.

The first time you click the Find tab, the Find Setup Wizard appears, as shown in Figure 6-5. This Wizard builds a database of keywords that the Find feature uses to search for help topics.

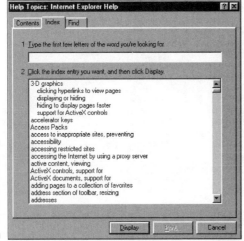

Figure 6-4:
Searching
the Help
Topics
Index.

Figure 6-5:
The Find
Setup
Wizard.

As shown in Figure 6-5, the Find Setup Wizard gives you three options that govern how the database is created:

- ✔ **Minimize database size:** The Find Setup Wizard suggests you pick this option.

- ✔ **Maximize search capabilities:** If you have scads of unused disk space and a really fast processor (like a 100 MHz Pentium or better), select Maximize search capabilities.

- ✔ **Customize search capabilities:** Check out the upcoming Technical Stuff paragraph to find out why you shouldn't need to bother with this option.

Choose the appropriate option and then click Next> to move to the second dialog box displayed by the Find Setup Wizard, shown in Figure 6-6.

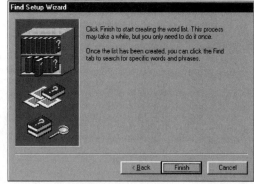

Figure 6-6:
The Find
Setup
Wizard is
ready to
build the
database.

If you're dying to know what options are available for the Find Setup Wizard, click the Customize search capabilities option and then click Next>. Instead of the dialog box shown in Figure 6-6, the Find Setup Wizard leads you through a series of dialog boxes that let you set various options for how the database is built. Most of these options will probably cause you to shrug your shoulders and grunt "huh?" which is why it's better to pick either Minimize database size or Maximize search capabilities and skip all the option screens.

When you click Next> again, the Find Setup Wizard scans Internet Explorer's help files and builds a database that you can use to search for help on specific topics. This process should take only a few seconds, as Internet Explorer's help files aren't that big.

After you use the Find Setup Wizard to build the Find database, you can then search for help topics using the Find tab. Here's the procedure:

1. **Open Internet Explorer Help and then click the Find tab.**

   The dialog box shown in Figure 6-7 appears.

2. **Type the word or words you want to find.**

3. **Select one or more of the matching words to narrow your search.**

   Matching words appear in the list box after you type the search word in Step 2.

4. **Double-click the help topic you want to view.**

   A Help window appears and shows the text of the help topic that you select.

For more precise control over how the help search works, you can click the Options button, which brings up the Find Options dialog box, shown in Figure 6-8.

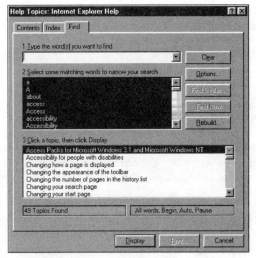

Figure 6-7:
Using Find
to locate
help topics.

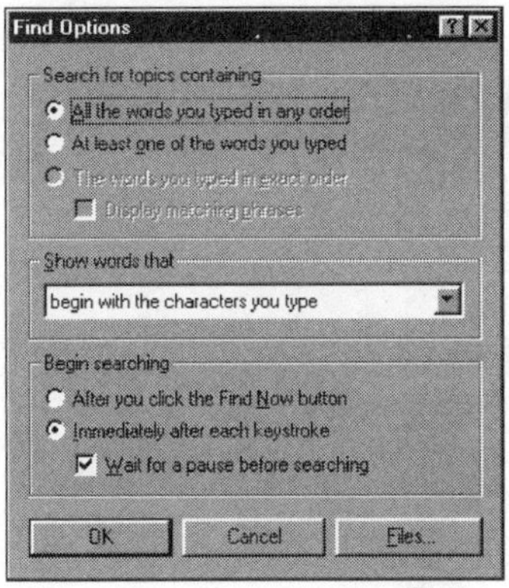

Figure 6-8:
The Find
Options
dialog box.

The Find Options dialog box lets you specify the following options:

✔ You can search for topics that contain all of the words you type or for topics that contain at least one of the words you type. In other words, if you search for the phrase *World Wide Web,* do you want to display all topics that contain any *one* of the words World, Wide, or Web? Or do you want to display only those topics that contain *all three words?*

✔ You can choose how closely the text you type must match the text in the help topic. The default setting is to search for words in the help text that *begin* with characters that exactly match the words you type. Other settings for this option allow the text to be located at the *end* or in the *middle* of words in the help text.

✔ You can select whether Find should start searching the help database immediately as you begin typing the search word, or whether Find should wait until you click the Find Now button.

Troubleshooting at Your Fingertips

If you don't find the answer you're looking for in Internet Explorer's Help feature, you may find the answer buried within the Help files that come with Windows 95 itself. In fact, the Windows 95 Help system includes several special troubleshooting features that can walk you through the most frequent causes of common problems.

To conjure up one of the Windows 95 troubleshooters, follow these steps:

1. Click the Start button located on the taskbar and then choose Help.

The Windows 95 Help screen appears, as shown in Figure 6-9.

Figure 6-9:
The Windows 95 Help screen.

2. Double-click Troubleshooting under the Contents tab.

A list of several troubleshooting topics appears.

3. Double-click the troubleshooting topic that interests you.

For solving Internet Explorer problems, the two troubleshooters you're most likely to find useful are the topics labeled `If you have trouble using your modem` and `If you have trouble using Dial-Up Networking`. Figure 6-10 shows the Modem Troubleshooter.

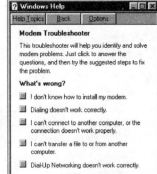

Figure 6-10:
The Modem
Trouble-
shooter.

4. **To use the troubleshooter, double-click the icon to open the topic and then answer each of the troubleshooter's questions by clicking the appropriate button.**

With luck, the troubleshooter leads you to the solution to your problem.

 If you've installed Microsoft Plus!, a popular add-on program for Windows 95, additional help for setting up an Internet connection is available in the form of the Internet Setup Wizard. Click the Start button and then choose Programs⇨ Accessories⇨Internet Tools⇨Internet Setup Wizard. The Internet Setup Wizard, shown in Figure 6-11 leads you step by step through the process of connecting your computer to the Internet. If you're having trouble connecting to the Net, the Internet Setup Wizard can sometimes correct the problem.

Figure 6-11:
The Internet
Setup
Wizard.

Getting Help Online

If you can't find help for a specific problem in the Internet Explorer Help files, you can always turn to your online comrades on the Internet. The first place to check for online help is Microsoft's own Web page devoted to Internet Explorer technical support. You can call up this Web page by starting Internet Explorer and then choosing Help⇔Online Support. Or, you can manually navigate to the Internet Explorer technical support Web site at www.microsoft.com/ iesupport.

The Internet Explorer Support Home page, shown in Figure 6-12, provides up-to-date information about the latest releases of Internet Explorer. This Web page also includes links to pages that list frequently asked questions (FAQs), known problems with Internet Explorer, a troubleshooting guide, and other helpful information.

You can also get help for specific Internet Explorer problems by visiting Microsoft's support newsgroups. Microsoft operates more than a dozen newsgroups that are devoted to Internet Explorer support. To access the newsgroups, click the Visit Our Newsgroups link on the Internet Explorer support page. This option brings up a page that lists the various Internet Explorer newsgroups. Click the newsgroup that seems most relevant to your problem. You can then post a question about the problem you're having with Internet Explorer, and odds are, by the following day you'll have half a dozen responses. For more information about using newsgroups, see Chapter 12.

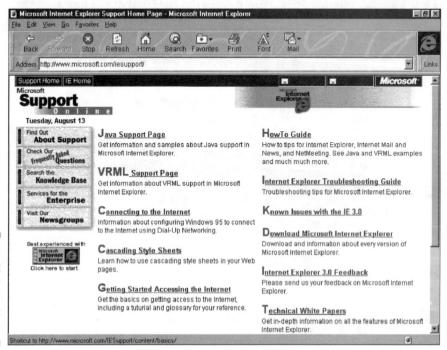

Figure 6-12:
The Internet Explorer online support page.

Part III

Customizing Your Explorations

The 5th Wave   By Rich Tennant

"NOW, THAT WOULD SHOW HOW IMPORTANT IT IS TO DISTINGUISH 'FERTILIZING PRACTICES' FROM 'FERTILITY PRACTICES' WHEN DOWNLOADING A VIDEO FILE FROM THE INTERNET."

In this part . . .

This is the part to turn to when you're tired of working with Internet Explorer the way it runs out-of-the-box, and you want to customize it to more closely suit your working style. These chapters show you how to set up your own customized start page, how to set the many Internet Explorer options, and how to create a Dial-Up Networking script so that you won't have to type your user ID and password every time you connect to the Internet.

Chapter 7

Personalizing Your Start Page

- -

In This Chapter

▶ Setting your own start page

▶ Customizing the msn.com start page

▶ Customizing other start pages

- -

*Y*our *start page* is the page that Internet Explorer automatically displays each time you begin an exploration of the World Wide Web. This chapter shows you how to designate any page of the Web as your start page and even how to create your own, customized start page.

Changing Your Start Page

Normally, Internet Explorer defaults to The Microsoft Network home page (called msn.com) as its start page. If you obtained your copy of Internet Explorer from a company other than Microsoft — CompuServe, for example — Internet Explorer may be configured with a different start page. Whatever your start page currently is, Internet Explorer lets you designate *any* page on the Web to be the first one you see. For example, if the only Internet site you're interested in is David Letterman's Top Ten List, you can set the Top Ten List site to be your start page.

 The start page is also the page that pops up whenever you click the Home button on the toolbar.

To change your start page, follow these steps:

1. **Navigate your way to the page you want to use as your new start page.**

   See Chapter 3 for details about getting around on the Web.

2. **Choose <u>V</u>iew⇨<u>O</u>ptions.**

   The Options dialog box appears.

3. **Click the Navigation tab.**

The Navigation part of the Options dialog box appears, as illustrated in Figure 7-1.

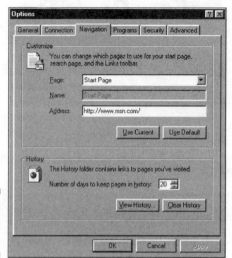

Figure 7-1:
Setting the
start page.

4. Make sure that the Page field indicates Start Page.

If necessary, scroll through the drop-down list to select Start Page.

5. Click the Use Current button.

The start page is now set to the current page.

6. Click OK to dismiss the Options dialog box.

You're done!

You can change back to the default start page by choosing View➪Options, clicking the Navigation tab, and clicking the Use Default button.

Customizing msn.com

One of the best things about the msn.com page is that you can customize it to include information you're interested in seeing every time you access the Internet. For example, you can add sports scores, daily news, links to your favorite Internet locations, weather reports, and other useful information.

Note: Customizing the msn.com start page is not the same as setting up your own home page that other Web users can see. When you customize the msn.com start page — or any start page — only *you* can see the custom options that you select.

Information you can add

The following is a list of the custom options that you can add to the msn.com customizable start page:

- ✔ **Links:** You can add up to six links to other Web sites.

- ✔ **Music:** You can customize the start page to automatically play a music clip of your choice when you display the page.

- ✔ **Search forms:** If you frequently use search services, you can put form fields for any or all of the search services that are displayed when you click the Search button: AltaVista, Yahoo!, Lycos, Excite, Magellan, Infoseek, and the Microsoft Web site.

- ✔ **Stock quotes:** You can display stock quotes for up to seven stocks.

- ✔ **Sports scores:** You can display scores for baseball, professional or college football, professional or college basketball, or hockey.

- ✔ **News:** You can display headline news from MSNBC or computer industry news from Ziff-Davis.

- ✔ **TV:** You can display network TV listings for your time zone.

- ✔ **Weather reports and ski information:** You can include detailed weather maps or local weather reports.

- ✔ **Web picks:** You can add links to cool Web sites picked by Microsoft staff.

You can also specify the colors for each element of the start page display, and you can indicate how much graphics detail to include (more detail requires longer download times).

Customizing the start page

To customize the msn.com start page, just follow these steps:

1. **Display the start page.**

   The easiest way is to click the Home button. Or, if MSN isn't your default home page, you can type in the address www.msn.com.

2. **Click the <u>Custom Start Page</u> link.**

   The page illustrated in Figure 7-2 comes up. This page serves as an overview of the options that subsequent screens present.

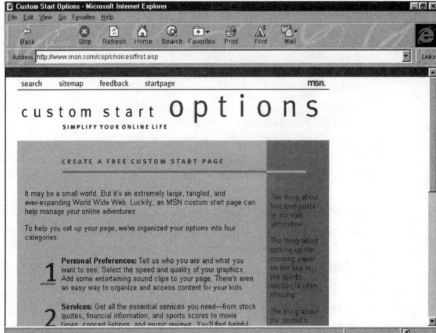

Figure 7-2:
Customizing
your
msn.com
start page.

3. Specify the custom options that you want to include on your start page.

To get started, scroll down to the bottom of the page shown in Figure 7-2 and click the Let's get customized button. You then see a sequence of four more pages that allow you to specify which options you want to include on your start page. These pages represent four basic categories of options:

- **Personal information:** Such as your name, city, and choice of music to be played each time you visit your start page

- **Services:** Such as stock quotes, sports scores, and movie times

- **News and Entertainment:** Including headline news, weather reports, TV listings, and comic strips

- **Internet Searches:** Lets you access the most popular search services right from your start page

4. Complete each of the four pages by selecting the options you want to include on your start page.

At the bottom of each page, you find a Set up this page button that you can click to proceed to the next page.

After you fill out all four pages of custom information, your customized start page appears, as pictured in Figure 7-3.

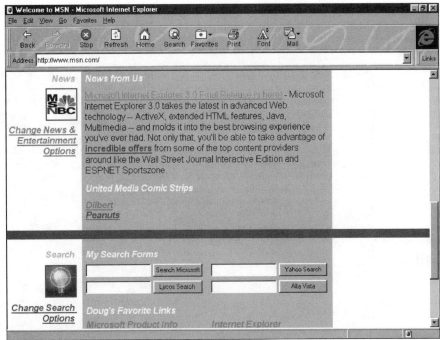

Figure 7-3:
A custom-
ized start
page.

Other Start Pages You Can Customize

Not to be outdone by Microsoft, several other companies are jumping on the
"customize your own start page" bandwagon. The following sections describe
two alternatives to the msn.com personalized start page.

Personal Excite

`home.excite.com/home`

Excite is one of the search services available from the Microsoft all-in-one
search page, which you can read about in detail in Chapter 4. Besides offering
an excellent Web search database, Excite also provides a customizable start
page called Personal Excite, which offers more custom options than msn.com.
Personal Excite even lets you choose a psychedelic background, as shown (but
not done justice) in black and white Figure 7-4.

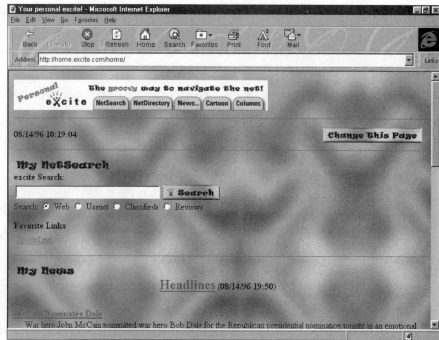

Figure 7-4:
Personal
Excite, with
an exciting
background.

Personal Excite lets you add the following custom features to your start page:

- **Event Reminders:** Warns you a day, week, or month before an important birthday, anniversary, or other event (you can set as many as ten such reminders)

- **Hot List:** Adds up to 20 links to your favorite Internet sites

- **Saved Searches:** Lets you add a search to your start page so you don't have to type the same search text over and over (you can create up to four saved searches)

- **Reference:** Adds links to 15 online references, including *Webster's Dictionary, Bartlett's Quotations,* and *AT&T's 800 Directory*

- **Reuters News:** Offers you Headlines, International, Business, Politics, Sports, or Entertainment options

- **Stock Quotes:** Lets you add up to seven ticker symbols to your start page

- **Sports Scores:** Gives you scores for baseball, NFL, NBA, college football, and college basketball

- **Ski Reports:** Displays ski conditions for any state in the Union

- **TV Listings:** Gives network TV listings for any area

✔ **Movie Times:** Lists movie times for major cities

✔ **Directory Topics:** Provides links to individual topics in the Excite Web directory

✔ **Cartoons:** Lets you chuckle along with *Bill Mitchell, Dilbert, Peanuts, Robotman, Committed, Reality Check,* and *Deep Thoughts*

✔ **Columns:** Links to the text of several popular newspaper columns

Infoseek Personal

`personal.infoseek.com`

Infoseek, another of the search services available at the Microsoft all-in-one search page, also offers a personalized start page. Its default setup, shown in Figure 7-5, provides quick access to Infoseek searches, plus a snippet of news, local TV, movies, weather, comics, and horoscope links.

One unique feature of Infoseek Personal is its Personal News, which works sort of like a news-clipping service. You can display newsworthy information about the following:

✔ **Companies and Products:** IBM, General Motors, the American Cancer Society, Saturn, Nordic Track, and so on

✔ **People and Places:** Bill Clinton, Whoopi Goldberg, Arnold Palmer, Taiwan, Texas, San Francisco, Africa, and so on

✔ **Sports and Personal Interests:** Football, the Chicago Bulls, aerobics, photography, nutrition, and so on

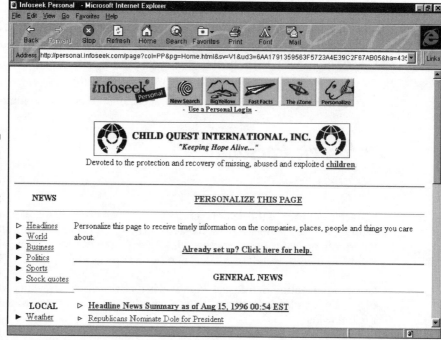

Figure 7-5:
Among
other
services it
provides,
Infoseek
Personal
can sort
through
news
clippings
for you.

Chapter 8

Opting for Options

- -

In This Chapter

▶ Getting to know Internet Explorer's options

▶ Changing option settings to suit your tastes

- -

Selecting View⇨Options opens the door to myriad options that affect the way Internet Explorer browses the World Wide Web. Of course, you can't use this command to pick your *real* preferences, such as playing golf instead of toiling with your computer. But you can do stuff that's almost as much fun, such as changing the colors used to display links you've already visited or setting the default start page.

Read this chapter after you've become comfortable with the out-of-the-box version of Internet Explorer and you're ready to find out what all those options really do. This chapter describes the most useful options, but what's more important, it tells you which options you can safely ignore so that you (unlike some people I know — me, for example) can catch up on your golf.

Note: I am aware, of course, that for some people golf is a more frustrating pastime than using your computer. And for some, golf is more boring than reading Internet Explorer's online help. If you're one of those poor, unenlightened souls, feel free to substitute your favorite nongolf pastime — and may I recommend *Golf For Dummies*?

What's with All the Options?

Selecting View⇨Options presents you with a killer dialog box that has tabs out the wazoo (whatever a *wazoo* is). Each of the tabs has its own set of controls. To switch from one tab to another, just click the tab label at the top of the dialog box.

Here's the lowdown on the six tabs that appear in the Options dialog box:

- ✔ **General:** Contains options that affect the general operation of Internet Explorer

- ✔ **Connection:** Indicates which dial-up connection to use to establish a connection to the Internet

- ✔ **Navigation:** Lets you customize your start page, search page, and Quick Links, and lets you specify how long to keep items in the history folder

- ✔ **Programs:** Lets you indicate which programs to use to read Internet mail and newsgroups, and lets you specify which program to use to display different types of files

- ✔ **Security:** Lets you indicate whether you want to be warned before doing something that may jeopardize your security and allows you to filter out pages with questionable content (see Chapter 9)

- ✔ **Advanced:** Holds a number of options that just didn't fit anywhere else

To set any of the preceding options, follow this general procedure:

1. **Choose View⇨Options.**

   The Options dialog box appears.

2. **Click the tab that contains the option you want to set.**

   If you're not sure which tab to click, just cycle through them all until you find what you're looking for.

3. **Set the options however you want.**

   Most of the options are simple check boxes that you click to check or uncheck. Some require that you select a choice from a drop-down list, and some have the audacity to require that you actually type something as proof of your keyboard proficiency.

4. **Repeat Step 3 until you've exhausted your options (or yourself).**

   You can set more than one option with a single use of the View⇨Options command.

5. **Click OK.**

   You're done!

Saluting the General Options

Back in the days of Internet Explorer 1.0, the options on the General tab were lowly Private Options. But they re-upped for version 2.0, and eventually decided to become Career Options. Now, with Internet Explorer 3.0, they've attained the rank of General. You'd better snap-to whenever you call up these options, shown in Figure 8-1.

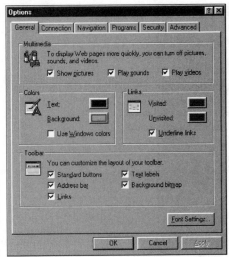

Figure 8-1:
The General
options.

The General options include the following four catagories:

- ✓ **Multimedia:** You can indicate whether graphics, sounds, and video are downloaded automatically whenever you go to a Web page. Disabling any or all of these options improves Internet Explorer's performance.

- ✓ **Colors:** You can set the colors used for text and background.

- ✓ **Links:** You can change the color used to display links you've already visited and links you haven't yet traversed.

- ✓ **Toolbar:** You can control the appearance of the toolbar. Choose whether to include various parts of the toolbar (such as the standard toolbar buttons, the address bar, and the Quick Links) and whether the toolbar should include text labels and a pretty background bitmap image.

For more viewing area, uncheck the Text Labels option.

Cajoling the Connection Options

The Connection options, shown in Figure 8-2, enable you to specify which dial-up connection you use to connect to the Internet. You may find yourself turning to this tab frequently if you have more than one Internet provider and you often switch from one to another. You should also visit this tab if you decide to change providers.

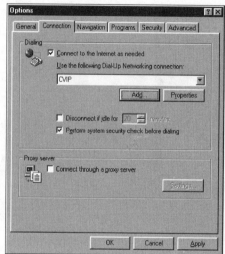

Figure 8-2:
The
Connection
options.

If you have not yet created a dial-up connection for your Internet provider, click the Add button. A Wizard creates a connection for you after asking basic questions such as the phone number to dial and your user ID.

If your Internet service provider charges you by the hour for connect time, consider checking the Disconnect if idle for option. That way, if you accidentally walk away from your computer without disconnecting from the Internet, Internet Explorer automatically disconnects after a certain amount of time has elapsed (the default is 20 minutes).

If you use a *proxy server,* the Connection tab is the place to set it. Click the Proxy server check box; then click the Change proxy settings button and enter the proxy settings. (Your Internet service provider should supply you with these settings.)

Nabbing the Navigation Options

Figure 8-3 shows the Navigation tab. This tab enables you to change the URLs of several default Web pages that Internet Explorer uses. It also lets you to specify how long pages are stored in the history folder.

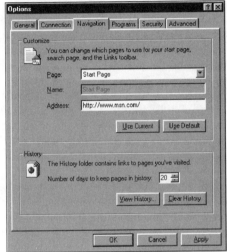

Figure 8-3:
The
Navigation
options.

The default pages that you can change are

- ✓ **The start page:** The page that's displayed when you first start Internet Explorer and when you click the Home button (see Chapter 7)
- ✓ **The search page:** The page that's displayed when you click the Search button (see Chapter 4)
- ✓ **The five Quick Links:** The pages you can access via the Links toolbar (see Chapter 5)

To change one of Internet Explorer's default pages, follow these steps:

1. **Navigate to the page you want to use as the default page.**

   It doesn't matter how you get to this page, just get there.

2. **Choose View⇨Options and select the Navigation tab.**

3. **In the Page drop-down list, select which page you want to set.**

   Your choices are Start Page, Search Page, or Quick Links #1 through #5.

4. **Click the Use Current button.**

You can also restore these settings to their default values by clicking the Use Default button.

Perusing the Programs Options

The Programs tab, shown in Figure 8-4, contains options that let you tell Internet Explorer what programs you want to use to read your e-mail and access Internet newsgroups. The default settings are Microsoft Internet Mail and Internet News, the e-mail and news programs that come with Internet Explorer (see Chapters 11 and 12).

You should leave the default Programs settings as they are unless you have installed some other e-mail or newsgroup program that is designed to work with Internet Explorer.

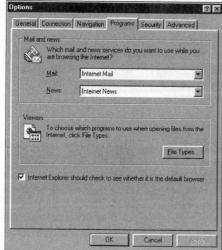

Within the Programs options, you can also click the File Types button to call up the dialog box shown in Figure 8-5. This dialog box displays a list of all the file types that are registered with Windows 95.

To be *registered* means that Windows 95 recognizes the file type and knows which program to use to open a file of this type. For example, Windows 95 knows to launch Microsoft Word to open a .doc file.

In most cases, file types are added automatically whenever you install a program. The only time you should mess with these settings is when you have two or more programs that are capable of opening a particular file type, and the program you prefer isn't the one that is being used. To change the program associated with a file type, select the file type and then click the Edit button. In the dialog box that appears, specify the program you want to use to open the file.

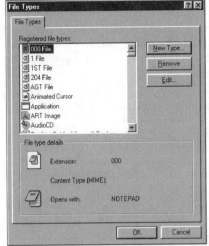

Figure 8-5:
The File
Types
dialog box.

Setting Security Options

Figure 8-6 shows the Security options, which are designed to protect you from Internet sites with offensive content, to protect your privacy, and to warn you about potential security problems.

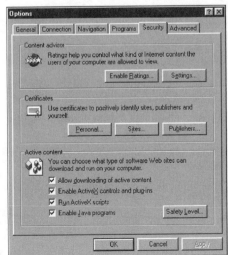

Figure 8-6:
The
Security
options.

The Security options include the following three security features:

- **Content advisor:** This feature allows you to screen out Internet sites that have potentially offensive content (see Chapter 9).

- **Certificates:** Certificates are a bleeding-edge method of ensuring secure communications between two Internet sites. The sites exchange specially encoded documents called *certificates,* which are like identification badges. Certificates guarantee that the computer you are connected to is what it claims to be. They also guarantee to the computer you are connected to that you are who you claim to be.

  The use of certificates hasn't quite caught on yet. Until it does, you probably don't need to mess with the Certificates options.

- **Active content:** These features allow you to selectively enable Microsoft's hot new ActiveX technology, which allows Web designers to fill their pages with all sorts of interesting new types of controls (see Chapter 15). If you want to visit pages that use ActiveX, you should enable all of these options.

Achieving Advanced Options

The Advanced options, shown in Figure 8-7, let you set several features that govern Internet Explorer's operation.

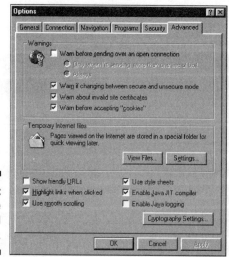

Figure 8-7:
The
Advanced
options.

Among the Advanced options are the following:

- **Warnings:** This option notifies you whenever certain actions are about to occur, such as sending information over an unsecured line. Most of these warnings are more annoying than helpful, so you'll probably end up turning them all off sooner or later.

- **Temporary Internet files:** This option lets you manage the temporary files that Internet Explorer downloads to your hard disk. By default, Internet Explorer uses as much as 10 percent of your disk drive to store these files. The more disk space you allocate to Internet Explorer, the less often Internet Explorer is forced to download files that you've already seen. Of course, the tradeoff is that increasing the amount of disk Internet Explorer can use decreases the amount of free disk space on your computer.

  You can empty the Temporary Internet files folder by clicking the Empty Folder button. But be warned that emptying this folder causes delays as Internet Explorer is forced to download files that were previously stored on your disk.

- **Show friendly URLs:** If this option is checked, Internet Explorer abbreviates URLs by eliminating the portions of the address that refer to the current page. This usually shortens the URLs and makes them easier to read. For example, suppose that you're currently viewing a page whose address is `http://www.somewhere.com`, and the page has a link to `http://www.somewhere.com/goodstuff.htm`. With Show Friendly URLs enabled, the link's address appears simply as `goodstuff.htm`.

- **Highlight links when clicked:** With this option enabled, Internet Explorer draws a box with dashed lines around a link that you have clicked. This option is pretty inconsequential, so don't bother changing it.

- **Use smooth scrolling:** You may have noticed that Internet Explorer scrolls its windows differently than most other applications, using an animated effect that makes scrolling appear smoother. On slower computers, you may want to disable this option to improve performance.

- **Use style sheets:** *Style sheets* are a new feature of Internet Explorer 3.0 that Web authors can use to create splashy Web pages (see Chapter 20). By all means, leave this option checked.

- **Enable Java JIT compiler:** This option enables you to view Web pages that have special little programs called *Java applets*. Leave this option checked unless you don't mind trading cool Web-page features for speedy access.

- **Enable Java logging:** If you're a Java expert, you can use this option to enable the Java log, which records all Java activity.

Chapter 9

Exercising Your Parental Controls

* * *

In This Chapter

▶ Activating the Content Advisor feature of Internet Explorer

▶ Determining your blush threshold

▶ Picking a secret password

▶ Requiring password access to restricted sites

* * *

*A*lthough the Internet can be a great resource for kids, it is also a notoriously unsafe place for kids to hang out unsupervised. For every museum, library, and government agency that springs up on the Internet, a corresponding adult bookstore, sex shop, or smutty magazine seems to appear. What's a parent to do?

Fortunately, Internet Explorer has a built-in feature called *Content Advisor,* which enables you to restrict access to off-color Internet sites. Content Advisor uses a system of ratings similar to the ratings used for movies. Although this system isn't perfect, it goes a long way toward preventing your kids from stumbling into something they shouldn't.

About Internet Ratings

Internet ratings work much like motion picture ratings: They let you know what kind of content you can expect at a given Internet site. The ratings are assigned voluntarily by the publisher of each individual Internet site.

Although movie ratings give you an overall rating for a movie (G, PG, PG-13, R, or NC-17), the motion picture ratings system doesn't give you a clue about *why* a movie receives a particular rating. For example, does a PG-13 rating mean that a movie is filled with foul language, almost-explicit sex, or excessive violence? It could be any of these — or all of them.

By contrast, Internet ratings give specific information about several categories of potentially offensive material. Several different ratings systems are currently being developed. The system that Internet Explorer uses was developed by a nonprofit organization called the Recreational Software Advisory Council, or RSAC. RSAC assigns a rating of 0 to 4 for each of the following four categories:

- ✔ Violence
- ✔ Nudity
- ✔ Language
- ✔ Sex

Table 9-1 shows the specific meaning for each rating number in an RSAC rating.

Table 9-1	What the RSAC Ratings Mean			
Rating	*Violence*	*Nudity*	*Language*	*Sex*
0	Harmless conflict; some damage to objects	No nudity or revealing attire	Inoffensive slang; no profanity	Romance; no sex
1	Creatures injured or killed; damage to objects; fighting	Revealing attire	Mild expletives	Passionate kissing
2	Humans injured or killed; small amount of blood	Partial nudity	Expletives; nonsexual anatomical references	Clothed sexual touching
3	Humans injured or killed; blood and gore	Nonsexual frontal nudity	Strong, vulgar language; obscene gestures; racial epithets	Nonexplicit sexual activity
4	Wanton and gratuitous violence; torture; rape	Provocative frontal nudity	Crude or explicit sexual references; extreme hate speech	Explicit sexual activity; sex crimes

With Internet Explorer, you can set a threshold value for each of the four categories. If any attempt is made to access a Web site that has a rating higher than the threshold value, Internet Explorer blocks the user from viewing the Web site.

The RSAC rating system was developed by a group of recognized experts who study the effects of the media on children. For more information about RSAC, check out its Web site at www.rsac.org. Figure 9-1 shows the RSAC Web page, where you can learn more about RSAC; if you're a Web publisher, you can find out how to provide a rating for your site.

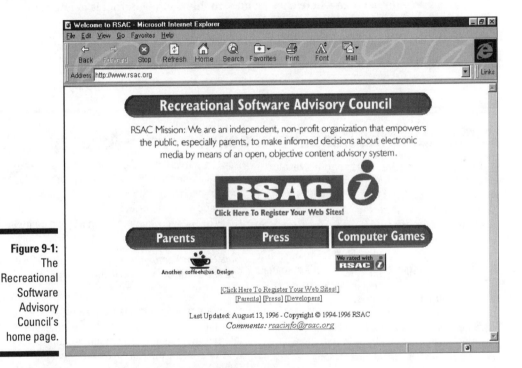

Figure 9-1:
The Recreational Software Advisory Council's home page.

Limitations of Internet Ratings

Before I show you how to activate and configure the Internet Explorer Content Advisor, I want to be sure that I don't lull you into a false sense of security, thinking that after you activate the Ratings feature, you won't have to worry about your kids getting into trouble on the Internet. Just to be sure, here are a few of the limitations of the RSAC rating system:

 ✔ Ratings are voluntary. No one can guarantee that a Web site publisher will give his or her site an accurate rating.

 ✔ Currently, Internet Explorer's Ratings feature applies only to the World Wide Web. However, some of the nastiest Internet content is found, not on the Web, but rather in Usenet newsgroups. Microsoft is working on a way to extend controls to newsgroups, but, as of now, RSAC ratings apply only to Web pages.

- Not all Web sites are rated. In fact, most are *not* rated. Internet Explorer allows you to either ban all unrated sites, or allow full access to unrated sites. Neither option is good: If you ban unrated sites, you'll be banning most of the Web. If you allow access to unrated sites, you'll let some garbage in. Sigh.

- Another area where kids get into trouble on the Internet is in Internet Relay Chats (IRCs). Ratings do not apply to IRCs.

- Kids are clever, and you can rest assured that some kids will figure out a way to bypass the ratings feature altogether. No security system is totally secure.

What about the Communications Decency Amendment?

Much attention has been given lately to a law passed by Congress called the *1996 Telecommunications Act,* which includes an amendment called the *Communications Decency Amendment,* or CDA. The CDA purports to protect children from abuse via the Internet. Unfortunately, this amendment does little to protect anybody, yet still manages to trample over the First Amendment rights of every Internet user. One of the main problems with the new law is that it uses the term *indecent* rather than *obscene* to describe the type of information that is considered illegal. *Obscene* is a fairly well-defined legal term. *Indecent* is not.

According to opponents of the CDA, the list of Internet sites that could be considered *indecent* is long, and includes such Web content as the *Venus de Milo,* and the text of Mark Twain's *The Adventures of Huckleberry Finn.* Other Web material that could be interpreted as indecent under the CDA are online discussions of health issues such as HIV and breast cancer, and even the text of the King James Bible, which contains words that fit the Supreme Court's criteria of indecency. Certain aspects of the CDA have already been found unconstitutional by the courts.

Many online information providers have joined a *Blue Ribbon Campaign* to protest the CDA. So if you see a little blue ribbon in the corner of a Web page, now you know what it means.

Voluntary ratings systems such as RSAC are an alternative solution to the problem of smut on the Internet. Ratings enable parents to control the type of content their children view, without infringing on anyone's First Amendment rights. Of course, ratings are not perfect. There's no guarantee that a site's ratings are accurate or that kids won't figure out a way to bypass the ratings system. But RSAC should make stumbling across offensive Internet content much more difficult for kids.

Activating Content Advisor

Out of the box, Internet Explorer does not check for Web site ratings. To screen out offensive Web sites, you must first activate the Content Advisor. Just follow these steps:

1. **Choose View⇨Options.**

   The Options dialog box appears.

2. **Click the Security tab.**

   The Security options shown in Figure 9-2 appear.

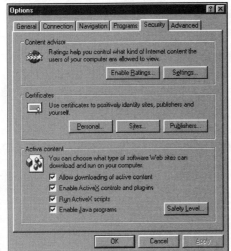

Figure 9-2:
The Security
options.

3. **Click the Enable Ratings button.**

   Internet Explorer asks you to create a supervisor password in the dialog box shown in Figure 9-3.

4. **Think up a good password.**

   Read the nearby sidebar "Open sesame" to get some guidelines for creating a good password.

Figure 9-3:
Creating a
supervisor
password.

Create Supervisor Password

To prevent children from changing their Content
Advisor settings or turning it off, you must create a
supervisor password.

Content Advisor settings can be changed or
turned on or off only by people who know the
password.

Password:

Confirm Password:

OK

Cancel

5. Type the password twice.

The password is not displayed on-screen as you type it. Therefore, Internet Explorer requires you to type your password twice, just to make sure that you don't make a typing mistake. Type the password once into the Password field and then type it again into the Confirm Password field.

6. Click OK.

The following message appears in its own little dialog box:

```
Content Advisor has been turned on.
```

7. Click OK.

You return to the Options dialog box. You can tell that Content Advisor has been turned on because the Enable Ratings button has been changed to Disable Ratings.

Open sesame

The Internet Ratings feature is only as good as the password you pick. Thus, you must make sure that you don't pick a password that your kids can easily figure out. Here are some passwords to avoid:

✔ Your name or your kid's name

✔ The names of your pets

✔ The name of your boat

✔ Your birthday or anniversary

✔ Your car license number

✔ The password you use to access the Internet

✔ Any other word or number that is important to you, and that your kids could easily figure out

The best passwords are random combinations of letters and numbers. Of course, these are also the hardest to memorize. Next best passwords are randomly chosen words. Just flip open the dictionary to a random page, point to a random word, and use it as your password.

Above all, do *not* write the password down on a sticky note attached to the computer monitor! If you must write the password down, put it in a secure place where only *you* can find it.

8. Click the Settings button.

You are required to enter your password via the dialog box shown in Figure 9-4.

Figure 9-4:
Content
Advisor
asks for
your
password.

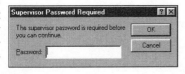

9. Type the password and then click OK.

The Content Advisor dialog box appears, as shown in Figure 9-5.

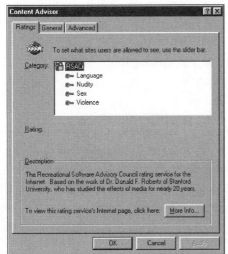

Figure 9-5:
The Content
Advisor
dialog box.

10. Set the rating for each category by clicking the category and then adjusting the slider bar for the rating you want to use.

The slider bar magically appears after you click the category. For example, Figure 9-6 shows the slider bar that appears after you click the Language category. Notice also that a description of what each rating level means appears beneath the slider bar; this description changes as you move the slider bar.

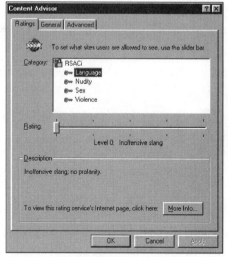

Figure 9-6:
Setting the
rating
for the
Language
category.

11. **After you have set the ratings to appropriate levels for your kids,
    click OK.**

    You return to the Options dialog box once again.

12. **Click OK to dismiss the Options dialog box.**

    Finally! You're finished!

After Content Advisor is in place, the dialog box shown in Figure 9-7 appears
whenever someone attempts to access a site that your ratings do not allow.

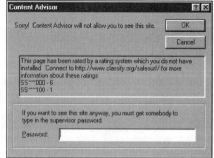

Figure 9-7:
Caught in
the act!

You can deactivate Content Advisor at any time by calling up the Security
options (choose View⇨Options and then click the Security tab) and clicking the
Disable Ratings button. You will, of course, be required to enter your password
in the process.

If you turn off Content Advisor so that you (a consenting adult) can use Internet Explorer without restriction, don't forget to turn it back on after you're finished!

Dealing with Unrated Sites

Internet ratings are a great idea. Unfortunately, not all of the sites on the Internet have yet rated themselves. When you enable Content Advisor, Internet Explorer bans access not only to sites whose ratings are above the threshold you set, but also bans access to any site that is not rated.

Unfortunately, most Internet sites are unrated. Even the Microsoft Web site (www.microsoft.com) is unrated, which means that if you enable Content Advisor, your kids won't be able to visit the Microsoft site or any other unrated site.

Fortunately, Internet Explorer lets you ease the ban on unrated sites. Here is the procedure:

1. **Choose View⇨Options and click the Security tab.**

   The Security options appear. (Refer to Figure 9-2.)

2. **Click the Settings button.**

   You are asked for your password. Type the password and then click OK. The Content Advisor dialog box appears.

3. **Click the General tab.**

   You see the General Internet Ratings options, as shown in Figure 9-8.

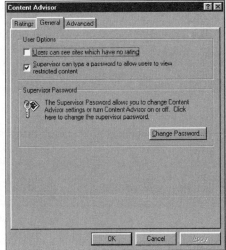

Figure 9-8:
The General
Content
Advisor
options.

4. **Check the Users can see sites which have no rating check box.**

5. **Click OK to dismiss the Content Advisor dialog box.**

   You return to the Options dialog box.

6. **Click OK to dismiss the Options dialog box.**

Now, you can view unrated sites without the constant `Sorry! Your ratings do not allow you to see this site` message.

To restrict access to unrated sites once again, repeat the procedure, but check (rather than uncheck) the Users can see sites which have no rating check box in Step 4.

Note that the General options dialog box also allows you to change the supervisor password. Simply click the Change Password button. A dialog box appears, into which you can type a new password. (As before, you must type the password twice to make sure that you don't make any typing errors.)

You can disable the feature that allows the user to view restricted sites by entering the supervisor password. Just uncheck the Supervisor can type a password option.

Chapter 10

Automating Your Log-in Procedures

Dial-up scripting is a feature of Windows 95 that I hope you don't have to use. It is the type of feature that requires you to don a pocket protector and assume the role of a computer geek. But after you have it set up, a Dial-Up Script can simplify your Internet sign-in procedures dramatically.

Dial-Up Scripting is designed for those whose Internet providers require them to go through a complicated log-in sequence whenever they access the Internet. If, when you dial up your provider, a terminal window pops up and greets you with a message such as `User-ID:` and a cold, blinking cursor, then Dial-Up Scripting is for you.

If your Internet provider launches you straight into Internet Explorer, you can fall down on your knees, give thanks, and skip this chapter.

What Is a Dial-Up Script?

A *Dial-Up Script* is a special file that contains text and commands that are automatically typed in for you when you log in to a computer network. If the computer system you use to connect to the Internet requires you to manually enter information before it sends you to the Net, you can create a Dial-Up Script to automate the process.

For example, my Internet provider requires me to type in my user ID and password. Then it displays the text menu shown in Figure 10-1. From this menu, I must select item 4. Then I am prompted to enter an *IP address* (whatever that is),

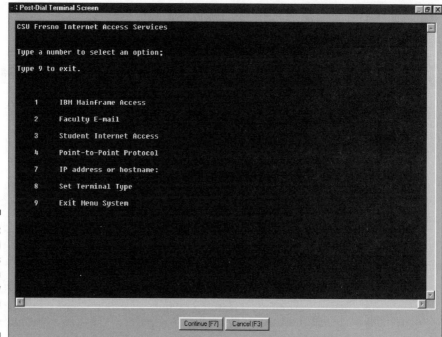

Figure 10-1:
The menu that appears when I sign in to my service provider.

to which I must reply, *Default.* Only then am I connected to the Internet so that I can use Internet Explorer.

By using a script, I can have the computer do all this typing for me. The script types in my name and password, waits for the menu to appear, chooses item 4, waits for the prompt, and then types *Default.* All I have to do is sit back and enjoy a sip of coffee while the script does all the work.

Unfortunately, you have to write the script yourself. The script is a simple text file that can be edited with ease, but it must contain certain commands, which I describe later in this chapter. In addition, you have to attach the script to the Dial-Up Connection so that Windows 95 knows to run your script when you dial in. I describe the procedure for attaching the script later in this chapter.

Installing Dial-Up Scripting

The first step in using Dial-Up Scripting is installing the Dial-Up Scripting tool. Dial-Up Scripting comes free with Windows 95, but many users don't have it installed on their computers. To find out whether you already have Dial-Up

Scripting, click the Start button and select Programs⇨Accessories. If you see a Dial-Up Scripting Tool command, Dial-Up Scripting has been installed. If not, follow this procedure to install it:

1. **Insert your Windows 95 CD in your CD-ROM drive.**

   Wait a moment to see whether the CD opens by itself. If it doesn't, open it by double-clicking My Computer and then double-clicking the icon for the CD drive.

2. **Click the Add/Remove Software button.**

3. **Scroll through the list of Windows 95 components to find and select SLIP and Scripting for Dial-Up Networking.**

   See Figure 10-2. If this option doesn't appear on your list, click the Have Disk button and then click Browse and locate the folder \admin\apptools\dscript on your CD-ROM drive. Click OK and then check SLIP and Scripting for Dial-Up Networking.

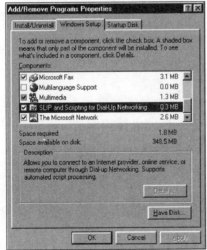

Figure 10-2:
Installing
Dial-Up
Scripting.

4. **Click OK.**

   Ta da! The Dial-Up Scripting tool is installed.

Planning a Script

The first step in creating a script file is to plan the contents of the script. Get a piece of paper and label two columns *Computer Types* and *I Type*. Then sit down at your computer and log in to your Internet provider. As you do, carefully write down in the *I Type* column everything you must type. Also indicate when you must press the Enter key. In addition, write down in the *Computer Types* column the last thing displayed on-screen before anything you must type.

For example, here's what I wrote down to create the script for my provider:

Computer Types	I Type
Username:	user ID (Enter)
Password:	my password (Enter)
Exit Menu System:	4 (Enter not required)
hostname:	default (Enter)

You will use the information as the basis for your script.

Creating a Script

To create a script, you must use a text editor such as Notepad. Here's the procedure for creating a script file:

1. **Click Start and choose Programs⇨Accessories⇨Notepad.**

   Notepad appears in its own window.

2. **Type whichever commands you need to type to establish your Internet connection.**

   The commands vary depending on your service provider's requirements. Figure 10-3 shows the script I use for my provider. I describe each of the commands in this script later in this chapter.

3. **Choose File⇨Save As to save the file.**

   Choose a filename that ends in .scp, and save the file in \Program Files\Accessories.

4. **Choose File⇨Exit to quit Notepad.**

Your script filename must end in .scp and reside in the \Program Files\Accessories folder.

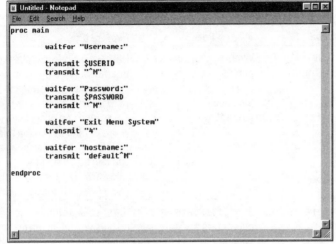

Figure 10-3:
The script I
wrote to log
in to my
service
provider.

Script Commands

The hard part of creating a script is knowing which commands to include in the script file. The following sections describe the commands that are used in the script in Figure 10-3 (these are the most commonly used commands), and Table 10-1 lists all of the commands that you can use.

Table 10-1	Dial-Up Scripting Commands	
Command	*What It Does*	*Explanation*
`proc main`	Begins the script	The script begins running at the main procedure and stops at the end of the main procedure. (Every script must start with `proc main`.)
`endproc`	Marks the end of the script	When your computer reaches this command, Dial-Up Networking starts PPP or SLIP.
`delay <n seconds>`	Pauses the script for n seconds before executing the next command	For example, `delay 4` pauses for four seconds.

(continued)

Table 10-1 *(continued)*

Command	What It Does	Explanation
waitfor "<string>"	Waits until the computer you are connecting to has received the specified characters	Here, *string* refers to the words your Internet service provider uses to prompt you for information (from the *Computer Types* column). Note that the string is *case sensitive*. Thus, if your provider sends the text USERNAME (in all capital letters), you must type waitfor "USERNAME" (not waitfor "Username") to wait for this string.
transmit "<string>"	Sends the specified characters to the computer to which you are connecting	Here, *string* refers to the words you type as you log in to your Internet service (from the *I Type* column).
transmit $USERID	Sends the user ID obtained from the Connect To dialog box	
transmit $PASSWORD	Sends the password obtained from the Connect To dialog box	
set port databits <integer>	Changes the number of bits in the bytes that are transmitted during the session, from 5 to 8	
set port stopbits <integer>	Changes the number of stop bits for the port during the session, either 1 or 2	
set port parity none | odd | even | mark | space	Changes the parity for the port during the session	
set ipaddr	Sets the IP address for the session	
set screen keyboard on | off	Enables or disables keyboard input to the terminal window	
getip <optional index>	Reads an IP address and uses it as the workstation address	

Command	What It Does	Explanation
halt	Causes Dial-Up Networking to stop running the script, but leaves the terminal window open so you can enter additional information manually	
;	Indicates a comment	All text after the semicolon is ignored — comments are for your reference only.

proc main and endproc

Every script must begin with a line that says proc main and end with a line that says endproc. It's a programming thing, required probably because the programmers at Microsoft who created the Dial-Up Scripting tool were in a bad mood that day and figured, hey, because we have to type stuff like *proc main* and *endproc* all day, everyone should have to, too.

So the first thing you should do when creating a script is add these two lines, as follows:

```
proc main



endproc
```

Notice that I left a few blank rows between these two lines. This space is where the meat of the script goes.

Waiting for stuff: waitfor

Before your script can type anything to the computer, it must wait until the computer is ready to accept the information. To tell the script to wait, you must make note of the text that is displayed as a prompt and then use a waitfor command to tell the script to wait until that text appears on the screen.

For example, the following line tells the scripting tool to wait until the prompt Username: appears:

```
waitfor "Username:"
```

The only trick in using a `waitfor` command is to make sure that the text you specify is unique; that is, that it doesn't occur anywhere else during your log-in procedure.

The script in Figure 10-3 uses four `waitfor` commands. In each case, I used the text that I had written down in the *Computer Types* column when I planned the script.

Typing text: transmit

To send text to the computer, you use a `transmit` command. In the script in Figure 10-3, you can see several variations of this command:

- ✔ `transmit $USERID:` This command transmits the user ID that I enter into the Connect To dialog box. By using this command in your script, you don't have to actually type your user ID into the script.

- ✔ `transmit $PASSWORD:` This command sends the password I enter into the Connect To dialog box. Once again, typing your command this way allows you to send the password without actually having to type your top-secret password into the script.

- ✔ `transmit "^M":` This cryptic command is equivalent to pressing the Enter key.

- ✔ `transmit "some text":` This command transmits some text as if you had typed it at the keyboard. Note that if the text includes ^M, the Enter key is sent as well.

`"^M"` is but one example of several special characters that you can send as part of a text string. Table 10-2 lists all of the special characters that can be included in strings.

Table 10-2	Special Characters for Strings
Character	*Explanation*
^M	Carriage return (Enter)
<cr>	Carriage return (Enter)
<lf>	Line feed
\"	Includes the quotation mark as part of the string
\'	Includes the apostrophe as part of the string
\^	Includes the caret (^) as part of the string
\<	Includes the less-than sign as part of the string
\\	Includes the back slash as part of the string

Attaching the Script to a Dial-Up Connection

After you have created your script, you must attach it to a dial-up connection so that the script plays automatically each time you start the connection. Here's the procedure for attaching a script:

1. **Click Start and choose Programs⇨Accessories⇨Dial-Up Scripting Tool.**

   The Dial-Up Scripting Tool comes to life, as shown in Figure 10-4.

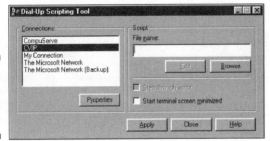

Figure 10-4:
The Dial-Up
Scripting
Tool.

If the Dial-Up Scripting Tool doesn't appear in the Start menu under Programs⇨Accessories, you can run the scripting tool by clicking Start, choosing Run, and typing **C:\Program Files\Accessories\scripter.exe** (where C is your hard drive).

2. **Select the connection to which you want to attach the script.**

3. **Click the Browse button.**

   An Open dialog box appears.

4. **Select the file you want to use as the script.**

   You may have to use the Open dialog box's navigation controls to find the correct drive and folder.

5. **Click the Open button.**

6. **Back in the Dial-Up Scripting Tool dialog box, click Apply.**

7. **Click Close to dismiss the Dial-Up Scripting Tool dialog box.**

You're almost there. You must make one more change in order for the script to work: You must turn off the terminal window that is displayed automatically after you start the connection. To suppress the terminal window, follow these steps:

1. **Click Start and Choose Programs⇨Accessories⇨Dial-Up Networking.**

   This command brings up a window that lists your connections.

2. **Right-click the icon for the connection you attached the script to and then choose Properties from the shortcut menu.**

   The dialog box shown in Figure 10-5 appears.

3. **Click the Configure button.**

   The dialog box shown in Figure 10-6 appears.

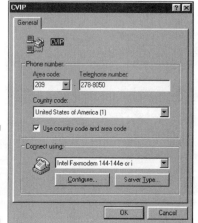

Figure 10-5:
The
Connection
Properties
dialog box.

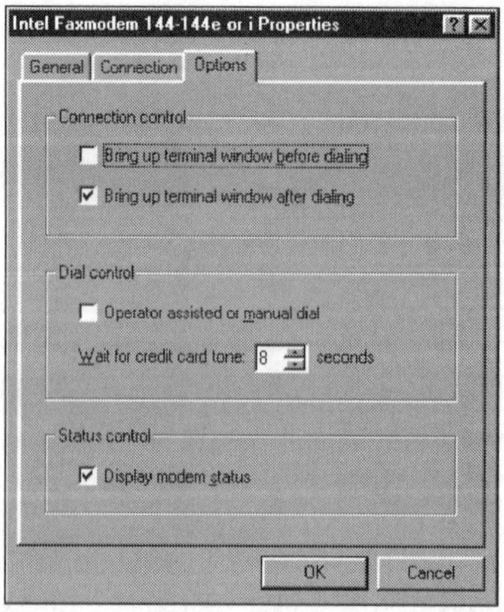

Figure 10-6:
The Modem
Properties
dialog box.

4. **Click the Options tab.**

5. **Click to *uncheck* both Connection control options.**

   These options include bringing up the terminal window before and after dialing.

6. **Click OK to dismiss the Modem Properties dialog box.**

7. **Click OK again to dismiss the Connection Properties dialog box.**

8. **Close the Dial-Up Networking window.**

Now, at long last, you are ready to run the script. When you open the Dial-Up Network connection, the script should run automatically. As the script runs, watch it carefully to make sure that it appears to be running correctly. If it doesn't run properly, double-check the script to make sure that you're transmitting the correct information and, just as importantly, waiting for the correct text before transmitting information.

Part IV
Ports of Call

"HOW SHOULD I KNOW WHY THEY TOOK IT OFF THE LIST? MAYBE THERE JUST WEREN'T ENOUGH MEMBERS TO SUPPORT AN 'AIREDALES FOR ELVIS' NEWSGROUP."

In this part . . .

1 nternet Explorer comes with two accessory programs, called *Internet Mail* and *Internet News,* that are designed to let you access the other two most commonly used portions of the Internet besides the World Wide Web: newsgroups and e-mail.

Besides these two programs, Microsoft also offers two other free programs which, although they don't work directly with the Internet Explorer browser, complement Internet Explorer's functions. The first of these programs, Comic Chat, lets you access one of the most popular areas of the Internet: Internet Relay Chat (or IRC), which allows you to engage in live conversations with other Internet users throughout the planet. The second program, NetMeeting, is sort of like IRC on steroids. In addition to chatting, NetMeeting gives you voice communication and the ability to actually share a program running on your computer with other Internet Users.

You can download all of these extra features when you first acquire Internet Explorer, or you can add them on later from the Internet Explorer Web page.

Chapter 11

Keeping in Touch with Microsoft Internet Mail

*O*ne of the main reasons many people use the Internet at all is for electronic mail, or *e-mail,* as it is called. You can think of e-mail as the high-tech equivalent of Mr. McFeeley, the friendly, bespectacled mailman on *Mr. Rogers' Neighborhood.*

Sending an e-mail message is much like sending a letter through regular mail. In both cases, you write your message, put an address on it, and send it off through an established mail system. Eventually, the recipient of the message receives your note, opens it, reads it, and (if you're lucky) answers by sending a message back.

But e-mail offers certain advantages over regular mail. For example, e-mail arrives at its destination in a matter of minutes, not days. E-mail can be delivered any day of the week, including Sundays. And, as a special plus, no way yet exists for your great-aunt to send you a fruitcake through e-mail.

About the only thing that keeps the post office in business anymore, other than transporting fruitcake, is that e-mail only works when both the sender and the receiver have computers that are connected to the Internet. In other words, you can't send e-mail to someone who isn't on the Internet.

Internet Explorer 3.0 comes with a nifty little Internet e-mail program cleverly called Microsoft Internet Mail. If you don't have Microsoft Internet Mail, run (don't walk) to the Microsoft download site at www.microsoft.com/ie/ download and obtain your copy of this cool little program. It's probably better than whatever puny little e-mail program your Internet service provider offers, and it's certainly better than The Exchange, the e-mail program that comes free with Windows 95.

Starting Microsoft Internet Mail

Like all Windows 95 programs, you can start the Microsoft Internet Mail program in any of several ways. Here are some of the most popular methods:

- Click the Start button and choose Programs⇨Internet Mail
- In Internet Explorer, choose Go⇨Read Mail.
- In Internet Explorer, click the Mail and News button and then choose Read Mail from the pop-up menu that appears.

However you open it, Internet Mail springs to life, displaying the window shown in Figure 11-1.

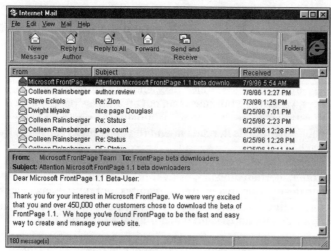

Figure 11-1:
Microsoft
Internet
Mail.

As Figure 11-1 shows, Microsoft Internet Mail has a similar user interface to Internet Explorer. For example, the toolbars in Internet Mail work the same way as the Internet Explorer tools. Notice that the Microsoft Internet Mail window is divided into two major sections, called *panes*. The top pane, called the *Inbox*, is a list of all the e-mail you have received. The bottom pane shows the text of the currently selected message.

Each time you start Microsoft Internet Mail, the program automatically checks to see whether you have received new mail. And provided that you leave Internet Mail open (you can minimize it if you wish), Internet Mail periodically checks to see whether new mail has arrived. Any new messages that you haven't yet read appear in boldface in the Inbox pane.

Sending Electronic Mail

To send electronic mail, all you have to do is follow these steps:

1. **Click the New Message button on the left side of the toolbar.**

   Or choose Mail⇨New Message or use the keyboard shortcut Ctrl+N. Whichever option you choose, the New Message dialog box shown in Figure 11-2 appears.

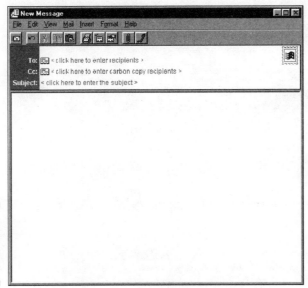

Figure 11-2:
The New Message dialog box.

2. **Click in the To: field and type the Internet address of the person to whom you want to send the message.**

   Click where you see the words `<click here to enter recipients>` and then type the complete address. Note that you can send mail to more than one recipient by typing more than one name or address in the To: field. Type a semicolon between each name.

For examples of different kinds of Internet addresses, check out the nearby sidebar, "Addressing your e-mail."

3. **If you want to send a copy of the message to another user, type that person's address in the Cc: field.**

   Click where you see the words `<click here to enter carbon copy recipients>` and then type the address or addresses of anyone to whom you want to send a copy of the message.

4. **Type a succinct but clear title for the message in the Subject field.**

   Click where you see the words `<click here to enter the subject>` and then type the subject of your message. For example, type **Let's Do Lunch** or **Jetson, You're Fired!**

5. **Type your message in the message area of the New Message dialog box.**

   Figure 11-3 shows what a message looks like with all this information typed in and ready to go.

Figure 11-3:
A message ready to be sent.

 6. **When you finish typing your message, click the Send button.**

   Internet Mail dismisses the New Message dialog box and places the message in your Outbox — a folder that contains messages you have created but that have not yet gone out to their intended recipients.

 7. **To send the message, click the Send and Receive button.**

   You can also press Ctrl+M or choose Mail⇨Send and Receive.

Addressing your e-mail

Just as with paper mail, before you send electronic mail, you have to know the address of the person to whom you're sending it. The easiest way to find out someone's e-mail address is simply to ask for it.

To send mail to a user of one of the major online services, compose the user's e-mail address as follows:

✔ For America Online users, type the user name followed by @aol.com. For example, Lurch@aol.com.

✔ For CompuServe users, type the numeric user ID followed by @compuserve.com. Be sure to use a period rather than a comma to separate the two parts of the numeric user ID. For example:

12345.6789@compuserve.com.

✔ For users of The Microsoft Network, type the user name followed by @msn.com. For example, BillG@msn.com. (No, that's not really Bill Gates's e-mail address. So please don't flood The Microsoft Network with hate mail — or love mail — for Bill!)

Note: You can skip this step if you first configure Internet Mail to send all mail messages immediately. To do so, choose Mail⇨Options, check the Send messages immediately option (found under the Send tab), and click OK.

If you're working in Internet Explorer and you want to send some quick e-mail without starting up Internet Mail, just click the Mail and News button in the toolbar and choose New Message from the pop-up menu that appears. This command takes you straight to a New Document window, where you can compose and deliver your message without starting Internet Mail.

Instead of typing a full Internet address, you can simply type the person's name if you have already created an entry for that person in your Address Book. For more information, see the section "Using the Address Book," later in this chapter.

If you're not sure that you've typed the names and addresses correctly, click the Check Names button. This feature checks the names you've typed against the Address Book to reveal any errors. (Internet Mail assumes that any name you type in the form of an Internet address rather than using the Address Book is correct.) Check Names checks to make sure that the address is in the correct format, but does not check to make sure that the address actually exists.

Using the Address Book

Most Internet users have a relatively small number of people with whom they exchange mail on a regular basis. Rather than retype their addresses every time you send mail to these people, you can store your most commonly used addresses in Internet Mail's Address Book. As an added benefit, the Address Book lets you refer to your e-mail friends by name (for example, George Jetson) rather than by address (george@spacely.com).

Adding a name to the Address Book

Before you can use the Address Book, you must add the names of your e-mail correspondents to it. The best time to add someone to the Address Book is after you receive e-mail from that person. Here's the procedure:

1. **Open an e-mail message from someone you want to add to the Address Book.**

   The message is displayed. For more information about reading e-mail, see the section "Receiving Electronic Mail" later in this chapter.

2. **Right-click the user's name and then choose Add to Address Book.**

   The address is added to the Address Book.

3. **Close the message.**

   Thereafter, you can access the person's address in the Address Book.

To add someone from whom you have not yet received mail to your Address Book, follow these steps:

1. **In Internet Mail, choose File⇨Address Book.**

   The Address Book window appears, as shown in Figure 11-4.

 2. **Click the New Contact button.**

   The Properties dialog box appears, as shown in Figure 11-5.

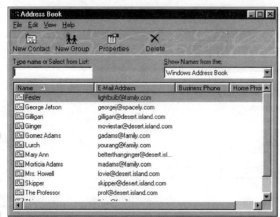

Figure 11-4: The Address Book in all its glory.

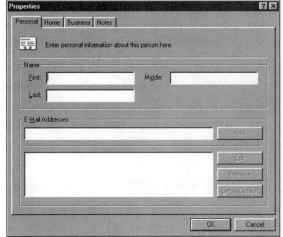

Figure 11-5:
The
Properties
dialog box
for an
Address
Book entry.

3. **Type the information for the new Address Book entry.**

At a minimum, type the person's first and last name and e-mail address.
If you want to, you can include additional information such as phone
numbers and addresses under the Home, Business, and Notes tabs.

4. **Click OK.**

The Address Book entry is created.

Using an address from the Address Book

To send a message to a user who is already in the Address Book, follow these
steps:

1. **In the New Message window, click the little Rolodex-card icon next to
   the To: field.**

   The Select Recipients dialog box appears, as shown in Figure 11-6.

2. **Double-click the name of the person to whom you want to send mail.**

   The person's name is added to the To: list on the right side of the dialog
   box. If double-clicking is against your religion, just click once on the
   person's name and then click the To button.

   Note: You can add more than one name to the To: list, and you can add
   names to the Cc: list by selecting the name and clicking the Rolodex-card
   icon next to the Cc: field.

3. **After you have selected all the names you want, click OK.**

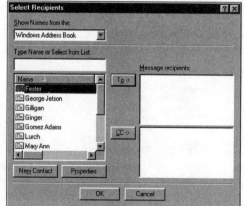

Figure 11-6:
The Select
Recipients
dialog box.

Poof! You're back at the New Message dialog box, and the names you selected appear in the To: and Cc: fields.

Changing or deleting Address Book entries

On occasion, one of your e-mail buddies switches Internet providers and gives you a new Internet address. Or you may lose touch with someone and decide to remove his or her name from your Address Book. Either way, the following steps guide you through the process of keeping your Address Book up to date:

1. **From Internet Mail, choose File⇨Address Book.**

   The Address Book dialog box appears (refer to Figure 11-4).

2. **Click the address you want to change or delete.**

3. **To delete the address, click the Delete button.**

4. **To change the address, click the Properties button.**

   When the Properties dialog box appears, make any necessary changes and then click OK.

5. **Click OK when you're finished.**

Checking your message for spelling errors

If you have Microsoft Office or any of its programs (Word, Excel, or PowerPoint), Internet Mail includes a bonus feature: a spell checker that is capable of catching those embarrassing spelling errors before they go out to the Internet. The spell checker checks the spelling of every word in your message, looking up the words in its massive dictionary. Any misspelling is brought to your attention, and the spell checker is under strict orders from Bill

Gates himself not to giggle or snicker at any of your misspellings, even if you insist on putting an *e* at the end of *potato*. The spell checker even gives you the opportunity to tell it that you are right and it is wrong — and that it should learn how to spell the way you do.

To spell check your messages, follow these steps:

1. **Choose Mail⇨Check Spelling.**

   The spell checker comes to life, looking up your words in hopes of finding a mistake.

2. **Try not to be annoyed if the spell checker finds a spelling error.**

   Hey, you're the one who told it to look for spelling mistakes; don't get mad if it finds some. When the spell checker finds an error, it highlights the offending word and displays the misspelled word along with a suggested correction, as in Figure 11-7.

Figure 11-7:
The spell
checker
points out
an embar-
rassing
spelling
error.

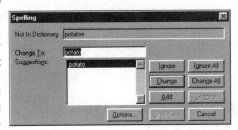

3. **Choose the correct spelling and then click Change, or click Ignore to skip to the next word the spell checker doesn't recognize.**

   If you agree that the word is misspelled, scan the list of suggested corrections and click the one you like. Then click the Change button.

   If, on the other hand, you prefer your own spelling, click Ignore. To prevent the spell checker from asking you over and over again about a particular word that it doesn't recognize (such as someone's name), click Ignore All.

4. **Repeat Steps 2 and 3 until the spell checker gives up.**

   When you see the message The spelling check is complete, your work is done.

Sending Attachments

An *attachment* is a file that you send along with your message. Sending an attachment is kind of like paper-clipping a separate document to a letter. In fact, Internet Mail uses a paper-clip icon to indicate that a message has an attachment, and the button you click to add an attachment sports a paper-clip design, as well.

Adding an attachment

Be aware that sending large attachments can sometimes cause e-mail troubles, especially for attachments that approach a megabyte or more in size. There's no predicting when and where such trouble will occur, and no one in the Internet business likes to admit that it happens, but it does. If you send a large attachment to someone, and your e-mail doesn't go through, try sending it again.

Here is the procedure for adding an attachment to an outgoing message:

1. **Click the Insert File button.**

   The Insert Attachment dialog box shown in Figure 11-8 appears.

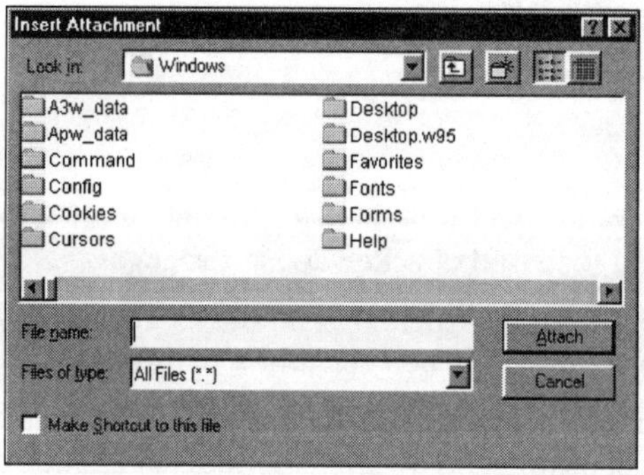

Figure 11-8: Inserting an attachment.

2. **Rummage through the folders on your hard disk until you find the file you want to insert.**

   When you find the file you want to attach, click the filename to select it.

3. **Click Attach.**

   The file is inserted into the message as an attachment. An icon appears in a separate pane in the New Message dialog box, as you see in Figure 11-9. Which icon appears depends on which program the attachment is associated with.

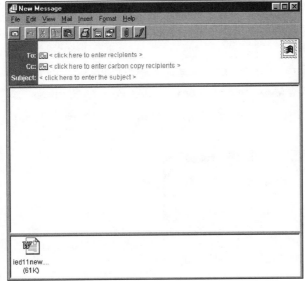

 4. **Finish the message and then click the Send button.**

Complete the rest of the fields in the New Message dialog box, and type a message to go along with the attachment. When you're message is complete, send it on its way.

Changing the encoding scheme

Internet e-mail was designed to send text-based messages, not messages that include binary data such as program files or graphics. To get around this limitation, most e-mail programs (including Internet Mail) let you send and receive encoded data. *Encoded data* is binary information that has been converted into a form that normal Internet e-mail can handle. When the mail arrives at its destination, the encoded data is decoded so that the recipient can access the binary file in its original form.

Two popular methods are used to send encoded data. By default, Internet Mail uses an encoding scheme called MIME. If the recipient of your message complains that he or she cannot read the attachment, you can change the encoding scheme to an alternate scheme called *Uuencode* (pronounced "you-you-encode"). Neither scheme appears to have an inherent advantage over the other, except that your recipient may be able to deal with Uuencode but not MIME, or vice versa.

To change encoding schemes, follow these steps:

1. **Attach a file according to the procedure described in "Adding an attachment."**

    Stop before completing the last step — sending your message.

2. **In the New Message dialog box, choose Format⇨Settings.**

    The Plain Text Settings dialog box appears, as shown in Figure 11-10.

3. **Change the Message format setting from MIME to Uuencode.**

4. **Click OK.**

The preceding steps change the format to Uuencode for the current message only. To change the default message format for *all* messages, choose Mail⇨Options from Internet Mail's main window. Then change the Mail Sending Format option in the Send tab of the Options dialog box.

Adding a Signature

As you surf the Net, you discover that many Internet users conclude all of their e-mail and newsgroup messages with a special *signature* — a line or two of text that includes their name, contact information such as their e-mail address and sometimes their phone or fax number, and often a witty saying. Special e-mail software automatically adds these people's signatures to the end of every message, so they don't have to type their signatures each time.

Internet Mail lets you tag your own signature on to the end of your e-mail messages. Follow these simple steps to set up your own signature:

1. **Choose Mail⇨Options and click the Signature tab.**

    The Signature options appear.

2. **Click in the Text button.**

3. Type the text you want to use for your signature.

Figure 11-11 shows an example.

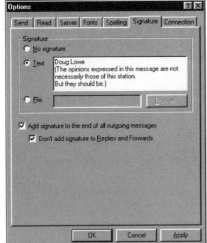

Figure 11-11:
A typical
signature.

4. Check the Add Signature options to make sure that they're to your liking.

The default settings are probably what you want to use: The signature will be automatically added to all new messages, but won't be added to replies or forwards.

5. Click OK.

If your signature is lengthy, you may want to create it in a separate file and choose the File option for the signature. This option is commonly used along with a program that automatically changes the signature file in some way each day — perhaps to add the date or to insert a random quotation. Such tricks are clearly in the realm of nerddom and best avoided by ordinary folk.

Receiving Electronic Mail

Electronic mail wouldn't be much good if it worked like a send-only set, sending out messages but not receiving them. (I once had an aunt who worked that way.) Fortunately, you can receive e-mail as well as send it — assuming, of course, that you have friends who write.

To read electronic mail that other users have sent you, follow these steps:

1. **Start Internet Mail.**

   Refer back to the section "Starting Microsoft Internet Mail," at the beginning of this chapter, if you're not sure how.

   After Internet Mail starts, it immediately checks to see whether you have any new messages. If you do, your computer beeps and the subject line and sender name for the new messages are displayed in boldface in the Internet Mail window.

2. **Double-click a new message to read it.**

   The message is displayed in its own window.

3. **Read the message.**

4. **After you read the message, dispense with it in one of the following ways:**

   - If the message is worthy of reply, click the Reply to Sender button. A new message window appears, allowing you to compose a reply. The To: field is automatically set to the user who sent you the message, the subject is automatically set to `RE: (whatever the original subject was)`, and the complete text of the original message is inserted at the bottom of the new message. Compose your reply and then click the Send button.

   - If the message was originally sent to several people, you can click the Reply to All button to send a reply to all of the original recipients.

   - If the message was intended for someone else, or if you think someone else should see it (maybe it contains a juicy bit of gossip!), click the Forward button. A new message window appears, allowing you to select the user or users to whom the message should be forwarded. The original message is inserted at the bottom of the new message, with space left at the top for you to type an explanation of why you are forwarding the message (`Hey Mr. Spacely, get a load of this!`).

   - To print the message, click the Print button.

   - To save the message, click the Save button.

   - If the message is unworthy even of filing, click the Delete button. Poof!

5. **If you have additional messages to read, click the Next or Previous buttons to continue reading messages.**

   Click the Next button to read the next message in sequence.

   Click the Previous button to read the previous message.

Saving an Attachment as a File

If someone is kind enough to send you a message that includes an attached file, you can save the attachment as a separate file by following these steps:

1. **Open the message that has the attachment.**

   You can tell which messages have attachments by looking for the paper-clip icon next to the message in the message list.

2. **Right-click the attachment icon and then choose the Save As command from the pop-up menu.**

   A Save As dialog box appears.

3. **Choose the location where you want to save the file.**

   You can use the controls on the standard Save As dialog box to navigate to a different drive or folder.

4. **Type a filename for the file.**

   Internet Mail, always trying to help you out, proposes a filename. You need type a new filename only if you don't like the filename that Internet Mail proposes.

5. **Click Save.**

   The attachment is saved as a file.

You can immediately view an attachment by double-clicking on it. If the attachment is a document, Windows 95 launches the appropriate application to open the document. If the attachment is a sound file, Windows 95 plays the sound — provided your computer is equipped with a sound card.

Beware of attachments from unfamiliar sources: They may contain a virus that could infect your computer. Unfortunately, Internet Mail doesn't have any built-in virus protection. So if you are concerned about viruses (and you should be), purchase and install separate virus protection software.

Using HTML Formatting

Internet Mail has a nifty feature that enables you to add formatting to your e-mail messages. To accomplish this feat, Internet Mail uses the same HTML formatting codes used to create pages on the World Wide Web. Of course, when you send an HTML-formatted message to another Internet user, that user must have a mail program that is capable of reading messages formatted with HTML. Otherwise, your beautiful formats will be for naught.

To use HTML formatting, call up the New Message window to compose a new message and choose Format⇨HTML. A new toolbar appears in the New Message window, as shown in Figure 11-12.

Formatting toolbar

Figure 11-12:
Formatting an e-mail message with HTML.

Table 11-1 shows how you can use the options on the formatting toolbar to enhance the text in your e-mail messages.

Table 11-1	Options on the New Message Formatting Toolbar
Button	*Format*
Arial	Changes the font
10	Sets the size of the text font
	Changes the text color
B	Makes the text bold
I	Makes the text italic
U	Underlines the text
	Creates a bullet list

Button	Format
	Left-aligns the text
	Centers the text
	Right-justifies the text

Internet Mail Keyboard Shortcuts

Several keyboard shortcuts are available to you as you compose an e-mail message. Most of these shortcuts, summarized in Table 11-2, are pretty much standard throughout Windows, so they should come as no surprise.

Table 11-2	Keyboard Shortcuts for Editing E-Mail Messages
Keyboard Shortcut	*What It Does*
Moving and Selecting	
Ctrl+Left arrow	Moves cursor left one word
Ctrl+Right arrow	Moves cursor right one word
Home	Moves cursor to the beginning of the line
End	Moves cursor to the end of the line
Ctrl+Home	Moves cursor to the beginning of the message
Ctrl+End	Moves cursor to the end of the message
Ctrl+A	Selects the entire message
Editing	
Ctrl+X	Cuts the selection to the clipboard so you can paste it in another location
Ctrl+C	Copies the selection to the clipboard
Ctrl+V	Pastes the contents of the clipboard to the location of the insertion point
Ctrl+Delete	Deletes to the end of the word
Ctrl+Z	Undoes the last action you did (not available for some actions, such as sending a message)

(continued)

Table 11-2 *(continued)*

Keyboard Shortcut	What It Does
Shortcuts for reading mail	
Ctrl+F	Forwards the message to another user
Ctrl+R	Replies to the sender of a message
Ctrl+Shift+R	Replies to the sender of a message and all the message's recipients
Ctrl+>	Skips to next message
Ctrl+<	Returns to previous message
Other shortcuts	
Alt+S	Sends the message
F7	Checks the spelling of the message
Ctrl+N	Composes yet another message
Ctrl+K	Checks the names listed in the To: and Cc: fields against the Address Book

Using Internet Mail Folders

Internet Mail includes a separate toolbar, called *Folders,* that gives you access to any of four message folders that are available in Internet Mail. Normally, only the Inbox folder is displayed. You can display other folders by clicking the word *Folders* on the toolbar to reveal the Folders drop-down list, which allows you to select the folder you want to display.

The four message folders are

- **Inbox:** Where your incoming messages are stored
- **Outbox:** Where messages you have written are stored until they are sent to their intended recipients
- **Sent items:** Where messages are placed after they have been sent
- **Deleted items:** Where deleted messages are stored (This folder enables you to undelete a deleted message if you later decide you want the message back.)

Internet Mail also lets you create your own message folders. For example, you may want to create separate folders for different categories of messages, such as work related, friends and family, and so on. Or you may want to create date-related folders for storing older messages. For example, you can create a 1996 folder to save all of the messages you received in 1996.

The following sections explain how to work with message folders.

Creating a new folder

Before you start saving important messages, you should first create one or more folders in which to save the messages. I use just a single folder, named Saved Items, but you may want to create several folders for saving messages according to their content. For example, you may create a Personal Items folder for personal messages and a Business Items folder for business messages. You have to come up with a good scheme for organizing saved messages, but my advice is to keep your method simple. If you create 40 folders for storing saved messages, you'll never remember which message is in which folder.

To create a new folder, follow these steps:

1. **From Internet Mail's main window, choose File➪Folder➪Create.**

   The Create New Folder dialog box appears, as shown in Figure 11-13.

2. **Type a name for the new folder.**

   For example, type **Work Related**.

3. **Click OK.**

Figure 11-13:
Creating a new folder for saving messages.

Moving messages to another folder

After you create a folder for your messages, moving a message to the folder is easy. Just follow these steps:

1. **From the Inbox, select the message you want to save.**

2. **Choose Mail⇨Move To.**

   A menu listing all of the available folders appears.

3. **Click the folder to which you want to move the message.**

   The message moves to the folder you selected and is deleted from the Inbox folder.

If you prefer, you can make a copy of the message rather than move the message. Just choose Mail⇨Copy To instead of Mail⇨Move To.

Chapter 12

Staying Informed with Microsoft Internet News

In This Chapter

▶ How newsgroups work

▶ Browsing newsgroups with Microsoft Internet News

▶ Reading and writing messages to newsgroups

▶ Downloading pictures and other binary files from newsgroups

*I*nternet Explorer has a companion program, called Microsoft Internet News, that enables you to access *newsgroups,* the Internet equivalent of a bulletin board. This chapter explains the ins and outs of using Microsoft Internet News.

Introducing Newsgroups

A *newsgroup* is a place where you can post messages (called *articles*) about a particular topic and read messages that others have posted about the same topic. People with similar interests visit a newsgroup to share news and information, find out what others are thinking, ask questions, get answers, and generally shoot the breeze.

The Internet has thousands of newsgroups — yea, *tens* of thousands — on topics ranging from astronomy to the Civil War. You can find a newsgroup for virtually any subject that interests you.

Newsgroups come in two basic types:

▸ **Moderated newsgroup:** In a moderated newsgroup, one person is designated as a *moderator,* and has complete control over what does and does not appear in the newsgroup. All new articles are submitted to the moderator for his or her review. Nothing is actually posted to the newsgroup until the moderator has approved it.

The moderator establishes the criteria for which articles get posted to the newsgroup. For some newsgroups, the criterion is nothing more than that the article must be somehow related to the subject of the newsgroup. Other newsgroups use more stringent criteria, enabling the moderator to be more selective about what gets posted. As a result, only the best postings actually make it into the newsgroup. This supervision may seem stifling, but in most cases, it dramatically improves the quality of the newsgroup articles.

✔ **Unmoderated newsgroup:** In an unmoderated newsgroup, anyone and everyone can post an article. Unmoderated newsgroups are free from censorship, but they are also often filled with blatant solicitations, chain letters, and all sorts of noise.

Using Usenet

The term *Usenet* refers to a collection of newsgroups that are distributed together to computers that run special software called *news servers*. Each Internet service provider (ISP) provides its own news server so that you can access the newsgroups that are a part of Usenet.

In theory, the Usenet servers share their new postings with one another, so all the servers contain the most recent postings. In practice, Usenet servers are never really quite up-to-date, nor are they always in sync with one another. When you post an article to a newsgroup, a day or so may pass before your article propagates through the Usenet and appears on all servers. Likewise, replies to your articles may take awhile to show up on your server.

Each Usenet site decides on its own which of the Usenet newsgroups to carry. As a result, you may find that a particular newsgroup isn't available from your Internet service provider.

Because the content of newsgroups, particularly the renegade alt newsgroups, is sometimes a bit offensive, your Internet service provider may not automatically grant you access to all newsgoups. If you find yourself locked out of these groups, consult your ISP to find out how to gain access.

Understanding Usenet newsgroup names

Usenet boasts thousands of newsgroups. Each newsgroup has a unique name that consists of one or more parts separated by periods. For example, `soc.culture.assyrian` is a newsgroup that discusses Assyrian culture, `sci.polymers` contains information on the scientific field of polymers, and `rec.food.drink.beer` is a place to discuss your favorite brew.

The first part of a newsgroup name identifies one of several broad categories of newsgroups, as described in the following list:

- ✔ `comp`: Discussions about computers (Many of the participants in the `comp` newsgroups wear pocket protectors and glasses held together by tape.)

- ✔ `news`: Discussions about the Usenet itself, such as help for new Usenet users, announcements of new newsgroups, and statistics about which newsgroups are most popular

- ✔ `rec`: Recreational topics, such as sports, fishing, basket weaving, model railroading, and so on

- ✔ `sci`: Discussions about science

- ✔ `soc`: Social topics, where people gather to shoot the breeze or to discuss social issues

- ✔ `talk`: Newsgroups that favor long-winded discussions of topics such as politics and religion

- ✔ `misc`: Topics that don't fit in any of the other categories

- ✔ `bit`: Bitnet is the network that supports Internet mailing lists (a *mailing list* is like a newsgroup, except that all messages are exchanged via e-mail). The `bit` newsgroups are the bitnet mailing lists presented in newsgroup form.

- ✔ `biz`: This prefix denotes a business-related newsgroup.

- ✔ `bionet`: Newsgroups with this prefix discuss topics related to biology.

- ✔ **Regional newsgroups:** Newsgroups that share regional interests are indicated by a short prefix (usually two or three letters), such as `aus` (Australia) or `can` (Canada). Most states have regional newsgroups designated by the state's two-letter abbreviation (`CA` for California, `WA` for Washington, and so on).

- ✔ `alt`: Hundreds of newsgroups using this prefix discuss topics that range from bizarre to X-rated to paranoid. These newsgroups are not officially sanctioned by Usenet, but some of the most popular newsgroups fall into this category. The most visited of the `alt` newsgroups fall under the `alt.binaries` designation. These newsgroups contain binary files (such as pictures, sounds, and actual programs) that are specially encoded to be sent via Usenet's text-only messages. Fortunately, Internet Explorer is able to automatically decode these attachments, so you don't have to worry about using a separate program to do so.

The Microsoft news server

Usenet is the most popular source of Internet newsgroups, but it's not the only source. For example, Microsoft itself has its own news server that contains several dozen newsgroups related to Microsoft products. The Microsoft news server is an important news server to know about, because it's where Microsoft provides official online support for its products.

All the support newsgroups on the Microsoft news server begin with the words `microsoft.public`, followed by the name of a Microsoft product (or an abbreviation of it). Here are some of the Microsoft newsgroups that are dedicated to supporting users of Internet Explorer and related products:

- `microsoft.public.internetexplorer.win95`
- `microsoft.public.internet.news`
- `microsoft.public.internet.mail`
- `microsoft.public.internet.netmeeting`

These newsgroups are not distributed on Usenet, so you won't find them listed in your Internet service provider's list of newsgroups. Instead, you have to sign directly in to the Microsoft news server to access them. (Unless, of course, your Internet service provider happens to use the Microsoft news server as its default news server. That's unlikely, though.)

Checking the Internet News

Microsoft Internet News makes accessing Internet newsgroups easy. You can start Internet News several ways:

- Click the Start button in the taskbar and then choose Programs⇨ Internet News.
- In Internet Explorer, click the Mail and News icon and select the Read News command from the pop-up menu that appears.
- In Internet Explorer, choose Go⇨Read News.
- In Internet Explorer, click a link to a newsgroup. (Newsgroup addresses begin with `news:`. For example, `news:rec.backcountry` refers to the newsgroup named `rec.backcountry`.)

Internet News begins with a screen similar to the one shown in Figure 12-1.

Notice that the Internet News screen shows a list of article subjects in one pane and a preview of the current article in a separate *preview pane*. You can sort the list of articles by subject, author, or date by clicking the appropriate header above each column.

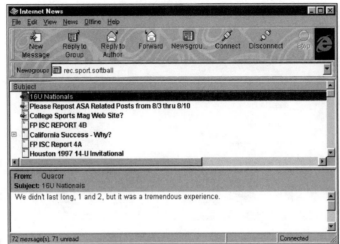

Figure 12-1:
The Internet
News
screen.

You can change the size of the preview pane by dragging the border between the preview pane and the subject list. You can relocate the preview pane by choosing View➪Preview Pane. You have three options:

✔ **Split Horizontally:** This is the default setting, in which the preview pane appears beneath the subject headers.

✔ **Split Vertically:** This option displays the preview pane alongside the subject list, allowing Internet News to display more subject lines.

✔ **None:** This setting improves performance because Internet News doesn't have to download article text as you select messages.

Accessing Newsgroups

When you start Internet News, the newsgroup you were last reading opens by default. You can switch to another newsgroup by following this procedure:

1. **Click the Newsgroups icon (or choose News➪Newsgroups or press Ctrl+W).**

   The Newsgroups dialog box appears, as shown in Figure 12-2.

2. **Scroll through the list to find the newsgroup you want to read.**

   The newsgroups are arranged in alphabetical order.

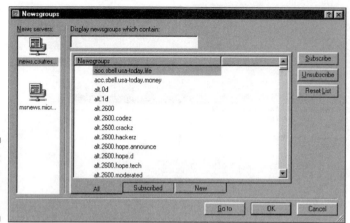

Figure 12-2:
The
Newsgroups
dialog box.

3. Click the newsgroup you want to read and then click the Go to button.

The newsgroup opens. You may have to wait a few moments as Internet News downloads the subject headers for the newsgroup.

If you find a newsgroup that you think you'll visit frequently, click the Subscribe button. Doing so adds the newsgroup to the list of newsgroups that appears in the main Internet News window in the Newsgroups drop-down list box (where your current newsgroup is listed).

You can type a word or phrase in the Display newsgroups which contain text box to display only those newsgroups whose names contain the word or phrase you type. For example, Figure 12-3 shows a list of all newsgroups that contain the word *startrek*. (As you can see, Usenet plays host to some pretty strange *Star Trek* fans.)

First come, first server

If you use more than one news server, the servers appear at the left of the Newsgroups dialog box. To switch to another news server, just click its icon. Each news server has a different set of newsgroups, so some newsgroups may not be available on your server.

If you need to configure Internet News to work with a different news server, choose News⇨ Options and click the Server tab. You can find buttons that enable you to add a new server, delete a server, or change the properties of a server.

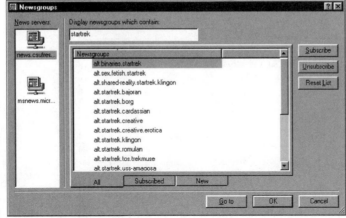

Figure 12-3:
Displaying
newsgroups
that contain
the word
startrek.

Reading Threads

A *thread* is a newsgroup article plus any articles that were posted as replies to the original article, articles posted as replies to the replies, and so on. Microsoft Internet News groups together all of the articles that belong to a thread. A plus sign next to a message title indicates that the article has replies.

The following are some of the ways you can expand or collapse threads:

- ✔ Click the plus sign to reveal the replies to an article.
- ✔ Click the minus sign to hide replies.
- ✔ Choose View➪Expand to expand a thread.
- ✔ Choose View➪Collapse to collapse an expanded thread.

Reading an Article

To read an article, double-click the article's title. The article appears in a separate window, as shown in Figure 12-4. After you finish reading the article, click the article window's Close button to close the window.

 To save an article to your computer, choose File➪Save As or click the Save button.

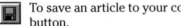 To print an article, choose File➪Print or click the Print button.

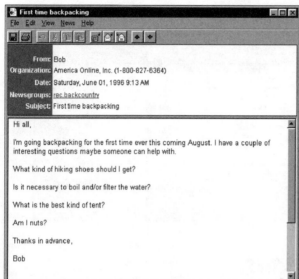

Figure 12-4:
A news-
group
article.

You can go to the next or previous articles by clicking the following buttons:

   ✔ Read the next article

   ✔ Read the previous article

Replying to an Article

To reply to a newsgroup posting, follow these steps:

1. Count to ten and then reconsider your reply.

Keep in mind that replying to a newsgroup is not like replying to e-mail. Only the intended recipient can read an e-mail reply. Anyone on the planet can read your newsgroup postings. If you don't really have anything to add to the discussion, why waste your time?

 2. After reading the article you want to reply to, click the Reply to Group button in the toolbar.

A new message window appears, with the subject line already filled in.

3. Type your reply.

 4. Click the Post button.

Your article is sent to the newsgroup.

5. You're about to become a published writer.

Hold the spam

No, I'm not referring to that canned meat product that was the butt of many jokes in the old TV series, *M*A*S*H.* I'm talking about a particular type of annoying newsgroup message. A *spam* is a message that has been bogusly posted to more than one — perhaps dozens — of newsgroups, all at the same time, in an effort to generate hundreds of responses. Spams often have subject headers like *Make money fast* or *Free X-rated pictures in your mailbox!*

You can spot a spam right away by looking at the newsgroups listed in the Newsgroups field at the top of the message window. If more than one

or two newsgroups are listed, you're probably looking at a spam.

The best way to deal with spams is to ignore them. You see, the main problem with spams is that they generate hundreds of responses, which may themselves generate hundreds of responses. Most of the responses are along the lines of "Quit spamming us, you idiot," but the responders don't realize that they themselves are helping the spammer by keeping his or her bogus thread alive. Better to ignore the spam altogether so it will go away.

By default, the complete text of the original message is added to the end of your reply. If the message is long, you may want to delete some or all of the original text. If you don't want the original message text to be automatically added to your replies, choose News⇨Options, click the Send tab, and deselect the Include original message in reply option.

 If you want to reply to several specific points of an article, you can intermingle your responses with the original message. The original message appears after greater-than signs, setting it off from your insightful responses. Figure 12-5 shows an example of what I mean.

Writing a New Article

When you have finally mustered the courage to post an article of your own to a newsgroup, follow these steps:

1. **Open the newsgroup in which you want to post a new article.**

 2. **Click the New Message button.**

    A new message window appears.

3. **Type a subject for the article in the Subject box.**

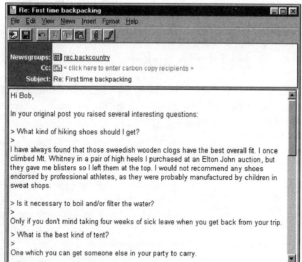

Figure 12-5:
Replying to
an article
point-by-
point.

Make sure that the subject you type accurately reflects the topic of the article — or prepare to get flamed. (Being *flamed* doesn't mean that your computer screen actually emits a ball of fire in your direction, singeing the hair off your forearm. It refers to getting an angry — even vitriolic — response from a reader.) If your subject line is misleading, at least one Internet user is sure to chew you out for it.

4. **Type your message in the message area.**

5. **If you're worried about your vice-presidential prospects, choose News⇨Check Spelling.**

   The spell checker gives you the option to correct any misspelled words.

 6. **Click the Post button when you're satisfied with your response.**

Adding a Signature

Like Internet Mail, Internet News allows you to attach a signature to the end of all your newsgroup postings. The signature can include any text you wish: your name, contact information, and perhaps a witty saying. The signature is automatically added to the end of your article postings, so you don't have to type it anew each time.

The procedure for adding a signature to a newsgroup article is the same as adding one to an e-mail message, so I humbly refer you back to Chapter 11 for the steps required to do so.

Dealing with Attachments

Internet newsgroups are text only; you cannot attach binary files (such as program, picture, and sound files) to newsgroup messages. Internet users are very resourceful, however, and they long ago figured out a way to get around this dilemma. They invented a technique, called *encoding,* that converts a nontext file into a series of text codes that you can post as a newsgroup article. Such an article looks completely scrambled when you see it. However, you can save the article to a file on your hard disk and then run the saved file through a special decoding program that converts it back to its original form, whether it's a program, picture, or sound file.

With Internet News, the decoding routine is built in, so you don't need a separate program. To save a binary file that has been attached to a newsgroup article, all you have to do is follow these steps:

1. **Open the article that has the attachment.**

   Unlike Internet Mail, Internet News does not indicate which messages contain attachments by displaying a paper clip next to the subject line. The only way to tell whether a message has an attachment is to open the message.

2. **Click the attachment icon with the right mouse button.**

   A shortcut menu appears.

3. **Choose the Save As command from the shortcut menu.**

   A standard Save As dialog box appears.

4. **Select the location where you want to save the file.**

   The controls in the Save As dialog box allow you to navigate to any drive or folder.

5. **Check the filename that is proposed for the file.**

   If you don't like it, change it.

6. **Click Save.**

   The file is saved.

You can view an attachment without saving it to disk by double-clicking the attachment.

Adding Formatting to Your Messages

Internet News gives you the option of adding fancy formatting such as **bold** or *italic* type to your newsgroup articles. To accommodate this special formatting, Internet News posts its articles in HTML format, using the same formatting codes that pages on the Web use.

To enable HTML formatting while composing a message, choose Format⇨ HTML. An additional formatting toolbar appears in the New Message window, as shown in Figure 12-6. The formatting toolbar is identical to the one you use to compose e-mail messages. To find out how to use it, check out Chapter 11.

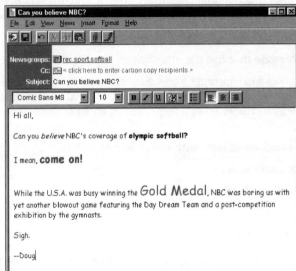

Figure 12-6:
Using HTML formatting in a newsgroup article.

Keep in mind that if you use HTML formatting in your newsgroup articles, many newsgroup users won't be able to see or appreciate your formatting. Sooner or later, though, most everyone will be using an advanced news-reader program (like Microsoft Internet News) that is capable of displaying HTML-formatted newsgroup articles. Until then, consider yourself on the cutting edge.

Working Offline

If you're unfortunate enough to use an Internet service provider that levies hourly connect-time charges, you may be reluctant to spend much time in newsgroups because charges can quickly add up while you read and write newsgroup articles.

Fortunately, Internet News provides an offline feature that lets you mark a batch of newsgroup articles to be downloaded all at once. After the articles have been downloaded to your computer, you can disconnect from your ISP and read the whole batch without worrying about connect-time charges accruing. You can even post as a batch any replies you make or new articles you compose while disconnected when you reconnect later.

To read newsgroup articles offline, follow these steps:

1. **Connect to the Internet and start Internet News.**

2. **Mark individual articles you want to download and read offline by selecting them and choosing Offline⇨Mark Message for Download.**

   Or you can mark entire message threads by selecting the top level of the thread and choosing the Offline⇨Mark Thread for Download command.

   You can select several articles to be marked at once by holding down the control key while clicking each of the articles you want to mark.

3. **When you are ready to download the articles you've marked, choose Offline⇨Post and Download.**

   Depending on how many articles you marked, the download process may take awhile.

4. **When all of the articles have been downloaded, disconnect from your ISP.**

   The easiest way to disconnect is to maximize the Connected To window from the Windows 95 taskbar and then click the Disconnect button.

5. **Read the articles you downloaded and post any replies or new articles.**

   You can take your time because you are no longer connected to the Internet. Any replies you create or new posts you compose are held until you complete the next step.

6. **When you're ready to post your replies, reconnect to the Internet.**

7. **In Internet News, choose Offline⇨Post and Download.**

   Your replies are posted automatically.

Chapter 13

See You in the Funny Papers: Microsoft Comic Chat

• •

In This Chapter

▶ Downloading and installing Comic Chat

▶ Chatting with other users using comic-book style characters

▶ Configuring Comic Chat

• •

*O*nline chatting is one of the most talked-about features of the Internet. Chatting enables you to communicate live with other Internet users throughout the world. Whereas e-mail and newsgroups have built-in communication delays, chatting gives you immediate feedback on your messages.

On the Internet, people chat using a special service called *Internet Relay Chat* (or IRC for short). IRC offers thousands of different *chat rooms* where people gather to discuss whatever is on their minds. Some chat rooms have just a few participants; others may have dozens or even hundreds of participants.

Although Internet Explorer does not provide a built-in method for accessing IRC, Microsoft does offer a free program called *Microsoft Comic Chat,* which enables you to participate in Internet chats.

As this chapter explains, Comic Chat is a bit unusual. Whereas most IRC programs are text based, Comic Chat presents IRC chats in a goofy comic-book format. Comic Chat uses a cartoon character to represent each Internet user participating in the chat. If this sounds weird, that's because it *is* weird.

Setting Up Comic Chat

The first step to using Comic Chat is to obtain a copy of the Comic Chat program and install it on your computer. Fortunately, Microsoft Comic Chat is

available free from the Microsoft Internet Explorer download page at
`www.microsoft.com/ie/download`. To download Comic Chat from this Web
page, follow these steps:

1. **From the drop-down list, select Additional Features & Add-ons and then
   click the Next> button.**

   You go to another page, in which a drop-down list displays several programs that work with or enhance Internet Explorer, including Comic Chat.

2. **Select Comic Chat and then click Next> again.**

   Up pops a page listing several Web sites from which you can download
   Comic Chat.

3. **Click the site that is geographically closest to you and then wait while
   Comic Chat downloads.**

   Be prepared to wait awhile — the Comic Chat download file is larger than
   1MB. Even with a fast 28.8 modem, you can expect the download to take 15
   minutes or longer.

   When the download begins, Internet Explorer displays a dialog box asking
   whether you want to open the file or save it to disk.

4. **Select Open or Save it to disk.**

   • Select Open if you want to install Comic Chat on your hard disk
     immediately after the download is complete.

   • Select Save it to disk if you want to wait to install Comic Chat later.
     Specify the folder where you want to save Comic Chat.

For more serious chatters only

If you find the Comic Chat interface annoying or
silly, you may want to try a different chat client
program. One of the most popular is the powerful
program mIRC, which you can download for free
for personal use from many Internet sites. For
the serious chatter, the client program mIRC has
many advantages over Comic Chat. Here are just
a few:

✔ mIRC doesn't use the cute-but-sometimes-
  tiresome comic-book style of Comic Chat.
  mIRC conversations appear in a simple, text-
  only format.

✔ mIRC gives you access to all of the commands that are available to chat users with

IRC. For example, IRC lets you use commands to grant operator privileges to other
users. But because Comic Chat won't let you
use IRC commands, you can't access this
feature with Comic Chat.

✔ mIRC enables you to carry on conversations
  in several chat rooms at once (although, in
  mIRC, chat rooms are called *channels*).

✔ mIRC allows you to carry on private conversations between you and another user.

If you're interested in trying out mIRC, you can
download it from `mirc.co.uk`.

If you select Save it to disk, you can install Comic Chat later by running the installation program you downloaded. To install Comic Chat after downloading and saving it, open My Computer, find the folder where you saved the downloaded Comic Chat file, and then double-click the file's icon.

Connecting to a Chat Server

After you download and install Comic Chat, the fun begins. Start Comic Chat by clicking Start and choosing Programs⇨Microsoft Comic Chat. After your computer grinds and whirls for a moment, the dialog box shown in Figure 13-1 greets you.

Figure 13-1:
The Comic Chat Connect dialog box.

In the Connect dialog box, you specify important information required for you to be able to initiate a chat with other Internet users. Here's the lowdown on the fields in the Connect dialog box:

- ✔ **Favorites:** As you use Comic Chat, you can add the chat rooms you visit most frequently to a list of favorite chat rooms. Initially, though, this list is empty. Microsoft doesn't presume to know what your favorite chat rooms are. (Kind of surprising, isn't it?)

- ✔ **Server:** Hundreds of chat servers exist throughout the world. Most are a part of the IRC system of chat servers. Microsoft provides several servers of its own, which you can use to chat with other Comic Chat users. Comic Chat is preconfigured to connect to these servers, which are named `comicsrv1.microsoft.com`, `comicsrv2.microsoft.com`, and so on.

  Comic Chat isn't limited to working with Microsoft's chat servers. You can connect to any IRC chat server you have access to. To connect to a different chat server, just type the name of the server in the Server field.

✔ **Port:** Ports are the entrance points to IRC chats. One of the funny things about IRC is that you have to specify a port number for your chat server, but the port number is almost always 6667. Don't ask me who chose the number 6667. I think maybe it was a practical joke by someone who picked 666 to imply that IRC was inherently evil, but then added a 7 to the end just to hedge the bet.

✔ **Go to chat room:** If everyone on the Internet chatted in the same place, the conversations would be incomprehensible. To keep conversations more manageable, chatting occurs in *chat rooms,* which are gathering places where people with common interests can meet to chat. If you know the name of a chat room you want to visit, select this option and type the name of the chat room in this field. Otherwise, select the next option.

✔ **Show all available chat rooms:** Select this option if you don't know the name of the chat room you want to visit, or if you aren't sure which chat rooms are available on the server to which you're about to connect.

After you've set all Comic Chat Connect options, click OK to connect to the chat server.

Selecting a Chat Room

If you select Show all available chat rooms from the Connect dialog box, you are greeted with a list of all the chat rooms available on the server you connected to, as shown in Figure 13-2.

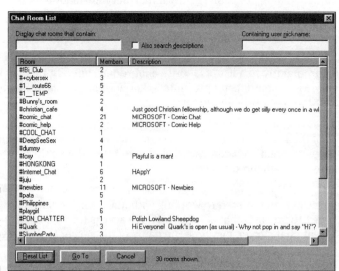

Figure 13-2:
The Chat
Room List
dialog box.

In the Microsoft chat server (`comicsrv1.microsoft.com`), Microsoft sets up several chat rooms where people can get help with Comic Chat. For example, #Comic_Help is a chat room where you can ask questions about using Comic Chat. Other chat rooms focus on interests such as sports and pets. You can also find a number of *unauthorized* chat rooms — rooms that Comic Chat users have created to discuss a variety of topics. Some of these chat rooms are on-the-level, but some are a bit sleazy.

If you find a chat room you like, you can add it to your Favorites by choosing Favorites⇨Add to Favorites. Or you can create a shortcut to the chat room by choosing File⇨Create Shortcut.

Chatting in Comic Chat

Most chat programs display the conversation in a chat room as a never-ending stream of text, but Comic Chat is different — it displays chats using comic-book style characters, as shown in Figure 13-3.

Your character ─┐

┌─Title frame Participants (by nickname)

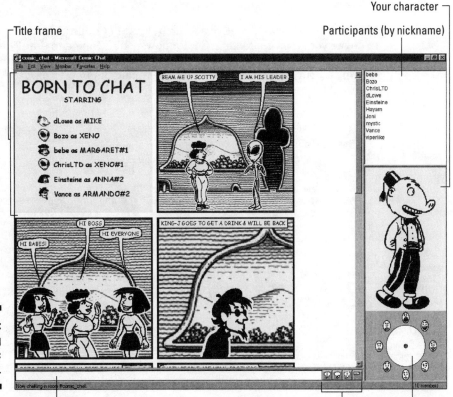

Figure 13-3:
Chatting
with Comic
Chat.

Message box   Send buttons   Emotion Wheel

The Comic Chat screen has a lot going on:

- ✔ The first frame of any chat shows the chat's title and lists the active chat participants (by nickname) and their character names.

- ✔ At the bottom of the screen is the *message box*, where you type messages to be sent to the chat.

- ✔ To the right of the message box are the send buttons (see the next section, "Sending a Message").

- ✔ The right side of the window lists the nicknames of all users who are in the chat room.

- ✔ Below the list of nicknames is a charming portrait of the character that represents you.

- ✔ In the lower-right corner of the screen is the *Emotion Wheel,* which lets you control your character's facial expressions.

Each person in the chat room is represented by one of 12 characters that come with Comic Chat. You can choose the character you want to represent you, but if you don't choose a character, Comic Chat chooses one for you — free of charge.

Microsoft has indicated that, in a future release of Comic Chat, you will be able to create your own characters. But for now, you're limited to the 12 characters that come with Comic Chat. Figure 13-4 shows these 12 characters. Read "Having It Your Way," later in this chapter, to find out how to pick the character you want to represent you.

Figure 13-4:
The 12 characters that come with Comic Chat.

ANNA   ARMANDO   DAN   HUGH   JORDAN   LANCE

MARGARET   MIKE   SUSAN   TIKI   TONGTYED   XENO

Each time you send a message in the chat room, Comic Chat adds your character to the comic strip and includes your message in a bubble. If possible, Comic Chat adds your character to the current comic strip frame, zooming back if necessary so that all of the characters in the frame are visible. Whenever the frame gets too crowded, Comic Chat creates a new frame and scrolls the entire comic strip so you can see the new frame.

Perhaps Comic Chat's most surprising feature is that it examines the text of each message and attempts to draw the characters accordingly. Here are some of the inferences Comic Chat makes about your messages:

✔ If you SHOUT something using all capital letters, Comic Chat draws your character with a wide-open, shouting mouth.

✔ When your message begins with the word "You" or contains a phrase such as "are you," "will you," or "did you," your character points to the other person.

✔ If your message begins with the word "I" or includes the words "I am," "I'm," "I will," or "I'll," your character points to itself.

✔ If you type "LOL" or "ROTFL," your character laughs.

✔ If you type an *emoticon* such as :) :-) :(or :-(, Comic Chat draws your character smiling or frowning.

✔ If you say "Hi," "Howdy," "Hello," "Welcome," or "Bye," your character waves.

Sending a Message

When you first enter a chat room, your best bet is to just eavesdrop for a while to figure out what's going on. When you get up the nerve to contribute your own messages to a chat, follow these simple steps:

1. **Compose a brilliant message in the message box.**

   The message box is at the bottom of the screen beneath the comic-book frames (refer to Figure 13-3).

2. **Pick your emotion from the Emotion Wheel.**

   The Emotion Wheel enables you to control the facial expression and body language of your character. To pick an emotion, just click somewhere in the Emotion Wheel. The sample character above the Emotion Wheel changes to show how your character's expression appears when you send your message. To return to a neutral expression, click in the exact center of the Emotion Wheel.

Note: Any emotion you pick from the Emotion Wheel overrides the facial expression that would have been selected based on your the text of your message.

3. Select one of the Send buttons that appear next to the message box.

The four Send buttons (shown in Table 13-1) determine how your message appears in the comic strip.

Table 13-1	The Four Faces of the Send Buttons	
Button	*When to Use It*	*How It Looks*
	To display an ordinary message that your character says	The message appears in a normal text balloon.
	To display a message that your character thinks	The message appears in a thought bubble.
	To display a message that your character whispers	The message appears in a special text balloon drawn with dashed lines.
	To display an action message, which is intended to suggest that your character is *doing* something (such as answering the phone or eating a donut)	The message appears in a box at the top of the comic frame.

When you compose an action message, keep in mind that Comic Chat always adds your name before the message. For example, if your name is John and you send the action message "sits back and enjoys a cold one," Comic Chat displays the message "John sits back and enjoys a cold one."

Getting Personal

In Microsoft Comic Chat, each user can fill out a Personal Information profile, which includes the user's real name and a description of the user. You compose your own description, which can include your interests, hobbies, hometown, gender, age, or anything else that may be interesting. In the following sections, I show you how to set your own Personal Information profile and how to display the profile for other users.

If you choose to fill out a Personal Information profile, you should limit the amount of personal information you give out. Most important, don't list your phone number or address.

Setting your Personal Information profile

To set your Personal Information profile, follow these steps:

1. **Choose View⇨Options.**

   The Options dialog box appears, as shown in Figure 13-5. (If the Personal Information options are not displayed, click the Personal Info tab.)

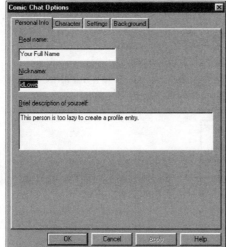

Figure 13-5:
Setting the
Personal
Information
options.

2. **Type your name in the Real name field.**

   Of course, there's nothing to stop you from typing "Elvis Presley" or "Jimmy Hoffa."

3. **Type the name you want to use in the chat rooms in the Nickname field.**

   Use your first name if you wish, or choose something more interesting, such as "Snoopy" or "Baby Cakes."

4. **Type a description of yourself in the Brief description of yourself field.**

   Type something interesting about yourself here if you want others to know more about you. You might include information such as what city you live in, what line of work you're in, what your favorite ...*For Dummies* book is, and so on.

5. **Click OK.**

   Your personal information is updated so that other users can view it.

Viewing another member's profile

Comic Chat enables you to find out information about the other users who are in a chat room with you, provided that those users have filled out the Personal Information profile. To display a chat user's personal information, follow one of these procedures:

 ✔ Right-click the user's nickname in the member list that appears at the right of the Comic Chat window. Then select <u>G</u>et profile from the quick menu that appears.

 ✔ Select the user's nickname in the member list and then choose <u>M</u>ember⇨ <u>G</u>et Profile from the main menu.

Comic Chat draws a new frame showing the user's character, with the user's personal information displayed at the top, as shown in Figure 13-6.

Figure 13-6:
Displaying
a user's
profile.

Ignoring Obnoxious Users

Every once in a while, you get into a chat room with someone who insists on dominating the conversation with a constant stream of obnoxious remarks. Or you may be pestered by a couple of chat users who go on and on about a topic that holds absolutely no interest for you.

Fortunately, Comic Chat gives you a way to tune these people out. Just follow these two steps:

 1. Select the nickname of the person you want to ignore from the nick-name list that appears at the right of the Comic Chat window.

2. Choose Member➪Ignore.

Any messages from the user you silenced are no longer displayed on your computer. The ignored user is still able to participate in the chat, and other users see the ignored user's messages as if nothing happened. In other words, ignoring a user is like putting on a selective set of ear plugs. The annoying user can talk all he or she wants, but *you* won't have to listen.

Alternatively, you can right-click the member's name in the member list and select Ignore from the pop-up menu that appears.

To reinstate someone you have ignored, just repeat the procedure.

 The person you tune out has no clue what you have done. He or she will keep babbling on, wondering why you never seem to answer. (Of course, if no one ever seems to answer you, it could be that *you* are the one who is being ignored!)

Having It Your Way

In Comic Chat, the View➪Options command enables you to customize the appearance of the chat comic strip in several ways:

- ✔ You can select one of the 12 comic characters to represent you in Comic Chat.
- ✔ You can change the background scenery.
- ✔ You can change the arrangement of comic strip frames used in the Comic Chat window.

Changing your image

Wouldn't it be nice if you could just click your button to instantly change your image? Politicians are deft at image makeovers, but most of us are not. Comic Chat offers a welcome chance to change your image, merely by following this procedure:

1. Choose View➪Options.

The Options dialog box appears.

2. Click the Character tab.

The Character options appear, as shown in Figure 13-7.

Figure 13-7:
Overhauling
your image.

3. Select the character you want to represent you.

As you click on each character name, a picture of the character appears in the Preview window of the dialog box. If you want to see how the character appears with various expressions, you can click in the Emotion Wheel at the bottom right corner of the Options dialog box.

4. Click OK.

Unfortunately, you are limited to the 12 characters provided with Comic Chat. Microsoft has hinted that, in a future release, you will be able to create your own characters. But until then, you'll have to be content with the stock characters.

A change of scenery

You can change the background scenery that Comic Chat uses. The scenery change applies only to your computer; you cannot change the background scenery that other users see on their screens. To change the comic strip background, follow these steps:

1. Choose View▷Options.

The Options dialog box appears.

2. Click the Background tab.

The Background options appear, as shown in Figure 13-8.

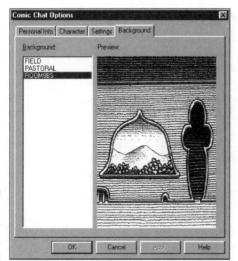

Figure 13-8:
Changing
the scenery.

3. **Select the background you want to use.**

   Microsoft provides three backgrounds with Comic Chat — FIELD,
   PASTORAL, and ROOM8BS.

4. **Click OK.**

Although you can't draw your own characters, Comic Chat does enable you to
create your own backgrounds. In fact, you can use any graphics file stored in
bitmap format (.BMP) as a background for Comic Chat. All you have to do
is copy the file you want to use as a background to the folder C:\Program
Files\CChat\ComicArt\Backdrop. Any bitmap files that appear in this folder
are displayed when you call up the Background options.

More settings

You can find additional settings for Comic Chat by choosing View⇨Options
and then clicking the Settings tab to display the Settings options, as shown in
Figure 13-9.

The following is a brief explanation of the settings available in this dialog box:

  ✔ **Page Layout:** You can tell Comic Chat to display the comic strip one, two,
     three, or four frames across. The width that looks best for you depends on
     the size of your monitor and the strength of your eyes. With a 14- or
     15-inch monitor, two frames across looks best to me.

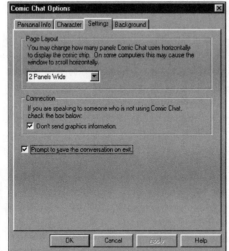

Figure 13-9:
So many
settings, so
little time.

↳ **Connection:** If you are conversing with other users who don't use Comic Chat, you can improve performance a bit by selecting Don't send graphics information. However, leave this setting unchecked if your chat buddies also use Comic Chat.

↳ **Prompt to save:** Check this option if you want Comic Chat to ask whether you want to keep a permanent record of your chats before quitting.

Opting for Plain, Old-Fashioned Text

Microsoft Comic Chat is one of the most interesting chat programs available. However, the comic-strip appearance of Comic Chat can be a bit annoying after a while, especially in a large chat room where 20 or more participants are sending a near-constant stream of text. In such busy chat rooms, you may want to switch Comic Chat to Plain Text mode, which displays chat messages in a simple text window, without the comic-book backgrounds and characters. Plain Text mode isn't as pretty as comic-strip mode, but it is sometimes easier to follow.

To switch to Plain Text mode, just choose View⇨Plain Text. You can switch back to comic-strip mode at any time by selecting View⇨Comic Strip.

Changing Rooms

When you get tired of chatting in a room, you can always leave and wander into another room. Just follow this procedure:

1. **Say good-bye.**

   It's rude to leave without saying good-bye, especially if you've been active in the conversation. Send a parting message. And, if you're in a silly mood, send an action message such as "exits stage right" or "leaves with a bang."

2. **Choose <u>V</u>iew⇨Chat Room <u>L</u>ist.**

   The Chat Room List dialog box appears, listing all of the chat rooms on your chat server. (Refer to Figure 13-2.)

3. **Double-click on the chat room you want to join.**

Unfortunately, Comic Chat won't let you visit two chat rooms at one time. However, you can chat in two or more rooms at once simply by running multiple copies of Comic Chat. For example, suppose that you're chatting in the #Comic_Chat chat room, and you want to also chat in #Sports. Rather than leave the #Comic_Chat room, click <u>S</u>tart and choose <u>P</u>rograms⇨Microsoft Comic Chat to start up a second Comic Chat window. Then select #Sports as the chat room. Arrange the windows so they appear side by side, so you can monitor both chats.

Chapter 14

Microsoft NetMeeting — Feel the Synergy

• •

In This Chapter

▶ Downloading and installing NetMeeting

▶ Placing a call to another NetMeeting user

▶ Drawing on the whiteboard

▶ Resorting to NetMeeting's Chat feature

▶ Sending files to NetMeeting participants

▶ Sharing your programs across the Internet

• •

*M*icrosoft NetMeeting is a highly touted new program that Microsoft says will revolutionize the way you communicate on the Internet. NetMeeting is a *computer telephony* program, which means that it turns your computer into a $3,000 telephone. Computer telephony is still in its infancy, with many glitches yet to be worked out. Still, NetMeeting is a cool program, one you should definitely look into if you're at all interested in cutting-edge Internet technology.

NetMeeting offers the following features in addition to voice communication:

✔ **Whiteboard:** This feature is similar to Windows Paint. Whiteboard displays a drawing area in which all the participants in a conference can doodle.

✔ **Chat:** This feature works similarly to Internet Relay Chat. NetMeeting chat allows more than two users to join together in a conference and type messages to one another. (Only two users can use voice communications.)

✔ **File transfer:** You guessed it — file transfer enables you to send files to other NetMeeting users.

✔ **Application sharing:** This feature enables other NetMeeting users to see on their screens an application that you are running on your computer. You can also share applications so that several NetMeeting users can work together on a single document over the Internet.

Although not technically a part of Internet Explorer 3.0, NetMeeting is often distributed with Internet Explorer. If you don't already have NetMeeting, you can obtain a copy free from the Internet Explorer download page at `www.microsoft.com/ie/download`. This chapter gives you a brief introduction to NetMeeting's major features.

Getting and Using NetMeeting

At its core, NetMeeting is an Internet telephone. NetMeeting enables you to conduct voice conversations with another Internet user.

The voice features of NetMeeting won't work unless your computer is equipped with all of the following:

- A sound card (any sound card that is compatible with Windows 95)
- Speakers
- A microphone

If you don't have these components, or if you aren't sure how to use them, pick up a copy of *Multimedia For Dummies*.

NetMeeting allows voice conversations between only two users at a time. If you want to start a conference call with more than two users, you have to limit yourself to NetMeeting's nonvoice features.

Downloading and installing NetMeeting

If NetMeeting is not already installed on your computer, you must download and install it before you can use it. Be prepared for the download to take awhile — the NetMeeting file is more than 2MB in size.

To download NetMeeting, start Internet Explorer and then go to the following Web address:

```
www.microsoft.com/ie/download
```

1. **From the drop-down list, select NetMeeting for Windows 95 and then click <u>N</u>ext>.**

   You get a choice of several language versions of NetMeeting: English, Chinese, and so on.

2. **Pick the language version you want and then click Next>.**

 You see a list of locations from which you can download NetMeeting.

3. **Start the download by clicking the filename at the site nearest to you geographically.**

4. **Click Open when Internet Explorer asks whether you want to open the file or save it to disk.**

When you click Open, NetMeeting automatically installs itself after the download is complete. If you prefer to wait and install the program later, choose Save to Disk, instead. You must then run the file to install NetMeeting. To run the file, double-click the My Computer icon on your desktop, navigate to the folder in which you saved the file, and double-click the file's icon.

Configuring the program

To start NetMeeting, click the Start button and then choose Programs↪ Microsoft NetMeeting. The first time you start NetMeeting, you have to wade through a sea of dialog boxes to configure the program for yourself and your computer. The first dialog box (shown in Figure 14-1) lists some of NetMeeting's nifty features. Reading about all the cool stuff you can do with NetMeeting takes the sting out of all the dialog boxes you have to fill out to configure the program!

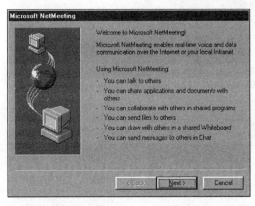

Figure 14-1:
This dialog box welcomes you the first time you start NetMeeting.

When you click Next>, NetMeeting asks you for information it can use to identify you to other NetMeeting users, as shown in Figure 14-2. You must enter at least your first and last name and your e-mail address. (You don't have to enter your real name here; Queen Victoria or Snow White will do.)

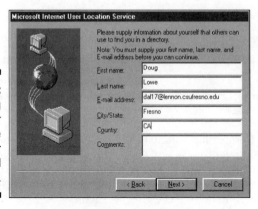

Figure 14-2:
NetMeeting
asks for
your name
and other
personal
information.

Click Next> to display the next configuration dialog box, shown in Figure 14-3. This dialog box asks for the name of the *User Location Service* (ULS) server to which you want to connect. A ULS server is a computer that keeps track of people who are using NetMeeting. In order to have a NetMeeting conference with another user, you must both be logged on to the same ULS server. The default ULS server is uls.microsoft.com, which should work just fine.

Figure 14-3:
Configuring
the ULS
server
information.

In addition, the ULS dialog box asks whether you want your name to be listed on the ULS. If you don't select this option, other NetMeeting users won't find your listing in the directory provided by the ULS server. When your number is unlisted, others can't call you, but you can call them.

After you fill in the ULS information, NetMeeting continues with a series of dialog boxes that automatically configure your sound card and modem. Follow the instructions on-screen to complete NetMeeting's configuration procedure.

Rest assured that all these configuration steps are required only the first time you run NetMeeting. After you've installed and configured NetMeeting, it starts right up whenever you click Start and choose Programs➪Microsoft NetMeeting.

Reaching out and touching someone

To call up another NetMeeting user for a voice conversation, connect to the Internet via your Internet service provider (if you haven't done so already) and then follow these steps:

1. Click the Start button and then choose Programs➪Microsoft NetMeeting.

NetMeeting comes to life, as shown in Figure 14-4.

The Place a call text box   The Call button

Figure 14-4:
NetMeeting
comes to
life.

If you already know the e-mail address of the person you want to call, you can skip Steps 2 through 4 and, instead, simply type the e-mail address of the person you want to call in the Place a call text box. Then click the Call button.

2. Click the Directory button (or choose Call➪Directory or press Ctrl+D).

A Directory window similar to the one shown in Figure 14-5 appears, listing all of the users who are logged on to your server.

3. Click the name of the person you want to call.

To make the search easier, you can sort the list on any of the columns by clicking the heading button at the top of the column. For example, click Last Name to sort the list by last name.

4. Click the Call button.

The Directory window disappears, and NetMeeting attempts to contact the user you selected. This process may take a few moments, so be patient.

E-mail	First Name	Last Name	City/State	Country	Comments
agolden@...	J, Allen	Golden	Wilmington, ...	USA	"Can we talk"
agough@r...	Andrew	Gough	Halifax/Nov...	Canada	
alex@micr...	Athanasios	Alexandrides	Lugano	Switzerland	64K, Audio
alex@tela...	Alex	Karchevsky	Minneapolis...	USA	VB developer [voice, can talk russian]
andersonr...	Dick	Anderson			
Any ladies...	Patrick	Adult Chat	_	US	
arek@ripc...	Arek	Atlasiuk	Chicago, Illin...	USA	
ariane@m...	Ariane	BETRISEY	Ecublens	Switzerland	
ati@topse...	Attila	Varga	Budapest	Hungary	No voice - GMT+1, (7:45-9:00 AM or 6:00-8:00 PM)
AusBenny...	James	Laird	Hoppers Cro...	Australia	talk to an Aussie!
bdoak@m...	Bob	Doak	Hotlanta, Ga	U.S.A.	Ya'll come back!
bdraper@...	Billie	Draper	Panama City	PANAMA	sexy senior citizen
bilhyd@ur...	Mahesh	AM	Bangalore	India	
billf@milan...	Bill	Foley	Deerfield Be...	USA	Milano Brothers

Figure 14-5:
A ULS
directory.

Messages appear at the bottom of the NetMeeting window to let you know the status of your call. If the person you are trying to call is already in another conference, NetMeeting offers to let you barge in on the conference. However, the members in that conference may decide not to let you in, so don't be surprised if your call goes unanswered.

When the connection is finally established, your name and the name of the person you are calling appear in the NetMeeting window, along with the status bar message In a call, as shown in Figure 14-6.

Figure 14-6:
NetMeeting
in a call.

└ Status bar

5. Talk into your microphone.

NetMeeting works just like a telephone. You talk into the microphone, and you can hear the person on the other end of the line through your computer's speakers.

6. When you're done, say good-bye and choose Call⇨Hang Up.

That's all there is to it!

You can redial a user whom you have recently called by selecting the user's name from the Place a call drop-down list. Just click the down-arrow button next to the text box labeled Place a call, select the name of the person you want to call, and click the Call button.

Drawing on the Whiteboard

Another way to communicate in NetMeeting is with Whiteboard, which is sort of like an Internet version of the venerable Paint accessory that comes with Windows 95. The difference between the two programs is that both you and your friend on the other end of the call can doodle on the whiteboard, and you can instantly see each other's doodles.

To use Whiteboard, follow these steps:

1. Establish a call to another NetMeeting user.

 2. Click the Whiteboard button (or choose Tools⇨Whiteboard or press Ctrl+W).

Whiteboard appears, as shown in Figure 14-7.

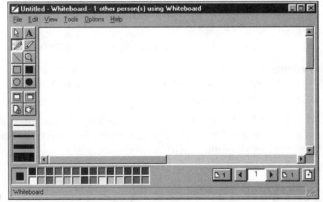

Figure 14-7:
Whiteboard
looks a lot
like Paint.

3. Draw something.

If you know how to use Microsoft Paint, you already know how to use Whiteboard. Just select one of the drawing tools in the toolbar on the left edge of the Whiteboard window and then doodle something in the drawing area.

4. **Gasp in amazement when Whiteboard appears to draw stuff all by itself.**

   Actually, Whiteboard isn't drawing that stuff, your counterpart on the other end of the NetMeeting call is. The whole point of Whiteboard is that any of the NetMeeting participants can draw on the whiteboard at the same time. Anything one person draws on NetMeeting's whiteboard automatically shows up on every participant's computer.

5. **If the drawing is worth hanging on to, choose File⇨Save to save the drawing or File⇨Print to print it.**

6. **When you're done, close Whiteboard by clicking the standard Windows 95 close button (you know, the one with the X on it, in the upper-right corner of the window).**

   Alternatively, you can choose File⇨Exit.

Although Whiteboard is similar to Paint, it has several features that are especially useful when working on the Internet:

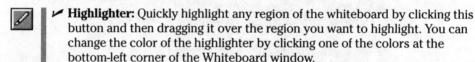

- ✔ **Highlighter:** Quickly highlight any region of the whiteboard by clicking this button and then dragging it over the region you want to highlight. You can change the color of the highlighter by clicking one of the colors at the bottom-left corner of the Whiteboard window.

- ✔ **Select Window:** Copy the contents of another window into the whiteboard by clicking this button and then clicking anywhere in the window you want to include. As soon as you click the mouse, the contents of the window you clicked are automatically pasted into the whiteboard.

- ✔ **Select Area:** You can copy a selected area from anywhere on your screen into the whiteboard by clicking this button and then dragging a rectangle over the area you want copied. When you release the mouse button, the area you selected is automatically pasted into the whiteboard.

- ✔ **Lock Contents:** Click this button to prevent other users from modifying the contents of the whiteboard. Click it again to unlock it. Note that any user in a conference can lock the whiteboard.

- ✔ **Remote Pointer:** Click this button to activate a special pointer that appears on everyone else's NetMeeting screen. You move the remote pointer around by dragging it with your mouse.

Using the NetMeeting Chat Feature

Although NetMeeting's voice features are interesting, voice communication is possible only between two users. For a conference with more than two users, you must resort to NetMeeting's Chat feature. You may even want to use Chat for two-way conversations, if you find that the sound quality of voice communications is less than adequate. (Sound quality is often a problem when using NetMeeting, depending on the speed of your Internet connection, the load on the server, and the quality of your sound card.)

To use Chat, follow this procedure:

1. Call up another NetMeeting user.

 2. Click the Chat button (or choose Tools⇨Chat or press Ctrl+T).

Up springs the Chat window, shown in Figure 14-8.

Read chat messages here

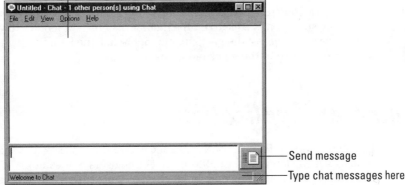

Figure 14-8:
The
NetMeeting
Chat
window.

Send message
Type chat messages here

3. Type something in the text box at the bottom of the Chat window.

4. Press Enter to send your message.

Or click the Send button shown in Figure 14-8. Messages that other NetMeeting users send are displayed automatically.

5. When you're finished chatting, choose File⇨Exit.

You can also close Chat by clicking the close button in the upper-right corner of the Chat window.

 Don't confuse NetMeeting's Chat feature with IRC (Internet Relay Chat), which I cover in Chapter 13. Although the two programs serve the same purpose, they are not compatible with one another. Thus, you can't use Microsoft Comic Chat or any other IRC program (such as mIRC) in a NetMeeting Chat session. Likewise, you can't use NetMeeting Chat for IRC chatting.

Sending a File

You can send a file to another NetMeeting user by following these steps:

1. **Call up another NetMeeting user.**

2. **Click the Send file button (or choose Tools⇨Send File or press Ctrl+F).**

   A dialog box appears, allowing you to select the file you want to send.

3. **Select the file you want to send.**

4. **Click OK.**

   That's all there is to it!

If you're in a conference with more than one other person, following the preceding steps sends a file to *all* the members of the conference. If you want to send a file to *just one* of the participants, right-click the icon for that person and select Send File from the quick menu that appears.

Sharing an Application

One of the coolest features of NetMeeting is that it enables you to share programs over the Internet with other NetMeeting users. For example, if you are discussing your marketing budget in a NetMeeting conference, you can call up Microsoft Excel, open the budget spreadsheet, and let everyone in the conference see and even edit the spreadsheet.

To share an application, just follow these steps:

1. **Start the application you want to share.**

   If you want to share a particular document, open the document you want to share, too.

2. **Click the Share Application button or choose Tools⇨Share Application.**

3. **Select the application you want to share from the list of applications that appears.**

4. **Use the application as you normally would.**

   Anything you do in the application is visible to the other members of the NetMeeting conference. However, other conference participants cannot take over and use the application until you complete the next step.

5. **Choose Tools⇨Collaborate.**

This command enables other users to take over and use the application you have shared. When another user takes over your application, you see your mouse pointer move magically by itself, with the other user's initials tacked onto the bottom of the mouse pointer so you can tell who's driving. You can wrest control away from the other user at any time by simply clicking the mouse.

6. **To stop the collaboration, choose Tools⇨Collaborate again.**

   This command toggles on and off each time you use it.

 7. **To stop sharing the application, click the Share Application button and select the application again.**

   The Share Application button also acts like a toggle, switching from On to Off each time you click it.

 Beware of security problems when you share an application, especially when you enable Collaboration. When you give someone access to your application from across the Internet, that person can delete files, open sensitive documents, and even plant macro viruses on your computer. You should enable the Collaboration feature in NetMeeting only with users you trust. And never leave your computer unattended — even for a moment — with Collaboration enabled.

Saving Time with SpeedDial

The SpeedDial feature lets you store the addresses of frequently called NetMeeting users for quick access. With the SpeedDial feature, you can call your best friend in San Diego without having to log in to a ULS server and wait for the directory to appear on your computer.

- ✔ To add a someone to your SpeedDial list, call up the user and then choose SpeedDial⇨Add SpeedDial. From then on, the user's name appears right on the SpeedDial menu.

- ✔ To call someone from your SpeedDial list, choose the SpeedDial command from the NetMeeting main menu and then select the person's name from the list of names that appears at the bottom of the menu.

- ✔ To edit your SpeedDial list, choose SpeedDial⇨Open SpeedDial Folder. When the folder opens, you can rename or delete items in the SpeedDial menu.

Part V

Multimedia and Interactivity on the Web

The 5th Wave   By Rich Tennant

ORIGINAL VAN-GOGH-OF-THE-MONTH CLUB

"SINCE WE BEGAN ON-LINE SHOPPING, I JUST DON'T KNOW WHERE THE MONEY'S GOING."

In this part . . .

Once upon a time, the Internet was a static, boring place. Then along came multimedia, and the boring, green-on-black Internet was transformed overnight into a magical place with sights and sounds and moving images. Web pages come alive as background sounds play and animated objects leap off the page.

Internet Explorer 3.0 is the most multimedia-friendly Web browser ever. The chapters in this part show you how to use Internet Explorer 3.0 to navigate the sights and sounds of the Web.

Chapter 15

The Sights and Sounds of the World Wide Web

*M*ultimedia is all the rage these days, as any computer salesperson can tell you. You can hardly find a new computer today that doesn't include a high-quality sound card and high-speed CD-ROM drive to take advantage of all the new multimedia software that is now available. In recent years, the Internet has gone multimedia too. In fact, one of the main advantages of the World Wide Web over older Internet technologies is its inherent — well, *almost* inherent — support for multimedia.

What Is Multimedia?

Strictly speaking, *multimedia* means information that is presented using more than one form of media. In the past, most information available on computers was in the form of text — a single, basic type of media. However, in addition to text, computers today can present information in a variety of media, including

✔ Pictures

✔ Sounds

✔ Movies

When the World Wide Web first became popular, the main type of media it relied upon (besides text) was pictures. Now, however, the Web is starting to delve into sounds and movies, too. To take advantage of these multimedia advancements on the Web, you have to have a Web browser capable of reading and displaying audio and video clips. As it just so happens, Internet Explorer 3.0 comes complete with *ActiveMovie,* an interface specially designed for handling multimedia on the Web.

If, after reading this brief introduction to multimedia, you find yourself fascinated by the topic and wanting to know more, I suggest you pick up a copy of *Multimedia For Dummies.*

Pictures

You've no doubt already encountered many different types of pictures in your Web explorations, and most of your graphic viewing sessions have probably gone by without incident. Although picture files can be stored in dozens of formats, the two most popular file formats are GIF and JPEG. Internet Explorer handles both of these file formats easily — all you have to do is sit back and watch.

Sounds

Although people use several different sound formats today, the most popular format is WAV, simply because Windows itself supports WAV and uses WAV files for its sounds. Internet Explorer can play WAV files without requiring that you load or run any other software. Whenever you open a page that includes a WAV file, Internet Explorer automatically plays the sound. In addition, Internet Explorer also supports other popular sound formats, including MIDI, AU, and AIFF.

Video

Microsoft and Apple are duking it out in the battle to determine which of several file formats will be the most popular for movies on the Internet. Several formats are currently being used:

- ✔ **AVI:** The format used by Microsoft Video for Windows
- ✔ **QuickTime:** A format developed by Apple for its Macintosh computers
- ✔ **MPEG:** A audio/video version of JPEG

Lucky for you, the Internet Explorer ActiveMovie interface supports all three of these video formats.

Internet Explorer 3.0 is the first Web browser with built-in playback support for MPEG audio and video clips. Microsoft recommends the MPEG format, which it says provides TV-quality video and CD-quality sound (not the blurry, fuzzy stuff Web browsers have settled for until now). MPEG also boasts smaller file sizes and shortered download times than other video and audio formats.

The Speed Dilemma

Multimedia on the Web has just one problem: It is s-l-o-w. Unfortunately, you can do little about the slowness of multimedia. The basic problem is that multimedia files are very large, and you have to download them to your computer before you can display or play them. Even with a fast 28.8 Kbps modem, movies that are much longer than 30 seconds require unreasonable download times. Who wants to wait 15 minutes to view a 30-second movie?

Because of its inherent speed problem, multimedia is still best viewed from CD-ROM discs loaded into your computer's CD-ROM drive. Don't make the mistake of assuming that a Web site that features multimedia can compare in any way with a CD-ROM multimedia title.

You can do some things to improve the speed of multimedia on the Web, however:

✔ Get the fastest Internet connection you can afford. If possible, use a 28.8 Kbps modem rather than a slower 14.4 Kbps modem. Better yet, use a high-speed connection such as ISDN, the new digital telephone service that lets you connect to the Internet up to four times faster than standard phone lines.

✔ Make sure that your computer has plenty of RAM — 16MB, at least — and plenty of free disk space on the C drive (or whatever drive houses Windows 95 or Windows NT).

✔ Disable automatic play of sound and video files by choosing View➪ Options and unchecking the Play sounds and Play videos options. With these options disabled, you won't have to wait for large sound and video files to download automatically.

If you're having trouble viewing pictures or playing sounds or videos, select View➪Options, select the General tab and then look in the Multimedia box, and make sure that Show pictures, Play sounds, and Play videos are all checked (see Figure 15-1).

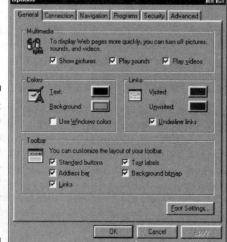

Figure 15-1:
For a true
multimedia
experience
on the Web,
enable
pictures,
sounds, and
videos.

Playing Sounds and Movies

If you find a Web site that includes a link to a sound or movie file, click the link to download the file. Internet Explorer asks whether you want to save the file to disk or open it. Select Open to play the sound or movie immediately after downloading.

When you play a sound, a small control appears with buttons that enable you to start and stop the sound playback, as shown in Figure 15-2. To play the sound, just click the Play button (the one with the right-facing arrow).

When you play a movie, the movie occupies a box within the Web page or is displayed in a separate window. Either way, Internet Explorer displays a set of controls similar to those shown in Figure 15-2, allowing you to start or stop the movie.

Internet Explorer 3.0 includes a new feature called *progressive playback,* which allows you to view a movie or sound clip as the clip is downloaded to your computer, without forcing you to wait until the entire clip has downloaded before starting to play it. Progressive playback works best if you have a high-speed Internet connection such as ISDN. With a standard 28.8 Kbps Internet connection (or slower), progressive playback doesn't help that much, especially for video clips.

Stop button

Play button

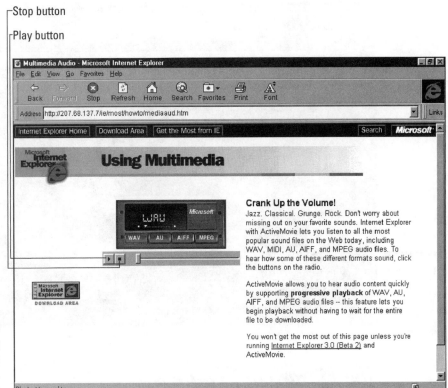

Figure 15-2:
Playing a
media file.

Where to Find Sounds and Movies

You can find multimedia files everywhere on the World Wide Web. However, certain sites exist solely to serve as repositories or catalogs of multimedia files. The following sections describe some of the best of these sites.

Simplex Knowledge Company

```
www.skc.com/ocean/index.html
```

The Simplex Knowledge Company maintains a site that contains hundreds of sound files with sound clips from movies and several popular television series, including *Star Trek* and *The Simpsons*. In addition, you can find several interesting sound effects. Figure 15-3 shows the Simplex Knowledge Company home page.

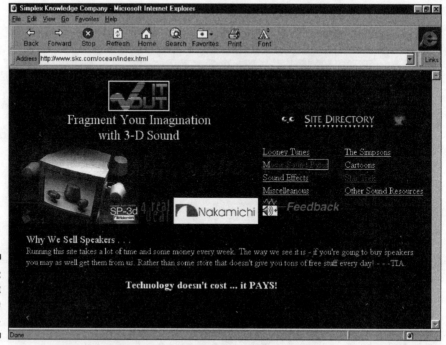

Figure 15-3:
Simplex
Knowledge
Company.

The Library of Congress

www.loc.gov

The Library of Congress has an excellent collection of pictures, sounds, and video files called American Memory, as shown in Figure 15-4. Here, you can find some fascinating collections, such as Civil War photographs, recordings of political speeches from the presidential election of 1920, and old movies made by Thomas Edison himself.

Be warned that many of the files in the American Memory collection are huge: 5MB, 10MB, some even more than 20MB in size. The larger of these files are overnight downloads.

Space Movie Archive

www.univ-rennes1.fr/ASTRO/anim-ewf.html

This site, shown in Figure 15-5, includes hundreds of space-related video clips, including shots of spacecraft and astronomical observations. The site is well organized, and most of the files are in the 1 to 2MB range, suitable for downloading with a 28.8 Kbps modem.

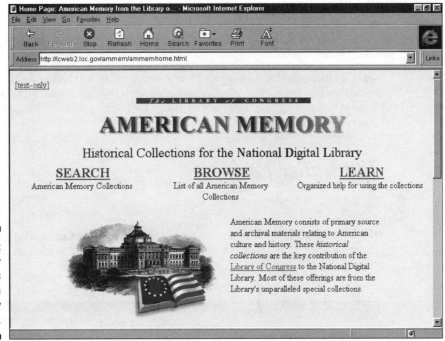

Figure 15-4:
The Library
of Congress
American
Memory
page.

Figure 15-5:
The Space
Movie
Archive.

Jesse's Movies

www.uslink.net/~edgerton/index.html

Jesse's Movies is not itself an archive of movie clips, but rather a catalog of links to dozens of sites on the Internet that contain movie archives. Thus, Jesse's Movies is a gateway to hundreds of movie files. It's a great starting point if you're looking for movies to download.

The Trailer Park

lyre.mit.edu/~deering/tpark.html

Many film producers publish theatrical trailers on the Internet. The Trailer Park contains links to hundreds of movie previews for current movies as well as classics. Figure 15-6 shows The Trailer Park's opening page.

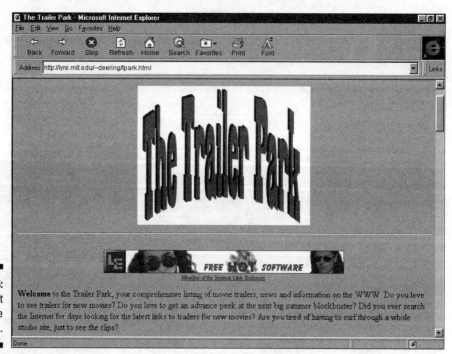

Figure 15-6:
Take a visit
to The
Trailer Park.

Chapter 16

Getting Virtual with VRML

• •

In This Chapter

▶ Discovering VRML

▶ Configuring Internet Explorer for VRML

▶ Exploring virtual worlds

▶ Checking out some cool VRML sites

• •

*V*irtual reality is one of the hottest buzzwords in computers today. In fact, more than a few major motion pictures in recent years have featured virtual reality in one form or another: *Lawnmower Man, Virtuosity,* and *Disclosure* to name but a few. Unfortunately (or fortunately, depending on your point of view), virtual reality on the Internet isn't nearly as well developed as it is in the movies. Still, the crude beginnings of virtual reality on the Net are here, in the form of VRML. This chapter shows how Internet Explorer's VRML support lets you explore virtually real worlds.

Before I begin, I better tell you that VRML stands for *V*irtual *R*eality *M*odeling *L*anguage. This won't help you use or understand VRML any better, but it won't hurt either. Also, to sound really in-the-know, don't spell out the letters *V-R-M-L.* Instead, pronounce VRML as the word *vermal.*

Entering the World of VRML

If your new computer came with Internet Explorer 3.0 already installed, it is probably already configured to support VRML. However, if you installed Internet Explorer by downloading it from Microsoft or some other Web site, you probably don't have VRML support installed. In that case, you must first download and install the VRML component of Internet Explorer 3.0 before you can explore VRML worlds.

Testing VRML support

The easiest way to test whether VRML support is enabled on your computer is to check into the Microsoft VRML page at www.microsoft.com/ie/most/howto/vrml.htm. This page includes a VRML world that represents the Microsoft campus in Redmond, Washington, as shown in Figure 16-1.

The terms *VRML world* and *VRML object* are used interchangeably to describe virtual reality scenes created with VRML. The only distinction is the type of scene that is represented. Single objects such as cars, trees, or geometric shapes are usually referred to as objects. Locations, which include buildings or rooms that you can wander around in, are referred to as worlds.

Click the picture of the Microsoft campus to see whether VRML has been enabled. If it has, a toolbar appears beneath the picture, and you should be able to use the mouse to explore the campus, as described in the following section, "Exploring Virtual Worlds."

If nothing happens when you click the picture of the campus, download and install the VRML add-on and then restart Internet Explorer to enable VRML support.

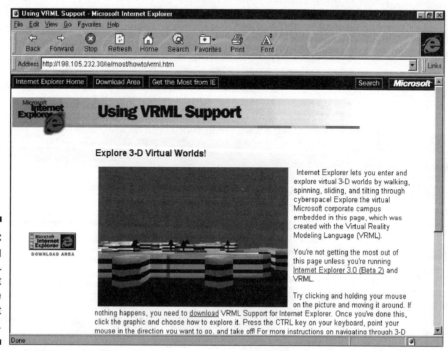

Figure 16-1: Testing VRML support at the Microsoft campus.

Downloading and installing VRML

Because of some bugs in the main Microsoft Internet Explorer download site, at the time of this writing, you must visit a special site to download VRML support for Internet Explorer. Here's how:

1. **Navigate to the following cumbersome URL:**

   `www.microsoft.com/msdownload/ieadd/0400.htm`

2. **Click the filename next to the site that's geographically closest to you.**

3. **Choose Open it.**

   If you want to install the file yourself later on, choose <u>S</u>ave it to disk. But I recommend opting for the automatic installation so that you can get virtual right away.

4. **Wait, wait, wait.**

   You can sit back and watch the pages float in slow motion from one folder to the other during the download (which is about 2MB). Or you can switch to another program and get some work done. Or you can go pop a frozen pizza in the oven. When the download is complete, a dialog box appears asking you whether you want to install the file you just waited for an eternity to download.

5. **Click <u>Y</u>es.**

6. **Read the license agreement and click <u>Y</u>es to signify that you agree to the terms.**

   A few dialog boxes fly by letting you know that your computer is initializing and extracting the files. A final dialog box announces that the VRML add-on has been installed.

7. **Click OK.**

After downloading the VRML add-on, visit the VRML test site at `www.microsoft.com/ie/most/howto/vrml.htm`. This time, you should be able to move around in the Microsoft campus.

Exploring Virtual Worlds

Internet Explorer VRML renders three-dimensional scenes and objects on your computer screen and allows you use your mouse to explore them. To move about within the VRML world, hold down the mouse button and drag the mouse around. The movement may seem strange at first, but after a little practice, you should be able to move around the three-dimensional objects with ease.

Figure 16-2 shows a VRML object with the VRML toolbar displayed. Table 16-1 describes the function of each of the buttons on this toolbar:

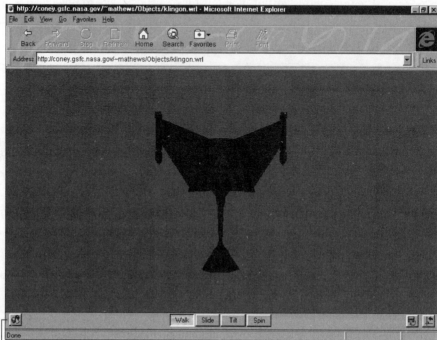

Figure 16-2:
A VRML
object.

└VRML toolbar

Table 16-1	Your Virtual Tools
Button	**What It Does**
Walk	Clicking the *Walk* button enables you to use the mouse to walk around within the VRML world. Simply hold down the mouse button and drag the mouse in the direction that you wish to walk.
Slide	Clicking the *Slide* button enables you to move the VRML object within the VRML window. Hold down the mouse button and drag the mouse in the direction you want to slide the object.
Tilt	Clicking the *Tilt* button enables you to tilt the VRML object by dragging the mouse in the direction you want the object to tilt.
Spin	Clicking the *Spin* button enables you to spin the VRML object about its center point in any direction by dragging the mouse in the direction that you want to rotate the object.

Table 16-1 *(continued)*

Button	What It Does
	Clicking the *Reset* button restores the VRML world to its original orientation. This button comes in handy if you tilt and spin the object to the point where you can't find your way around anymore.
	Clicking the *Straighten* button restores the original starting orientation to the VRML object, but does not move you back to the starting position. Use this button when you have maneuvered yourself into the position you want, but find that the object has become tilted or spun out of kilter.
	Clicking the *Menu* button opens a shortcut menu that provides several options for working with VRML objects.

Some Cool VRML Worlds to Explore

VRML is a relative newcomer to the Web, so you may not find too many VRML worlds out there yet to explore. However, you can find a few sites that maintain links to interesting VRML objects. The following sections describe the best of these sites.

Interactive Origami

```
www.neuro.sfc.keio.ac.jp/~aly/polygon/vrml/ika
```

This Web site provides a step-by-step VRML view of a simple origami project, in which a piece of paper is folded in a certain way to create an object. Figure 16-3 shows a project under way. In case you're unsure of how to make a particular fold, VRML origami enables you to change your view of the paper to get a closer look or to look at the paper from a different angle.

PointWorld

```
www.pointcom.com/vrml/home.wrl
```

Point is a Web index similar to Yahoo! or Excite, but with a twist: It includes PointWorld, a three-dimensional version of its index. PointWorld, shown in Figure 16-4, allows you to wander through a virtual city that features links to various categories of information, such as Entertainment, Education, and Kids. The 3-D PointWorld index is a bit slower than a text-based index, but it's also a lot more fun.

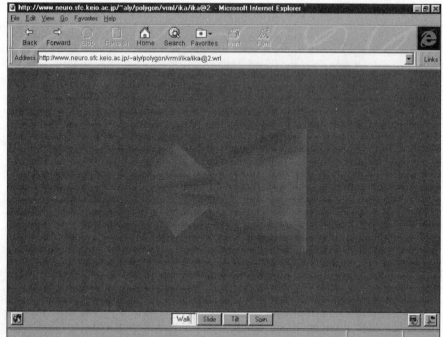

Figure 16-3:
Interactive
Origami.

Figure 16-4:
PointWorld,
a 3-D Web
index.

Planet 9 Studios

www.planet9.com

Planet 9 Studios hosts a Web page that features several virtual cities, including New York, San Francisco, New Orleans, Denver, and San Diego. Figure 16-5 shows a portion of Virtual San Francisco. The large diamonds represent areas that you can click to view even more detailed renderings.

VRML catalogs

You can turn to several sites on the Internet that contain catalogs of dozens or even hundreds of VRML objects you can explore. Here are two catalog sites you can investigate:

✔ The VRML Page at OCR, Inc., at www.ocnus.com/vrml.html, contains links to more than 350 VRML worlds.

✔ The VRML Legit List at www.geom.umn.edu/~daeron/bin/ legitlist.cgi is a list of dozens of VRML worlds that have passed a *VRML Authenticator* program, which verifies that all the VRML used to create the VRML world is in order.

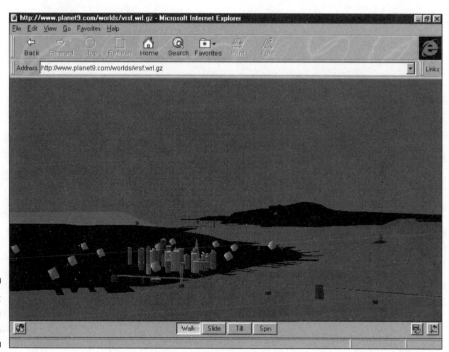

Figure 16-5: VRML San Francisco.

Chapter 17

Balancing Interactivity with Security

Most Web pages are static displays of information. They can show you great information, but they can't get information *from* you. But special types of Web pages, called *forms,* don't suffer from this limitation. A *form* is any Web page that includes input fields that work similarly to standard Windows dialog boxes. You type information into the fields and then click a button to send the information to the form's host system. The host system then processes the information in some way and displays a result. In other words, a form is an *interactive* Web page.

Interactivity is one of the latest and greatest breakthroughs on the World Wide Web, but it also carries some risks. By all means, take advantage of all that Internet Explorer has to offer. But be sure to read this chapter so that you explore safely.

Working with Forms

You can find an excellent example of a form at the U.S. Postal Service's zip+4 Lookup page, at the following URL:

```
www.usps.gov/ncsc/lookups/lookup_zip+4.html
```

As you can see in Figure 17-1, this Web page contains a space for you to type in an address. Then, when you click the Process Address button, the database at the post office's host computer searches for and displays the proper Zip code for the address you entered.2

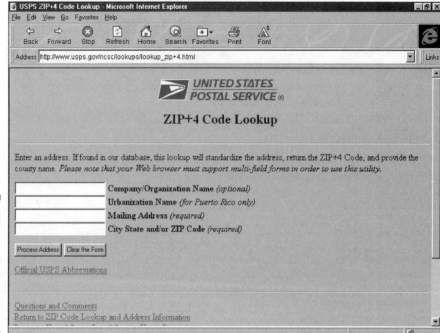

Figure 17-1:
The U.S.
Postal
Service's
zip+4
Lookup page
uses a
simple form.

Taking the controls

Forms can include the following different types of controls, which are similar to the controls found in Windows dialog boxes:

- ✔ **Single-line text boxes:** This type of control lets you enter a single line of information such as a name, phone number, or credit card number. This is the most common type of form currently on the Web.

- ✔ **Password boxes:** This control is like a normal single-line text box except that the information you type into the box is not displayed as you type it (perfect for sending super-secret passwords that the person standing behind you would love to peek at).

- ✔ **Multiline text boxes:** This control lets you enter several lines of information. The multiline text box includes a scroll bar if the information that has been entered into the control won't fit in the text box.

✔ **List boxes:** This control lets you select one of several options from a list of choices.

✔ **Check boxes:** This control lets you indicate whether an option or choice should be enabled or selected. Click the check box to change its status from checked to unchecked or vice versa.

✔ **Radio buttons:** These buttons let you select one of several options.

✔ **Push buttons:** These buttons come in two flavors. A *submit button* sends the information you have entered into other controls on the form to the host computer for processing. A *reset button* clears any information you have entered into the form so that you can start over.

When you click the Submit button, the information you entered into the other controls on the form is sent back to the host computer on which the form resides. There, the information is processed by a program that runs on the host computer. That program can do just about anything it wants to with the information you entered. In the case of the post office's zip+4 lookup page, the information is processed by a program that looks up the address in a huge database and returns the result to your computer.

Keyboard shortcuts

Although the normal way of working with Web pages is with the mouse, Internet Explorer lets you use the keyboard to work with forms. For example, you can use the Tab key to move from one form control to the next.

Table 17-1 summarizes the keyboard shortcuts you can use in forms with Internet Explorer.

Table 17-1	Keyboard Shortcuts to Use with Forms
Keyboard Shortcut	*What It Does*
Tab	Moves forward to the next control on the form
Shift+Tab	Moves backward to the previous form control
Enter	Equivalent to clicking the Submit button
Ctrl+Delete	Deletes from the insertion point to the end of the field
Home	Moves the insertion point to the beginning of the field
End	Moves the insertion point to the end of the field
Shift+Home	Selects from the insertion point to the beginning of the field
Shift+End	Selects from the insertion point to the end of the field

Are Forms Secure?

Forms are the one area of using the Web in which security becomes a major factor for most Web users. For example, suppose you find a shirt you want to buy from a company that lets you order directly from the Web. Should you type your credit card number into a form field and click the Submit button to order the shirt? Not if you are anything less than absolutely certain that the shirt company — and only the shirt company — will have access to the credit card number.

Unfortunately, guaranteeing that someone else won't see your credit card number on its way to the shirt company is difficult. The Internet often creates an illusion that you are directly connected to the computers that host the Web pages you are viewing. Actually, information may travel through several computers on its way from the Web host to your computer, and vice versa. Who knows who may be listening in on your electronic exchanges?

You should be very wary about sending sensitive information over the Web, especially your credit card number, Social Security number, bank account number, phone number, or address.

Scrambling: It's not just for breakfast anymore

All is not lost as far as Internet security goes, however. Internet Explorer includes the most recent security protocol, designed to enable secure communications over the Internet so that bad guys can't steal your credit card number when you send it over the Internet. This protocol is called SSL, and it effectively scrambles your information before sending it over the Internet, and unscrambles it at the other end. The scrambling is done in such a way that other users who might intercept your message cannot unscramble it.

With SSL, sending credit card numbers and other personal information over the Internet is safe — provided that the party to whom you are sending the private information also uses SSL. And herein lies the rub: Not everyone on the Internet is using SSL. So before you send any sensitive information over the Internet, make sure that the party you're sending it to uses SSL to protect your data.

Most companies that are using SSL are happy to brag about the fact that they offer secure communications. For example, Figure 17-2 shows a page from the Lands' End Web site, assuring customers that they can safely place online orders without worrying about someone stealing their credit card numbers. Most sites that use SSL include similar pronouncements. If you don't see such an assurance, don't send sensitive information to the site.

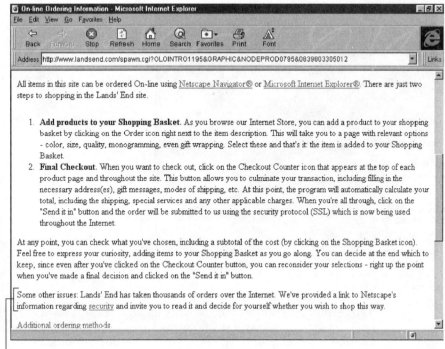

Figure 17-2:
A Web page
that brags
about its
capability to
securely
process
online
orders.

└ Look for security features

Beefing up your security

If you're nervous about sending information over the Internet, you can beef up the security protection built in to Internet Explorer by asking it to warn you whenever you are about to do something that may be a security risk. To set your security level, choose View⇨Options and click the Security tab. Up pop the security options shown in Figure 17-3.

The security options are a Catch-22. If you uncheck these options, you open yourself up to the possibility that your computer may fall victim to a virus or other destructive program masquerading as a cookie or an ActiveX or Java control. On the other hand, if you leave these security options checked, you'll be bombarded by what seems to be a constant procession of annoying warning messages. If you decide to be prudent and don't disable the security restrictions at first, you may sing a different tune after you see the warnings a few hundred times.

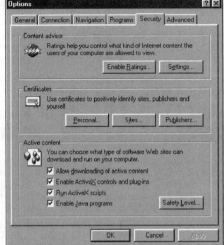

Figure 17-3:
Setting the
Internet
Explorer
security
options.

Certifying your security

The Certificates section of the Security dialog box contains options that let you control how your browser treats certificates. *Certificates* (also called *digital IDs*) are the computer equivalent of your driver's license. Certificates help guarantee that you are who you say you are, and more importantly, that the Web sites you send information to are what they say they are.

A complete explanation of how certificates work would span pages and require you to take a couple of Maalox before reading. But the basic concept is that an independent company, called a *credentials agency,* issues three types of certificates:

- **Personal:** This certificate identifies you so that you can access Web sites that require positive identification (such as banks that allow online transactions). When you first install Internet Explorer, you have the option of acquiring a personal certificate free from a credentials agency known as VeriSign. If you decline the certificate at that time, you can obtain a certificate by going to digitalid.verisign.com.

- **Sites:** These certificates insure that the site you are visiting is not a fraud. Internet Explorer automatically checks site certificates to make sure that they're valid.

- **Publishers:** These certificates enable you to trust software, such as ActiveX controls, that you download. Internet Explorer maintains a list of software companies whose certificates are trustworthy.

Jumping into Java

Microsoft ActiveX wasn't the first tech-nology that enabled Web developers to create pages that interacted with users through program-mable objects. Before ActiveX, there was Java — a system developed by Sun Micro-systems. In many ways, Java is similar to ActiveX, but it also has many differences. The most important difference is that ActiveX is a Microsoft product, specially designed to be used with Microsoft's Windows operating systems (although Microsoft plans to create a Macintosh version of ActiveX). Java, by contrast, is a more open system; it works with Windows 95, Windows 3.1, Macintosh, UNIX, and other operating systems.

Only time will tell how the battle to be king of the Web hill between Java and ActiveX will turn out. For now, there are many pages on the Web that require Java for best viewing, and there are also many that require ActiveX. Lucky for you, Internet Explorer can handle both technologies. Just be sure to enable both the ActiveX and Java op-tions on the Security option tab.

Click the three buttons in the Certificates section of the Security dialog box for a review the certificates that Internet Explorer is able to recognize.

Getting active

One big advancement in version 3.0 of Internet Explorer is that it supports Java and ActiveX — two exciting Web developments that standard HTML browsers can't handle. Both Java and ActiveX endow the otherwise static Web with active content such as background sounds, moving pictures, and enhanced interactivity.

According to some people (mostly those who work for Bill Gates), ActiveX is the best thing to happen to the Internet since the invention of the Web itself. Instead of being limited to forms with only a few types of controls, such as text boxes and radio buttons, Web-page designers can use ActiveX controls to create charts, graphs, spin wheels, progress bars, animated buttons, menus, and who knows what else.

ActiveX controls are stored on your hard disk, so you don't have wait for them to download over the Internet each time you access a page that includes the control. The first time you view a page that has a particular ActiveX control, your computer automatically downloads the control and stores it on your hard disk. Because some ActiveX controls are quite large, you may have to wait a few minutes for the download to finish. This delay is annoying, but happens only once for each different type of control.

Internet Explorer 3.0 comes with a small collection of ActiveX controls that pop up in many Web forms. Figure 17-4 shows one of these ActiveX controls in action, in this case a menu control. The menu control works like any other menu in Windows: When you click the menu, a drop-down list appears from which you can select any of several options. ActiveX-powered menu controls are designed to mimic standard Windows 95 menus, so Web developers can now create Web pages that have menu bars just like real programs.

Here are some other ActiveX controls that come with Internet Explorer:

- **Timer control:** Allows the Web page to change its appearance after a certain time period has elapsed

- **A pop-up window control:** Lets the Web developer display information in a separate window

- **An animated button control:** Brings clickable buttons to life

Check out Chapter 21 if you're interested in enhancing your own Web page with some of these ActiveX controls.

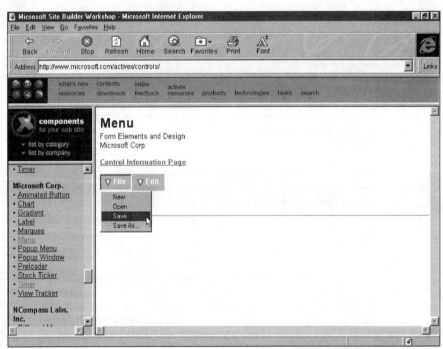

Figure 17-4:
An ActiveX
control.

Without Java and ActiveX, the Web is a quieter, stiller, less interactive place. If none of the Web sites you visit seem to have active content, choose View➪Options, click the Security tab, and make sure that the `Allow down loading of active content` option is enabled. If this option is enabled, check with your online service provider to make sure that it can handle ActiveX.

Getting advanced warning

In addition to the Security tab, the Options dialog box contains one more place you can go to set security options: the Advanced tab (shown in Figure 17-4).

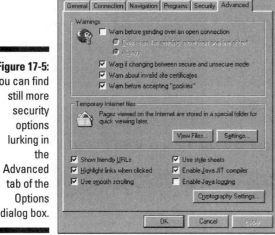

Figure 17-5:
You can find still more security options lurking in the Advanced tab of the Options dialog box.

The Warnings section of the Advanced options enable you to tell Internet Explorer whether to warn you about four potential types of security problems:

✔ `Warn me before sending over an open connection:` When you check this option, you get a warning anytime you send information to an account that doesn't have SSL security in place. The warning can get annoying after a while, so most users leave it off. You may want to turn it on, however, whenever you are about to order something over the Internet, so that you can make sure that SSL security indeed being used.

Internet Explorer allows you to select one of two variations of this option: You can elect to be warned only when you are sending more than one line of text, or you can elect to be warned whenever you send any amount of text. If you're going to use this option, I suggest you specify Al_ways. After all, you only need one form field to send a credit card number.

✔ Warn if changing between secure and unsecure modes: When you check this option, you get a warning any time your information passes through an unsecure server. I recommend that you leave this option checked.

✔ Warn about invalid site certificates: Always leave this option checked to make sure that you don't access a site that tries to send you a bogus certificate. (Refer to "Certifying your security," earlier in this chapter, for the lowdown on certificates.)

✔ Warn before accepting "cookies": This option doesn't have anything to do with chocolate chips or macadamia nuts. Instead, it refers to information that certain sites store on your computer's hard disk, to be used later. The most common example of a cookie is the information that customizable start pages such as www.msn.com store on your computer to keep track of how you have configured the page. Checking this option causes Internet Explorer to warn you whenever a Web site attempts to store a cookie on your hard disk. However, many sites rely on cookies to perform their magic.

Part VI
Adding New Internet Explorer Features to Your Own Web Page

The 5th Wave   By Rich Tennant

TECHNICAL STUFF

In this part . . .

This may be the first time an entire part of a *...For Dummies* book has been branded with the Technical Stuff icon. But the truth is, many of Internet Explorer's best new features are designed for the enjoyment of those who are not content to just view other people's Web pages, but insist on creating Web pages of their own. The chapters in this part highlight the new Web-page-creation features of Internet Explorer 3.0. Discover enhanced HTML features and, best of all, the newest kid on the Internet block: ActiveX.

A word of warning: Everything in this part is on the technical side. Grab your pocket protector and propeller cap before reading on.

Chapter 18

Best Experienced with
Internet Explorer 3.0

In This Chapter

▶ Flashy new features that require Internet Explorer 3.0

▶ Using the Microsoft Internet Explorer 3.0 logo in your Web pages

▶ Accessing the Microsoft online help for creating Web pages that use these new features

*I*n the battle for Web browser dominance, both Microsoft and Netscape have recently begun to introduce new features for their browsers. Typically, each new release of Internet Explorer or Netscape Navigator supports all of the features in the most recent version of the competitor's browser. Thus, Internet Explorer now supports features that once required Netscape Navigator 2.0, and Netscape Navigator now supports features that once required Internet Explorer 2.0. But Internet Explorer 3.0 now sports new features that the latest release of Netscape doesn't support, and vice versa.

What Microsoft really hopes is that you and thousands of other Web-page developers will commit to using Internet Explorer 3.0 and then stick a "Best Experienced with Internet Explorer 3.0" logo at the bottom of your Web page (see Figure 18-1). If Web surfers see the Internet Explorer logo more often on Web pages, they may be more inclined to download Internet Explorer and toss their old copies of Netscape into the closet.

This chapter presents an overview of the Web features you can take advantage of if you decide to commit your Web site to Internet Explorer 3.0 browsers. Read on to find out how your site can earn the "Best Experienced with Internet Explorer 3.0" merit badge and what you need to do before you stick the Internet Explorer logo on your Web page.

Figure 18-1:
Microsoft
marks its
territory.

This chapter assumes that you have a basic understanding of how Web pages are developed, including at least a rudimentary knowledge of *Hypertext Markup Language* (HTML), the programming language behind all Web pages. If you've never created a Web page, or if you're just starting out with HTML, check out *HTML For Dummies,* 2nd Edition, by Ed Tittel and Steve James, for some really great tips on creating Web pages.

Web Features Specially Designed for Internet Explorer 3.0

This section describes several different elements you can incorporate into your Web pages — elements your viewers must use Internet Explorer 3.0 to experience. As time goes on, other browsers — most notably, Netscape — will probably come to support some or all of these features. But for the time being, Web pages with these features are best viewed with Internet Explorer 3.0.

New HTML tags and attributes

Microsoft has introduced quite a few new HTML elements with Internet Explorer 3.0. Some of these features involve entirely new HTML tags; others involve new attributes that you can use with existing HTML tags. The most important of these new features include the following:

- **Style sheets:** Style sheets give you precise control over the layout of text on your Web page. With style sheets, you can specify fonts, font sizes, line spacing, text alignment, indentation, and other layout information. Style sheets are implemented using a new HTML tag (you guessed it: ⟨STYLE⟩).

- **Advanced tables:** Internet Explorer 3.0 supports several new HTML attributes that you can use with the standard table tags such as ⟨TABLE⟩, ⟨TR⟩, and ⟨TD⟩. These new attributes enable you to create tables that have different backgrounds and give you better control over table features such as borders, text alignment, and colors.

✔ **Advanced frames:** Frames have been around for a while, but only Internet Explorer 3.0 lets you create borderless frames, giving your Web pages a seamless appearance. Internet Explorer 3.0 also includes a floating frame feature that allows you to position a frame anywhere on the Web page.

✔ **Scrolling marquees:** Marquees allow you to display text that slides across the screen like a fancy theater marquee.

✔ **Background sounds:** You can attach a sound file to a page so that the sound plays automatically whenever the page is viewed.

✔ **Inline video:** You can now include a video directly on a Web page and have it play automatically when the user first displays the page.

To find out more about style sheets, point your nose at Chapter 20. Check out Chapter 19 to find out more about the rest of these HTML enhancements.

ActiveX

An important new feature of Internet Explorer is its support for a new Internet object architecture called *ActiveX,* which allows Web authors to create pages that go beyond the static nature of standard HTML. With ActiveX, you can create Web pages that truly interact with users.

ActiveX follows close on the heels of Sun Microsystems' Java, which provides a similar capability for creating dynamic content and interactivity on the Web. Like Java, ActiveX lets Web developers create Web pages that don't just sit there, but move around, make noise, jump up and down, and do all sorts of interesting things.

ActiveX Controls

ActiveX Controls are a new breed of OLE (object linking and embedding) objects that you can incorporate into Web pages. An *ActiveX control* is an object that you can include on your Web page using an HTML <OBJECT> tag. Most ActiveX controls display information on the Web page in one form or another: as a chart or graph, or maybe as text formatted at an angle or in three dimensions.

Internet Explorer 3.0 comes with a small set of useful ActiveX controls. However, thousands of other ActiveX controls are available, some from Microsoft, some from other companies. Some of these controls you can use for free, but others require that you pay a license fee to use them.

When an Internet Explorer browser encounters an HTML <OBJECT> tag that calls for an ActiveX control, the browser first looks to see whether the ActiveX control is already present on the user's hard disk. If the ActiveX control is not present, Internet Explorer locates the ActiveX control on a Web site that is specified in the <OBJECT> tag and downloads the control to the user's hard disk. This process happens automatically, without your knowledge, unless of course the control happens to be very large. In that case, you might get up for a cup of coffee while the control downloads.

Figure 18-2 shows an example of a typical ActiveX control. In this case, the Web-page author has added an ActiveX pop-up menu to the Web page. The pop-up menu appears when you click the word *products* in the menu at the top of the Web page.

ActiveX Control Pad

The ActiveX Control Pad, shown in Figure 18-3, is a point-and-click tool for adding ActiveX controls to your Web pages. The Control Pad greatly simplifies the task of working with ActiveX controls. Best of all, you can download the Control Pad for free from the Microsoft Web site at the following address:

```
www.microsoft.com/workshop/author/cpad/
```

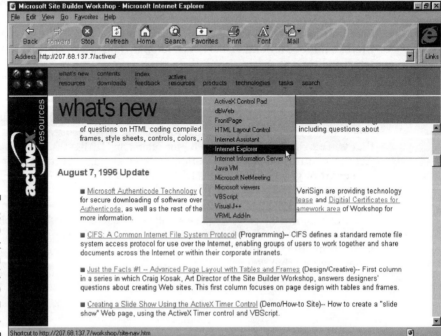

Figure 18-2:
A Web page that includes an ActiveX pop-up menu control.

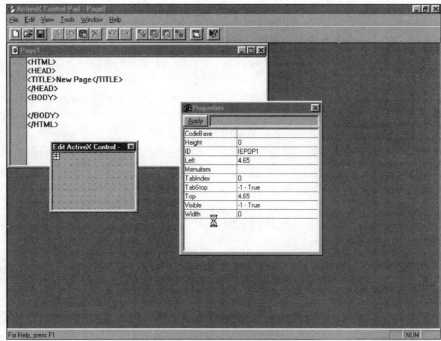

Figure 18-3:
Using the
ActiveX
Control Pad.

ActiveX scripts

ActiveX scripts are programs that you can embed in an HTML document.
ActiveX scripts work together with ActiveX controls to create interactive Web
pages. For example, if you put an ActiveX control on a Web page, you can create
an ActiveX script that runs whenever the user moves the mouse over the
control. You can even have a different script run if the user actually clicks the
control.

You can use one of two scripting languages to create ActiveX scripts: Visual
Basic Scripting Edition (known as *VBScript*) or JScript, Microsoft's implementation of the popular Java programming language. Of course, Microsoft hopes
you'll choose VBScript as your scripting language of choice. But if you are
already an experienced Java programmer, JScript works just as well.

For more information about incorporating ActiveX controls and scripts in your
Web pages and using the ActiveX Control Pad, refer to Chapter 21.

Java or ActiveX?

One of the biggest battles in the computer world today is the fight to see whether ActiveX or Java ends up dominating the Web world. ActiveX is, of course, Microsoft's offering. Java originated with Sun Microsystems, but its more open nature means that Java pretty much represents the rest of the computer industry.

Java has many things going for it. Some of the arguments in favor of Java include

- Java was designed from the ground up as a network-capable object-oriented programming language. In contrast, ActiveX is merely a recycled version of the 8-year-old Microsoft OLE technology.

- Java is *open,* which means that it is not dependent on one hardware platform, operating system, or manufacturer. ActiveX, on the other hand, is primarily for Intel-based computers running Microsoft Windows.

- Java was there first, so more Web sites are currently using Java than ActiveX.

Some of the arguments in favor of ActiveX include:

- ActiveX has the weight of Microsoft behind it. It will quickly catch up and surpass Java in acceptance.

- Because ActiveX is based on OLE, it is a proven technology.

- ActiveX is a more comprehensive object technology than Java. Java is merely a programming language; ActiveX is a complete object framework. Sun is working on a Java object framework, called *Java Beans,* but Java Beans doesn't exist yet.

One of Microsoft's strategies for winning this battle is to subsume Java into ActiveX, in typical Borg fashion. ("Resistance is futile; you will be assimilated.") ActiveX includes JScript, which allows Java scripts to interact with ActiveX controls. In addition, Microsoft has produced a Java compiler called Visual J++, which lets developers use the Java language rather than C++ to create ActiveX controls.

HTML Layout Control

HTML Layout Control is an ActiveX control that comes with Internet Explorer 3.0. True, thousands of ActiveX controls are available. But the HTML Layout Control is special because it provides a critical feature that HTML by itself does not: the ability to precisely control the position of other ActiveX controls on the page. You can think of the HTML Layout Control as sort of like a container that holds other ActiveX controls and displays them in precise locations on the page.

Figure 18-4 shows a sample Web page that uses Layout Control to create a complicated page layout. To find out more about Layout Control, flip over to Chapter 21.

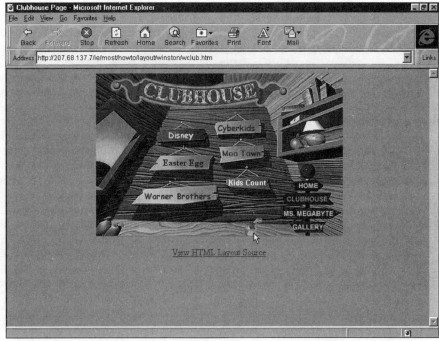

With Layout Control, you can incorporate the following layout features into your Web documents:

- ✔ **Exact placement:** You can place objects on a Web page accurately using x and y coordinates.

- ✔ **Overlapping:** You can stack objects and control how objects on top obscure the objects beneath them.

- ✔ **Transparency:** Objects can overlap other objects so that the ones beneath show through.

- ✔ **Scripting:** You can give a Web page some very interesting effects, such as a door opening when the mouse is moved over it or a flower blooming when the mouse is moved over an image of the sun. Note, as shown in Figure 18-4, that the little worm won't appear until you point your mouse at the apple.

The HTML Layout Control works in concert with the ActiveX Control Pad to provide a visual programming environment for ActiveX controls. This interaction allows you to build Web pages in much the same way as you build forms in Microsoft Visual Basic: by dragging and dropping controls onto the page, positioning them exactly where you want them to appear.

Using the Internet Explorer Logo

As you may expect, the legal eagles at Microsoft have, in their infinite wisdom, decided that not just anyone can incorporate the Internet Explorer logo into their Web pages. If you want to use the logo, you must first register your site with Microsoft and obtain its permission to use the logo.

Fortunately, the requirements for using the Internet Explorer logo are pretty modest, and Microsoft doesn't charge a fee for its use. The basic requirement for using the Internet Explorer logo is that your Web site feature at least *one* of the flashy new features of Internet Explorer, such as style sheets, ActiveX scripts, or HTML Layout Control. You must submit your page to Microsoft for review before getting permission to use the logo.

Two versions of the Internet Explorer logo are available for inclusion in your Web site: a static logo and an animated logo. The static logo is for Web pages that incorporate Internet Explorer's new HTML extensions such as scrolling marquees, floating frames, and enhanced tables. The animated logo (which looks just like the static logo, except that little E is replaced by a spinning globe) is for sites that incorporate ActiveX controls.

To find out more about using the Internet Explorer logo, and to register for the logo, check out the Microsoft Internet Explorer Logo Program page at www.microsoft.com/ie/logo, shown in Figure 18-5.

Online Help for Internet Explorer Developers

The Microsoft Web site (www.microsoft.com) includes several pages devoted to providing online help for using the new features of Internet Explorer 3.0 to create Web pages. You may want to mark many of these pages as Favorites, and some may even be useful enough to place on your Quick Links toolbar.

For general information about developing Web pages that work with Internet Explorer 3.0, consult the following Web page:

```
www.microsoft.com/workshop
```

This URL takes you to the Site Builder Workshop, as shown in Figure 18-6. The Workshop page includes links to many other useful pages, plus news about new development tools for Internet Explorer 3.0.

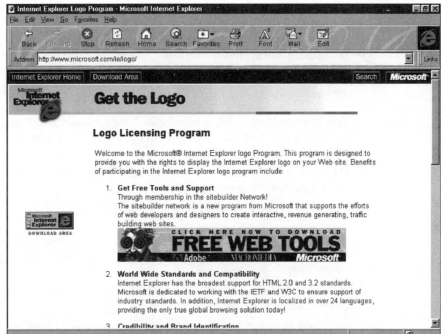

Figure 18-5:
The
Microsoft
Internet
Explorer
Logo
Program
Web page.

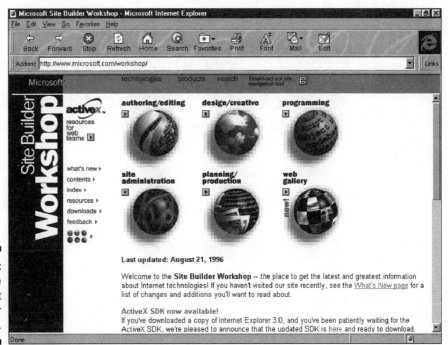

Figure 18-6:
The
Microsoft
Site Builder
Workshop.

Here are just a few of the pages you can access from the Site Builder Workshop page, all of which contain valuable information for Web authors:

- **HTML Reference:** Find a complete reference for Internet Explorer's HTML features at the following address:

   ```
   www.microsoft.com/workshop/author/newhtml/default.htm
   ```

   This is a complete HTML reference for Internet Explorer 3.0. You can look up tags by category (for example, Tables, Frames, or Image Maps) or alphabetically.

- **HTML FAQ:** Find a list of commonly asked HTML questions and their answers at the following address:

   ```
   www.microsoft.com/workshop/author/newhtml/default.htm
   ```

   For example, you can find answers to questions such as "How do I create a marquee that scrolls vertically?" and "How can I display small animations on my page?"

- **Style Sheets User Guide:** Find a complete explanation of the new style sheets feature at the following address:

   ```
   www.microsoft.com/workshop/author/newhtml/default.htm
   ```

   Here, you can find basic information about using style sheets, an HTML style sheet reference, and tips and tricks. (Style sheets are also covered right here in this very book, in Chapter 20.)

- **ActiveX Controls FAQ:** Find answers to frequently asked questions about incorporating ActiveX controls into your Web pages at the following address:

   ```
   www.microsoft.com/intdev/controls/ctrlfaq-f.htm
   ```

   For more information about ActiveX Controls, check out Chapter 21.

Chapter 19

Marquees, Background Sounds, and Other Flashy Tricks

· ·

In This Chapter

▶ Creating marquees that scroll across the screen

▶ Giving your Web page a voice

▶ Adding colors to a Web page

▶ Using TrueType fonts

▶ Creating fancy tables and floating frames

· ·

*T*his chapter presents some of the new HTML features that were introduced with Internet Explorer, some with Version 2.0, others with Version 3.0. These new features are either new tags, such as the `<MARQUEE>` tag used to create a marquee, or new attributes that work with existing standard tags, such as the `BGSOUND` attribute, which you can use with the `<BODY>` tag to add a background sound to a page.

Should you use these features in your Web pages? The answer depends on whether you think the possibility of losing some users is worth the benefits that these features provide. If you do use these features, your Web page could be eligible to receive the coveted Best Experienced with Internet Explorer 3.0 logo. (See Chapter 18 for a discussion of how you can include this logo in your Web site.)

If losing viewers who don't have Internet Explorer 3.0 is a big concern for you, you can provide alternate content for browsers that don't support the new HTML features covered here. But I wouldn't worry too much. Before long, other Web browsers besides Internet Explorer will support these new HTML features as well.

This chapter is *not* a tutorial on how to use *Hypertext Markup Language* (HTML). If you are experienced with HTML, this chapter can provide you with enough information to incorporate the new HTML features that are available with Internet Explorer 3.0 into your Web page. If you are new to HTML, I recommend that you check out a good primer on HTML — *HTML For Dummies,* 2nd Edition, by Ed Tittel and Steve James.

Making Magnificent Marquees

The `<MARQUEE>` tag lets you create a line of text that scrolls across the screen as the user views the page. This feature creates an interesting appearance and definitely draws attention to the scrolling text. Microsoft uses this feature in many of its pages at `www.microsoft.com`. If you've visited the Microsoft Web site, you've probably seen the `<MARQUEE>` tag in action.

Strictly speaking, the `<MARQUEE>` tag was first introduced in Internet Explorer 2.0 and is now also supported by Netscape's Navigator 3.0. I am covering this tag here because it is a still relatively new HTML feature. Browsers that don't support the `<MARQUEE>` tag simply ignore the tag when they encounter it and display the text in normal fashion, without any scrolling or other fancy effects.

Building a basic marquee

To create a basic marquee, you simply sandwich the text you want to scroll between a pair of `<MARQUEE>` and `</MARQUEE>` tags, like this:

```
<MARQUEE>This text will scroll across the screen!</MARQUEE>
```

When a browser reads this code, it scrolls the words "This text will scroll across the screen!" from right to left. When the text reaches the left edge of the monitor, it scrolls off the screen and reenters the screen from the right side.

Only *text* that appears between the `<MARQUEE>` and `</MARQUEE>` tags scrolls. Wrapping `<MARQUEE>` tags around an `<IMG>` tag doesn't cause the image to scroll. Even if you place an `<IMG>` tag in a marquee, the image remains stationary.

Formulating a fancy marquee

You can achieve several interesting effects by using attributes along with the `<MARQUEE>` tag. *Attributes* are simply keywords that appear within a tag to modify the tag's basic behavior. An attribute consists of a keyword followed by an equal sign and a value, as in `DIRECTION=LEFT` or `LOOP=3`.

Setting scrolling behavior

The `BEHAVIOR` attribute changes the scrolling behavior of the marquee. This attribute has three options:

✔ SCROLL: This option, which is the default, creates a marquee that scrolls across the screen repeatedly. When the marquee reaches the edge of the screen, it scrolls off and reenters at the opposite edge of the screen.

✔ SLIDE: Using this parameter causes the marquee text to enter the screen from one edge and scroll across until it reaches the other edge, where it stops.

✔ ALTERNATE: Using this parameter causes the marquee to bounce back and forth from one edge of the screen to the other.

Changing direction

You can change the direction in which the marquee travels by using the DIRECTION attribute with one of the following settings:

✔ DIRECTION=LEFT: This default setting causes the marquee to scroll from right to left.

✔ DIRECTION=RIGHT: This setting enables the marquee to scroll from left to right.

The following code causes the words "A right-sliding marquee!" to enter the screen from the left, scroll until they hit the right edge of the screen, and then stop:

```
<MARQUEE BEHAVIOR=SLIDE DIRECTION=RIGHT>A right-sliding
          marquee!</MARQUEE>
```

Scrolling across part of a Web page

You can create a marquee that scrolls within an area smaller than the full width of the Internet Explorer window by using the WIDTH attribute in the <MARQUEE> tag. The WIDTH attribute specifies the width of the area in which the marquee should scroll, in terms of number of pixels. The WIDTH attribute can also designate the width of the area that a marquee scrolls, in terms of a percentage of the page width. For example, consider these two <MARQUEE> tags:

```
<MARQUEE WIDTH=100>
<MARQUEE WIDTH=30%>
```

The first tag introduces a marquee that scrolls across an area that is 100 pixels wide. The second tag introduces a marquee that scrolls through an area 30 percent of the total width of the page.

Counting your loops

The LOOP attribute lets you specify how many times the marquee repeats its scrolling action. The default LOOP setting varies with the BEHAVIOR setting:

> ✔ For scrolling and alternating marquees, the default option is for the marquee to repeat *indefinitely*.
>
> ✔ For sliding marquees, the default setting is for the marquee to slide across the screen *just once*.

You can direct the marquee to scroll a specified number of times by using the `LOOP` attribute. For example:

```
<MARQUEE LOOP=1>This marquee will scroll only once!</MARQUEE>
```

In this example, the marquee scrolls across the screen only one time and then stops.

Turning some marquee tricks

You can accomplish some interesting tricks using marquees. For example, although the marquee must be text only, you're not restricted to using only letters and numerals. Consider the following snippet of HTML code:

```
<TT><MARQUEE DIRECTION=RIGHT BEHAVIOR=SLIDE WIDTH=25%>-&gt;
        </MARQUEE></TT>
Here is something pretty important!
```

In the preceding code, the `<MARQUEE>` tag creates an arrow using three hyphens and a greater-than sign. You have to use the silly `&gt;` code to create a greater-than sign in your HTML documents. Also, I use the `<TT>` tag to format the marquee arrow using TeleType text, which in Internet Explorer formats the text in the Courier New typeface.

The marquee enters from the left and slides to the right, pointing at the text "Here is something pretty important!" Because this HTML code uses the `SLIDE` attribute, the marquee stops when it gets to the right side of the screen. Figure 19-1 shows how this text appears in Internet Explorer. (In the figure, the arrow has already begun its journey across the screen toward the text.)

Another good marquee trick is to use a series of periods with spaces between them to create the effect of chasing lights. For example:

```
<MARQUEE BEHAVIOR=ALTERNATE WIDTH=20%>.   .   .   .   .   .
        </MARQUEE>
```

To get the effect to look right, you have to play around a lot with the marquee width and the spacing between periods. But when you set it up right, it looks pretty nifty.

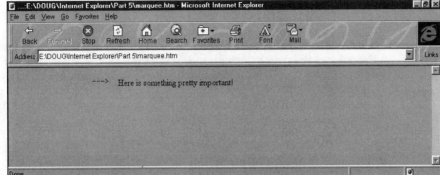

Figure 19-1:
This
marquee
slides from
left to right.

Adding Background Sounds

Internet Explorer 3.0 lets you use the <BGSOUND> tag to specify a background sound to play automatically whenever the Web page is displayed. This feature allows you to create transition sound effects that play when the user goes from one page to another. Whereas most older browsers only allow you to access sound files by clicking them, Internet Explorer 3.0 makes adding a background sound to a page an almost trivial exercise.

To add a background sound, include a <BGSOUND> tag similar to the following one near the beginning of the HTML document body:

```
<BGSOUND SRC="sound.wav">
```

The sound.wav file can be any .wav file you have available. Many music clips are available on the Internet — just look around for one that meets your needs. Or you may already have some music files you can use. For example, if you own Microsoft Office for Windows 95, you can find a large collection of sample music files on the Office CD, located in the ValuePack folder.

You can also use MIDI files, which are typically smaller than .wav files. *MIDI files* are not actual recordings of sounds, but rather files that contain the electronic equivalent of sheet music, which the synthesizer that's built in to your sound card can play.

If you want the sound to repeat, you can use a LOOP attribute to specify a number (for example, LOOP=3) or LOOP=INFINITE. The infinite option causes the sound to play as long as the page is displayed — if that happens to be for an infinite amount of time, well. . . .

Even short .wav files can be 200K or larger. You don't want to force people to tap their fingers for three or four minutes while your sound downloads. Use sound sparingly, and use MIDI files if possible because they're so much smaller.

Splashing on Some Color

HTML allows you to specify the color of the text on your Web page, as well as the color of the page's background. Standard HTML enables you to indicate the color to use as three hexadecimal numbers that represent the color's red, green, and blue levels. For example, red is specified as FF0000, green is 00FF00, and blue is 0000FF. This color-coding scheme lets you specify more than 16 million distinct colors, but it's kind of hard to tell exactly what color you'll wind up with when you specify a number such as 194E2B or C04A92.

To simplify color specification, Internet Explorer 3.0 allows you to use 16 color names in attributes that call for a color. This approach may be more limiting than using the standard hexadecimal color attributes, but specifying COLOR=RED is a lot less confusing than specifying COLOR="#FF0000". The color names permitted by Internet Explorer are as follows:

AQUA	BLACK	BLUE	FUCHSIA
GRAY	GREEN	LIME	MAROON
NAVY	OLIVE	PURPLE	RED
SILVER	TEAL	WHITE	YELLOW

For example, the <BODY> tag (used to mark the main body of your document) includes two attributes for setting colors:

- ✔ TEXT: Sets the color of your document's body text
- ✔ BGCOLOR: Sets the page's background color

To set the body text color to white and the background color to teal, use a <BODY> tag like this:

```
<BODY TEXT=WHITE BGCOLOR=TEAL>
```

Or to display a word in red type, use a <FONT> tag like this:

```
This word is <FONT COLOR=RED>red.</FONT>
```

Choosing Fonts

HTML does not allow you to control the fonts used to display text. Instead, each Web browser decides which font to use to display text. In many cases, HTML authors have resorted to using graphic images of text headings as the only method of displaying fonts other than the defaults used by the Web browser.

With the latest versions of Internet Explorer, Microsoft has introduced a new `FACE` attribute for the `<FONT>` tag so that you can control the fonts that other people see when they view your site with the Internet Explorer 3.0 browser. The new `FACE` attribute of the `<FONT>` tag lets you select a font in which to display your text. Thus, you can specify that you want a heading to appear in Arial font, while the body text of your Web page should appear in Century Schoolbook font.

The only problem with the `FACE` attribute is that you have no guarantee that a user will have a particular font on his or her computer. For this reason, the `FACE` attribute allows you to specify a list of font names rather than a single font. If the first font in the list isn't available on the viewer's computer, Internet Explorer displays the heading or text using the second font on the list. If that font is not available, Internet Explorer selects the third font named in the list, and so on.

Using the FACE attribute

The `FACE` attribute lets you specify a list of fonts from which Internet Explorer can choose to display text. You enclose the entire list in quotes and separate the font names from one another with commas.

The following example shows how you might use the `<FONT FACE>` tag:

```
<FONT FACE="Bookman Old Style,Times New Roman">Some text.
</FONT>
```

Internet Explorer browsers that encounter the preceding line of code display the words "Some text" in the Bookman Old Style font — if Bookman Old Style is available on the viewer's computer. If Bookman Old Style is *not* available, the browser uses the next option, Times New Roman.

The following HTML snippet shows one way to use the `<FONT FACE>` tag to change the fonts on your Web page. You can see the resulting page in action, as displayed by Internet Explorer, in Figure 19-2.

```
<BODY BGCOLOR=WHITE>
<FONT FACE="Comic Sans MS,Arial" SIZE=7>
"English Poets Who Couldn't Spell" for $200<P>
</FONT>
<FONT FACE="Bookman Old Style,Times New Roman" SIZE=4>
Whan that Aprill with his shoures soote<BR>
The droghte of March hath perced to the roote,<BR>
And bathed every veyne in swich licour<BR>
Of which vertu engendred is the flour;<P>
</FONT>
</BODY>
```

In Figure 19-2, notice that the heading *"English Poets who couldn't Spell" for $200* is displayed using the Comic Sans MS typeface, whereas the remaining text is displayed in Bookman Old Style.

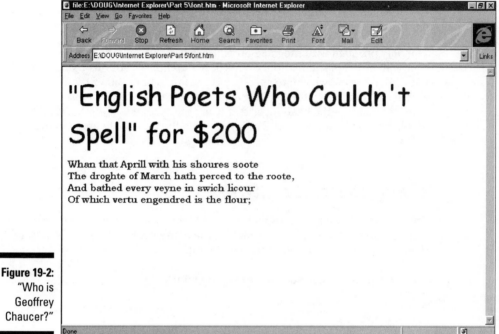

Figure 19-2:
"Who is Geoffrey Chaucer?"

Deciding which fonts to use in a Web page

When using the FACE tag, restrict your font choices to those fonts you can be reasonably sure that most Web users have at their disposal. For example, all Windows users have Times New Roman, Arial, and Courier New fonts. In addition, Microsoft distributes several other fonts with Internet Explorer: Arial Black, Comic Sans MS, Comic Sans MS (Bold), Impact, and Verdana (regular, bold, italic, and bold italic). The first four are designed for use in headings and other short text you want to draw attention to. The Verdana fonts work well for headings or body text. You can take a peek at how these Internet Explorer fonts look in Figure 19-3.

Many Web users also have Microsoft Office installed, which includes a number of additional fonts; other software programs come with even more fonts. Nevertheless, the only fonts you can count on a user having are the ones that come with Windows and Internet Explorer 3.0.

Figure 19-3:
Fonts you
can expect
viewers
using
Internet
Explorer to
have.

Arial Black
Comic Sans MS
Comic Sans MS (Bold)
Impact
Verdana
Verdana (Bold)
Verdana (Italic)
Verdana (Bold Italic)

If a browser that doesn't support the FACE attribute encounters your page, it simply ignores your typeface specifications. In that case, the typeface reverts to the default settings based on the tags used to format the text (<H1>, <P>, and so on).

Using New Table Features

Tables are one of the most important elements used in HTML documents. Internet Explorer 3.0 supports all of the table tags you've come to know and love (such as <TABLE>, <TR>, and <TD>), plus adds a few new capabilities of its own. In particular, newer versions of Internet Explorer enable you to customize your tables in the following ways:

- ✔ You can use a different color and background for each cell in a table.
- ✔ You can align text along a baseline so that cells with different font sizes line up properly.
- ✔ You can turn off internal or external borders.
- ✔ You can create cells that span more than one column or row in a table.

Remember: You use the following three tags to set up a table in HTML:

- <TABLE>: Marks the beginning of the table, with a corresponding </TABLE> tag marking the end of the table
- <TR>: Marks a row in the table, with a corresponding </TR> at the end of each row
- <TD>: Marks an individual table cell, with everything falling between the <TD> tag and its corresponding </TD> being considered to be a part of the cell

The following sections explain how to use each of the new table features for Internet Explorer 3.0.

Adding cell colors and backgrounds

Internet Explorer 2.0 first introduced the ability to vary the background color and image for each cell in a table by adding the BGCOLOR (to set a background color) and BACKGROUND (to specify a background image) attributes to the <TD> tag. For example, the following HTML code creates a table, using a different background color for each of the table's 16 cells:

```
<BODY BGCOLOR=WHITE>
<TABLE BORDER=3 CELLPADDING=10>
<TR>
  <TD BGCOLOR=AQUA>Aqua</TD>
  <TD BGCOLOR=BLACK><FONT COLOR=WHITE>Black</FONT></TD>
  <TD BGCOLOR=BLUE><FONT COLOR=WHITE>Blue</FONT></TD>
  <TD BGCOLOR=FUCHSIA>Fuchsia</TD>
</TR>
<TR>
  <TD BGCOLOR=GRAY>Gray</TD>
  <TD BGCOLOR=GREEN>Green</TD>
  <TD BGCOLOR=LIME>Lime</TD>
  <TD BGCOLOR=MAROON><FONT COLOR=WHITE>Maroon</FONT></TD>
</TR>
<TR>
  <TD BGCOLOR=NAVY><FONT COLOR=WHITE>Navy</FONT></TD>
  <TD BGCOLOR=OLIVE>Olive</TD>
  <TD BGCOLOR=PURPLE><FONT COLOR=WHITE>Purple</FONT></TD>
  <TD BGCOLOR=RED>Red</TD>
</TR>
<TR>
  <TD BGCOLOR=SILVER>Silver</TD>
  <TD BGCOLOR=TEAL>Teal</TD>
  <TD BGCOLOR=WHITE>White</TD>
  <TD BGCOLOR=YELLOW>Yellow</TD>
</TR>
</TABLE>
</BODY>
```

Figure 19-4 shows how this table appears when viewed by Internet Explorer 3.0. I tried to get IDG Books to splurge for color printing so that you could see the brilliant colors in this figure. They said they'd be happy to, and would deduct the additional cost of color printing from my first royalty check. So as far as the color goes, you'll just have to use your imagination.

Note that browsers that don't support the BGCOLOR attribute can display this the table just fine — but, of course, without any special background colors.

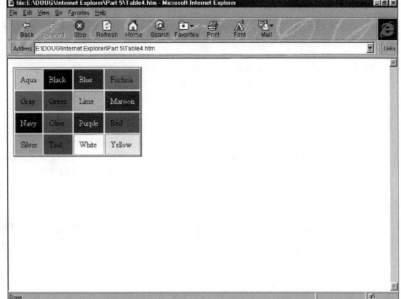

Figure 19-4:
A table with different background colors in each cell. Trust me.

Aligning cells to a baseline

By default, the text within each cell is vertically aligned to the middle of the cell. So before Internet Explorer 3.0 hit the streets, table rows that contained several cells with different text sizes often didn't look right. Such tables would look much better if you could align the text in each cell along a baseline.

Well, guess what! Internet Explorer's new VALIGN=BASELINE attribute for the <TD> tag, which defines individual table columns, lets you do just that. Now you can use this attribute to align your table text along a baseline, making your tables look neater and your Web pages more professional. Take a look at how the following code affects the text in the table shown in Figure 19-5:

```
<BODY BGCOLOR=WHITE>
<TABLE>
<TR>
  <TD><FONT SIZE=4>Big</FONT></TD>
  <TD><FONT SIZE=5>Bigger</FONT></TD>
  <TD><FONT SIZE=6>Biggest</FONT></TD>
</TR>
<TR>
  <TD VALIGN=BASELINE><FONT SIZE=4>Big</FONT></TD>
  <TD VALIGN=BASELINE><FONT SIZE=5>Bigger</FONT></TD>
  <TD VALIGN=BASELINE><FONT SIZE=6>Biggest</FONT></TD>
</TR>
</TABLE>
</BODY>
```

In the table created by the preceding HTML code, the first row consists of three cells using the default vertical alignment, with text sized at 4, 5, and 6. (Don't forget HTML's klutzy text-size attribute, which forces you to specify text size as a number from 1 to 7, with no control over how large the text is actually displayed.) The second row, however, consists of the same text, but uses the VALIGN=BASELINE attribute. Figure 19-5 shows this table as viewed with Internet Explorer 3.0. Notice how the second line of text aligns on a common baseline rather than in the middle of each cell, as does the first line of text.

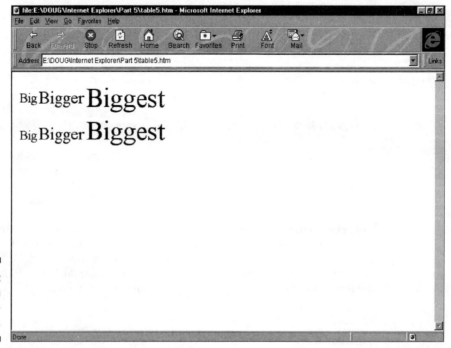

Figure 19-5:
A table with baseline-aligned text.

Controlling internal and external borders

Two of the new attributes added to the `<TABLE>` tag in Internet Explorer 3.0 —
`FRAME` and `RULES` — give you greater control over how you can display borders
in a table. `FRAME` controls the outside border drawn *around* the entire table, and
`RULES` controls the borders drawn *between* cells within the tables.

The `FRAME` attribute has the following settings to modify the border around a
table:

- `VOID`: No outside border is used
- `ABOVE`: A border appears above the table
- `BELOW`: A border appears below the table
- `HSIDES`: A border appears above and below the table
- `LHS`: A border appears on the left side of the table
- `RHS`: A border appears on the right side of the table
- `VSIDES`: A border appears on the left and right sides of the table
- `BOX`: A border appears on all sides of the table
- `BORDER`: Same as box

The `RULES` attribute has the following settings to modify the borders between
cells in a table:

- `NONE`: No inside borders are displayed
- `ROWS`: Displays horizontal borders between all rows of the table
- `COLS`: Displays vertical borders between all columns of the table
- `GROUPS`: Displays horizontal borders between all table groups, as identified
  by `THEAD`, `TBODY`, `TFOOT`, and `COLGROUP` tags
- `ALL`: Displays an interior border for all rows and columns

As an example, consider the effects of the following HTML code on the table
that appears in Figure 19-6:

```
<BODY BGCOLOR=WHITE>
<TABLE BORDER=3 FRAME=HSIDES RULES=ROWS CELLPADDING=10>
<TR ALIGN=CENTER>
   <TH>Name</TH>
   <TH>How They Measure Up</TH>
</TR>
<TR ALIGN=CENTER>
   <TD>Michael Banks</TD>
   <TD>Extremely stubborn and suspicious.</TD>
```

(continued)

(continued)

```
</TR>
<TR ALIGN=CENTER>
  <TD>Jane Banks</TD>
  <TD>Rather inclined to giggle, doesn't put things away.</TD>
</TR>
<TR ALIGN=CENTER>
  <TD>Mary Poppins</TD>
  <TD>Practically perfect in every way.</TD>
</TR>
</TABLE>
</BODY>
```

The <TH> tags used in the preceding example create table heading cells, and the CELLPADDING attribute in the <TABLE> tag adds additional space between the cells.

Figure 19-6 shows how this table appears when you view it using Internet Explorer 3.0. Notice the frame above and below the table, as specified by the FRAME=HSIDES attribute, and the rules drawn between the rows as a result of the RULES=ROWS attribute.

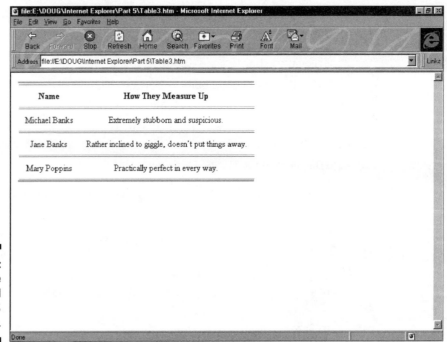

Figure 19-6:
Using the
FRAME and
RULES
attributes.

Spanning rows and columns

Internet Explorer 3.0 also lets you create table cells that span more than one row or column. You typically use this option to create a heading that covers more than a single row or column.

To create a cell that spans two or more columns, use the COLSPAN attribute in the cell's <TD> tag. For example, specify <TD COLSPAN=3> to create a cell that spans three columns.

Likewise, you can use the ROWSPAN attribute to create a cell that spans several rows. For example, <TD ROWSPAN=2> creates a cell that is two rows deep.

You can use COLSPAN and ROWSPAN together to create a cell that spans both rows and columns. For example, <TD COLSPAN=2 ROWSPAN=2> creates a cell that is two columns wide and two rows deep.

The following HTML code creates a table that includes a spanned cell:

```
<BODY BGCOLOR=WHITE>
<TABLE BORDER=2 CELLPADDING=10>
<TR ALIGN=CENTER>
  <TH COLSPAN=2>How They Measure Up</TH>
</TR>
<TR ALIGN=CENTER>
  <TD>Michael Banks</TD>
  <TD>Extremely stubborn and suspicious.</TD>
</TR>
<TR ALIGN=CENTER>
  <TD>Jane Banks</TD>
  <TD>Rather inclined to giggle, doesn't put things away.</TD>
</TR>
<TR ALIGN=CENTER>
  <TD>Mary Poppins</TD>
  <TD>Practically perfect in every way.</TD>
</TR>
</TABLE>
</BODY>
```

Figure 19-7 shows how this table appears in Internet Explorer. Notice that the first row (which contains the heading "How They Measure Up") consists of just one cell, but the COLSPAN attribute causes the heading row to span two columns.

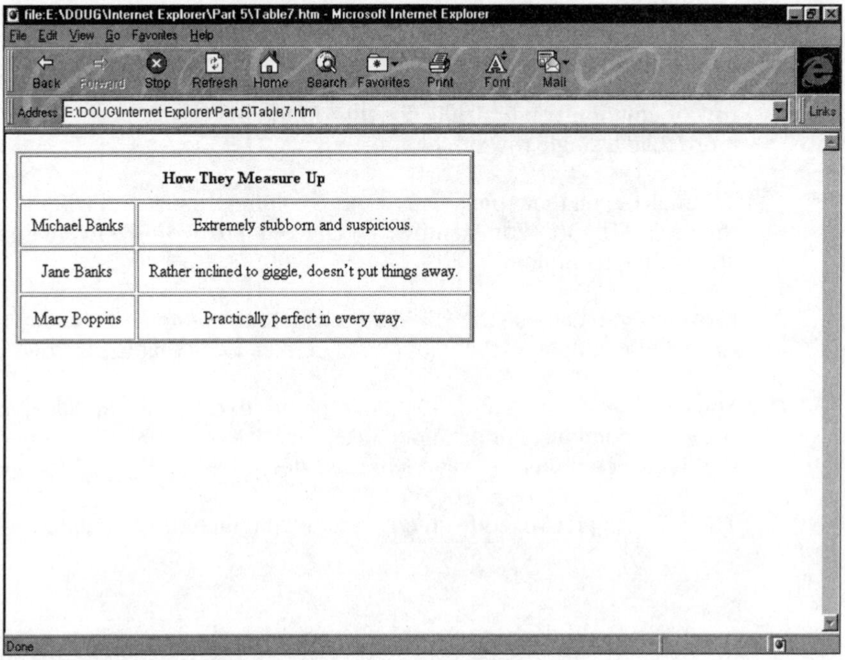
file:E:\DOUG\Internet Explorer\Part 5\Table7.htm - Microsoft Internet Explorer
File Edit View Go Favorites Help
Back Forward Stop Refresh Home Search Favorites Print Font Mail
Address E:\DOUG\Internet Explorer\Part 5\Table7.htm
Links
How They Measure Up
Michael Banks
Extremely stubborn and suspicious.
Jane Banks
Rather inclined to giggle, doesn't put things away.
Mary Poppins
Practically perfect in every way.
Done

Figure 19-7: The top cell spans two columns in this table.

Getting Framed

Frames are one of the newest features to become popular with Web authors. Frames allow you to divide a Web page into several distinct areas, each of which displays unique information, obtained from different HTML files. Visitors to your site can manipulate the area within each frame independently.

Frames rely on two HTML tags: `<FRAMESET>` and `<FRAME>`. A complete tutorial on how to use these tags is beyond the scope of this book. Instead, I want to focus on several new attributes that Microsoft has added to the `<FRAME>` tag to let you create frames that don't have borders or scroll bars. I also want to show you how to use a new tag called `<IFRAME>`, which is unique to Internet Explorer 3.0. The new `<IFRAME>` tag provides a much simpler method of creating frames and positioning them on the page.

Creating invisible frames

Normally, frames created with `<FRAMESET>` and `<FRAME>` tags are pretty obvious to the end user because they are delineated with a border. If the content of the HTML document doesn't fit entirely within the frame, a scroll bar appears along the border. The frame feature is great for creating frames that contain scrollable text, but it renders frames next to useless as a design tool because you have no control over the placement or appearance of the frame.

With Internet Explorer 3.0, Microsoft has added several attributes to the <FRAME> tag that make frames much more useful. These attributes include

- ✔ FRAMEBORDER=0: Results in a frame without a border, so the frame isn't visually separated from the rest of the page
- ✔ NORESIZE: Prevents the user from resizing the frame
- ✔ SCROLLING=NO: Draws the frame without a scroll bar, even if the HTML file displayed in the frame doesn't fit in the window

Together, these new attributes allow you to create an invisible frame. Visitors to your Web page can see the text contained in the frame, but the frame is indistinguishable. Here is an example of a <FRAME> tag that creates a stationary frame with no border or scroll bar:

```
<FRAME FRAMEBORDER=0 NORESIZE SCROLLING=NO>
```

Note that, to be complete, the preceding tag must be accompanied by appropriate <FRAMESET> and </FRAMESET> tags, and the <FRAME> tag needs a SRC attribute to specify the HTML file used for the frame.

Floaters

A *floating frame* is a frame that doesn't require an elaborate construction of <FRAMESET> and <FRAME> tags, as is normally used. Instead, a floating frame is handled similarly to an inline graphic that you insert using an <IMG> tag. Text and other elements on the Web page simply wrap around the floating frame as necessary.

To create a floating frame, you can use the new <IFRAME> tag. The <IFRAME> tag lets you create a frame whose contents are filled in by another HTML file. The <IFRAME> tag has several attributes:

- ✔ ALIGN: Sets the alignment for the frame relative to the surrounding text (settings include TOP, MIDDLE, BOTTOM, LEFT, and RIGHT)
- ✔ FRAMEBORDER: A value of 0 suppresses the border that would otherwise be drawn around the frame; a value of 1 adds a border
- ✔ HEIGHT: Controls the height (in pixels) of the frame
- ✔ MARGINHEIGHT: Sets the margin height (in pixels) for the frame
- ✔ MARGINWIDTH: Sets the margin width (in pixels) for the frame
- ✔ NAME: Specifies a target name that can you use in other HTML tags to refer to the frame
- ✔ NORESIZE: Prevents the user from resizing the frame

✔ SCROLLING: A value of NO suppresses the scroll bar; a value of YES shows the scroll bar

✔ SRC: When given a URL as a value, indicates the HTML file to be displayed in the frame

✔ WIDTH: Controls the width (in pixels) of the frame

As an example of how the <IFRAME> tag works, take a look at the following HTML file:

```
<BODY BGCOLOR=TEAL>
<FONT COLOR=WHITE>
Floating frames let you insert content from another HTML file
anywhere you want, like, for example, right here:<P>
<IFRAME WIDTH=600 HEIGHT=300 FRAMEBORDER=0 SRC=font.htm>
</IFRAME>
</BODY>
```

This HTML document displays some text, and then displays a floating frame that specifies the HTML file named font.htm as its source file. In this example, the font.htm file contains the following HTML:

```
BODY BGCOLOR=WHITE>
<FONT FACE="Comic Sans MS,Arial" SIZE=7>
"English Poets Who Couldn't Spell" for $200<P>
</FONT>
<FONT FACE="Bookman Old Style,Times New Roman" SIZE=4>
Whan that Aprill with his shoures soote<BR>
The droghte of March hath perced to the roote,<BR>
And bathed every veyne in swich licour<BR>
Of which vertu engendred is the flour;<P>
</FONT>
</BODY>
```

Figure 19-8 shows how this floating frame appears in Internet Explorer 3.0.

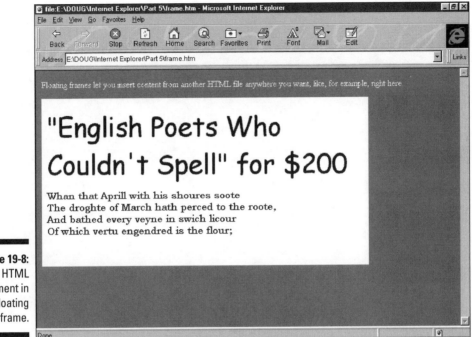

Figure 19-8:
An HTML
document in
a floating
frame.

Chapter 20

Formatting Web Documents Using Style Sheets

● ●

In This Chapter

▶ Understanding styles sheets

▶ Choosing formatting for style sheets

▶ Using embedded style sheets

▶ Linking to external style sheets

▶ Using inline styles to format chunks of text

● ●

I remember when I first learned HTML. Having 20 years of computer programming experience, I figured HTML programming would be a piece of cake. After all, HTML's whole purpose in life is simply to create documents that are formatted for the World Wide Web. How hard can *that* be? I figured the fun part would be using cool formatting codes that let you lay out pages any way you want.

Wrong! After a few hours of trying to use HTML, I began wondering, "Where's the <FONT> code? How do you set the typeface and point size? How do you control margins and indentation?"

Then it occurred to me that just about every page I had ever seen on the Web used the same fonts, the same text sizes, the same margins, and the same indentation. That's because HTML doesn't have any codes to control such basic layout elements. When it comes to layout and design, HTML is pretty pathetic. Until now.

Internet Explorer 3.0 is the first Web browser to implement a new HTML feature called *style sheets*. Style sheets provide all the page-formatting features that word processing users and desktop publishers have come to know and love. In this chapter, I show how style sheets work and how you can use style sheets to add formatting pizzazz to your own Web pages.

Discovering Style Sheets

HTML applies only rudimentary formats by using *paragraph tags* which associate a paragraph with a particular format. For example, headings are formatted using tags such as ⟨H1⟩, ⟨H2⟩, and ⟨H3⟩; block quotations are formatted with ⟨BLOCKQUOTE⟩ tags; and normal paragraphs are formatted with ⟨P⟩ tags.

All Web browsers apply simple, basic formatting to your Web page text based on these HTML tags. For example, headings are always displayed with a larger type size than normal text. A *style sheet,* however, lets you add additional formatting information to these standard HTML tags.

For example, with a style sheet, you can create a Web page in which all first level headings (using the ⟨H1⟩ and ⟨/H1⟩ tags) are centered on the page and appear in 26-point Arial Bold font. Or you can create regular paragraphs (using the ⟨P⟩ and ⟨/P⟩ tags) that are formatted as 9-point Century Schoolbook font with a first line indent of $1/2$ inch. You can make your text different colors, italicize words you want to emphasize, or highlight sections of your Web page — you can really make your Web pages come alive using style sheets.

To give your Web pages life, color, and personality, Internet Explorer lets you choose from more than a dozen formatting attributes that you can include in your HTML style sheets. Table 20-1 provides a nice, little summary of these formatting attributes:

Table 20-1	**Formatting Properties for Style Sheet**		
Attribute	*What It Does*	*Allowed Values*	*Example*
FONT-FAMILY	Sets the font	Any TrueType font name	{FONT-FAMILY: Arial}
FONT-SIZE	Sets the font size	Measurement in points (pt), inches (in), centimeters (cm), or pixels (px)	{FONT-SIZE: 12pt}
FONT-WEIGHT	Sets the thickness of the type	extra-light, light, demi-light, medium, demi-bold, bold, or extra-bold	{FONT-WEIGHT: bold}
FONT-STYLE	Controls italics	normal or italic	{FONT-STYLE: italic
TEXT-DECORATION	Adds underlining or strikethrough	none, underline, italic, or linethrough	{TEXT-DECORATION: none}

Attribute	What It Does	Allowed Values	Example
COLOR	Sets the text color	Color value (Refer to Table 19-1)	{COLOR: red}
LINE-HEIGHT	Sets the baseline text height	Measurement in points (pt), inches (in), centimeters (cm), pixels (px), or a percentage of the font size (%)	{LINE-HEIGHT: 18pt}
MARGIN-LEFT	Sets the left margin	Measurement in points (pt), inches (in), centimeters (cm), or pixels (px)	{MARGIN-LEFT: 1in}
MARGIN-RIGHT	Sets the right margin	Measurement in points (pt), inches (in), centimeters (cm), or pixels (px)	{MARGIN-RIGHT: 1in}
MARGIN-TOP	Sets the top margin	Measurement in points (pt), inches (in), centimeters (cm), or pixels (px)	{MARGIN-TOP: 1in}
TEXT-ALIGN	Sets the text alignment/ justification	left, center, or right	{TEXT-ALIGN: center}
TEXT-INDENT	Sets the indentation for the first line	Measurement in points (pt), inches (in), centimeters (cm), or pixels (px)	{TEXT-INDENT: .5in}
BACKGROUND	Sets a background image or color	color value or URL	{BACKGROUND= yellow}
FONT	Combines multiple font attributes in a single setting	See text	{FONT: 18/20 Arial bold}

Finding Your Style

You can apply style sheets to your HTML documents in the following three ways. Each method is appropriate in different situations.

✔ The first type of style sheet is an *embedded style sheet,* which you include in the `<HEAD>` section of your Web document. The embedded style sheet contains codes that specify the formats that should be applied to all text marked with a specific tag, which allows you to apply consistent text formatting throughout an entire HTML document. For example, if you specify in an embedded style sheet that headings (`<H1>` tags) should be formatted in 36-point Arial font, then *all* `<H1>` headings in a Web document are formatted with 36-point Arial font.

✔ The second method is to use a *linked style sheet* file. This method lets you store the style sheet itself as a separate file. With a linked style sheet, several HTML documents can share the same style sheet file so that any changes to the style sheet file affects the appearance of *all* the HTML documents that link to that style sheet. This method makes creating a consistent appearance for all pages in a Web site easy.

✔ The third method is to use *inline style,* in which you include formatting information directly in the body of an HTML document wherever you want the format to be applied. The inline-style method allows you to apply special formatting to individual bits of text.

Saving keystrokes with the FONT attribute

The FONT attribute lets you combine several basic font characteristics into a single setting. The format for the FONT setting is as follows:

```
{FONT: [bold] [italic] [size]/
   [leading] [font names]}
```

The size/leading pair indicates the typeface size in *points* (which is how publishing geeks measure text size — this font size is 8-point, for example), followed by the amount of spacing between lines (which typographers call *leading*). For the font names, you can specify more than one font name by separating the names with commas. That way, visitors to your Web page whose computers don't have the first font you specify see the second font, instead. For a user who doesn't have any of the fonts you list, the browser determines the font that's used.

Here are some examples of valid FONT attributes:

```
{FONT: 12/14 Times New Roman}
{FONT: 12/14 Century Schoolbook,
   Times New Roman}
{FONT: bold 24 Arial}
{FONT: bold italic 9/10 Times New
   Roman}
```

By using the FONT attribute, you can avoid the FONT-SIZE, FONT-FAMILY, FONT-WEIGHT, FONT-STYLE, and LINE-HEIGHT attributes altogether, and make your style sheets much more concise and easy to construct.

Creating an embedded style sheet

The easiest and most common way to use style sheets is to use the embedded style sheet technique, in which a style sheet is included at the beginning of an HTML document. With an embedded style sheet, the styles apply only to the HTML document that contains the style sheet. If you want to create a style sheet to format several HTML documents, use a linked style sheet instead.

To create an embedded style sheet, all you have to do is place a pair of `<STYLE> </STYLE>` tags at the beginning of your document, following the `<HTML>` tag but before the `<BODY>` tag. Then, between the `<STYLE>` tags, you include one or more *style definitions,* which consist of the name of any HTML tag and a list of formatting properties to be applied to any text affected by that tag. The formatting properties are contained within curly braces, and consist of the following items:

- An attribute name
- A colon
- An attribute value

If you have more than one attribute, you must separate the properties with semicolons.

Whew! What a mouthful. I'd better throw in an example before you toss this book in the fireplace and decide to take up brain surgery instead. This simple example of a style sheet specifies the typeface and font size to use for text that appears between `<H1>` and `<H2>` tags:

```
<STYLE>
H1 {FONT-FAMILY: Arial; FONT-SIZE: 36pt}
H2 {FONT-FAMILY: Times New Roman; FONT-SIZE: 24pt}
</STYLE>
```

That's all there is to it. With this style sheet placed at the beginning of a document (after the `<HTML>` tag and before the `<BODY>` tag), any `<H1>` heading appears in 36-point Arial typeface, and any `<H2>` heading appears in 24-point Times New Roman typeface.

For a complete example of an embedded style sheet in action, take a peek at the following HTML code:

```
<HTML>
<STYLE>
  BODY {FONT: 16/18 Century Schoolbook}
  H1   {FONT: 36/40 Comic Sans MS}
```

(continued)

(continued)

```
</STYLE>
<BODY BGCOLOR=WHITE>
<H1>"English Poets Who Couldn't Spell"<BR>for $200</H1>
Whan that Aprill with his shoures soote<BR>
The droghte of March hath perced to the roote,<BR>
And bathed every veyne in swich licour<BR>
Of which vertu engendred is the flour;<P>
</BODY>
</HTML>
```

Figure 20-1 shows how this sample of fine medieval poetry appears in Internet Explorer 3.0.

Note that applying formatting to text marked with a particular tag applies that style to all text in that section. However, if another tag marks text in that section, these formatting codes override the initial formatting.

For example, in Figure 20-1, all the text contained within the <BODY> section of the document appears as 16-point Century Schoolbook. However, the text formatting for the <H1> tags overrides the <BODY> formatting, so the heading "English Poets Who Couldn't Spell for $200" appears in 36-point Comic Sans MS font.

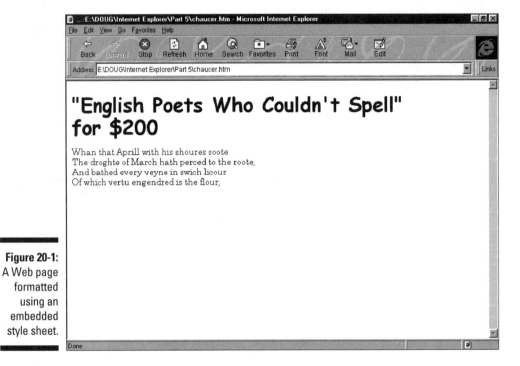

Figure 20-1:
A Web page formatted using an embedded style sheet.

Using a linked style sheet

A linked style sheet contains a set of style definitions and exists as a separate file with a .css filename extension. You use a <LINK> tag in an HTML document's <HEAD> section to link the Web document to the style sheet.

For example, suppose that you store your style sheet in a file named styles.css, located at http://freedonia.gov/styles.css. The style.css file looks like this:

```
BODY {FONT: 16/18 Century Schoolbook}
H1   {FONT: 36/40 Comic Sans MS}
```

Notice that the <STYLE> and </STYLE> tags aren't required in the .css file.

To link an HTML document to the style.css style sheet, you include the following lines between the <HEAD> tags of the HTML file:

```
<HEAD>
<TITLE>This document uses a linked style sheet</TITLE>
<LINK REL=STYLESHEET
HREF="http://freedonia.gov/styles.css" TYPE="text/css">
</HEAD>
```

That's all there is to it. The REL attribute indicates that the LINK applies to a stylesheet, and the HREF attribute supplies the filename for the stylesheet to be used. As a result, this Web document is formatted using the style definitions found in the styles.css file.

Using inline styles

Occasionally, you may want to override one of the formatting options provided by the embedded style sheet or the linked style sheet. For example, suppose that your style sheet formats <H1> headings as 36-point text, but you have one heading that you want to emphasize by displaying it as 44-point text. You can override the style sheet settings by applying an *inline style*. You first apply an <H1> tag to the heading and then add an inline STYLE attribute. This code overrides the FONT-SIZE attribute of the <H1> tag (which is specified in the embedded style sheet, for example) and specifies the new, larger type size.

To override a formatting attribute for a tag, you add a STYLE attribute to the tag, as in this example:

```
<H1 STYLE="FONT-SIZE: 44pt">
```

Notice that the STYLE attribute's value is a standard style definition enclosed in quotation marks. (See the "Discovering Style Sheets" section to find out everything you want to know about defining styles.) Thus, any of the formatting properties that can be used in a style sheet can also be used in a STYLE tag on *any* HTML tag.

The override formatting specified by an inline style attribute applies *only* to the tag in which the attribute appears. In the preceding example, for instance, all subsequent <H1> headings appear in the font size designated in the style sheet (that is, 36-point text).

To apply formatting to only a portion of a paragraph, you can use the <SPAN> tag along with a STYLE attribute. For example, suppose that you want to change the background color of a few words of text to yellow in order to give the text a highlighted appearance. You can format a portion of text using the <SPAN> tag, as shown in the following code:

```
<HTML>
<BODY BGCOLOR=WHITE STYLE="FONT: 18/20 Times New Roman">
This is <SPAN STYLE="BACKGROUND: yellow">some text</SPAN>
that has been highlighted.
</BODY>
</HTML>
```

In the preceding code, the <SPAN> tag includes a STYLE attribute that changes the background color to yellow for the words "some text." Notice also that I use a STYLE attribute in the <BODY> tag to apply font formatting to the body text. Figure 20-2 shows the effect of this HTML code on the Web document text.

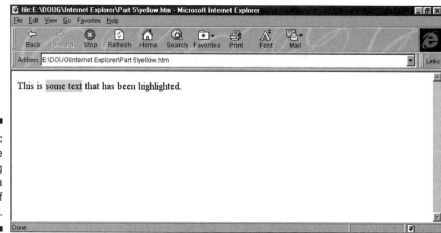

Figure 20-2:
Using the <SPAN> tag to format a portion of text.

Chapter 21
Diving into ActiveX

● ●

In This Chapter

▶ Understanding ActiveX
▶ Adding a layout control
▶ Using the Script Wizard
▶ Using the ActiveX Control Pad
▶ Adding a hot spot
▶ Creating a slide show

● ●

*A*ctiveX is the most exciting Internet advancement to come on the scene since the invention of HTML — at least, so Microsoft would have us all believe. Whether ActiveX lives up to its hype depends mostly on whether Web authors around the world decide to embrace ActiveX and incorporate its cool features into their Web pages. Only time will tell.

ActiveX is a far too complicated subject to cover thoroughly in a single chapter of a *...For Dummies* book. But I do want to give you a feel for what ActiveX can do and how you can use ActiveX to add some simple but impressive features to your Web pages. For more detailed information about ActiveX, visit the Microsoft Site Builder Workshop on the Web at `www.microsoft.com/workshop`.

What Is ActiveX?

Simply put (as if anything that comes from Microsoft can be put simply), ActiveX is a new Internet version of the Microsoft object technology OLE (which stands for *object linking and embedding*). OLE allows packaged objects — such as custom controls or complete documents — to communicate and work together to create complex and customizable applications that are based on the World Wide Web. In short, ActiveX enables you to create Web applications that resemble Windows applications coded in Visual Basic or C++.

Microsoft Visual Basic, one of the most popular programming languages ever introduced, relies on object controls to create complete applications. ActiveX controls are similar to Visual Basic controls, which are programmable objects that you can place on forms or dialog boxes to create interactive programs. With ActiveX, you can use the handful of stock ActiveX controls provided by Microsoft to assemble complicated applications that can run over the Web. For example, you can create a Web page that includes ActiveX controls, such as text entry fields, list boxes, and command buttons.

So how are ActiveX controls different from ordinary HTML forms? The most important difference between ActiveX controls and HTML is that ActiveX controls are programmable, whereas normal HTML forms are not. That is, in ActiveX you can write a program that runs whenever a Web surfer clicks a button. That program can, in turn, change the properties of other controls on the page. For example, an ActiveX control may change the URL of an image control so that a different picture appears in a window. Or an ActiveX control may reveal a control that was previously hidden. The options are almost endless.

ActiveX currently works only with Internet Explorer 3.0. Previous versions of Internet Explorer, as well as other browsers such as Netscape Navigator, cannot view ActiveX controls.

VBScript

The glue that holds ActiveX controls together is a scripting language called *VBScript,* which is short for Visual Basic Scripting Edition. If you are an experienced Visual Basic programmer, you're well on your way to developing active content for the Internet, because VBScript is very similar to standard Visual Basic.

VBScript enables you to attach Visual Basic procedures to specific events that are directed at ActiveX controls. For example, you can specify a Visual Basic procedure that is executed if a Web surfer clicks on a control or moves the mouse over a control. VBScript also allows Visual Basic modules to modify ActiveX controls. For example, a script can change the text displayed by a text label control, or add an item to a drop-down list box control.

Yes, you can also program ActiveX controls with Java. But to simplify matters, I stick to a discussion of VBScript in this chapter. For more information about using Java, check out *Java For Dummies,* by Aaron Walsh or, if you're an experienced programmer, try *Java Programming For Dummies,* by Donald and David Koosis.

ActiveX controls

ActiveX *controls* are special objects that you can insert into your Web pages using a new HTML tag: `<OBJECT>`. An ActiveX control is really a special type of program that must be downloaded to the viewer's computer before he or she can experience the control on your Web page.

Most ActiveX controls are user-interface objects such as clickable buttons, drop-down lists, menus, and so on. But ActiveX controls don't have to be related to the user interface aspects of an application. For example, one commonly used ActiveX control is a timer that allows a Visual Basic module to execute automatically after a certain time period elapses. The user needn't even be aware that the page contains a timer object.

The first time you view a page that contains an ActiveX control, the control automatically downloads to your computer from the Web site specified in the HTML code. Because many ActiveX controls are relatively large (50K or more), downloading a control noticeably slows down the display of the Web page. But after the control downloads to your computer, it remains on your hard disk for use every time you view a Web page that contains that ActiveX control.

ActiveX Control Pad

Microsoft provides a free program called the *ActiveX Control Pad,* which you can use to create Web pages that include ActiveX controls. The bulk of this chapter shows you how to use the ActiveX Control Pad to add ActiveX content to your Web pages. You can download the ActiveX Control Pad from the Microsoft Web site at the following URL:

```
www.microsoft.com/workshop/author/cpad
```

The ActiveX Control Pad comes with many built-in controls that you can use in your Web pages. Table 21-1 lists the ActiveX controls that you are most likely to want to add to your Web pages.

Table 21-1	**Useful ActiveX Control Pad Controls**
ActiveX Control	*What It Adds to Your Web Page*
ActiveMovie Control	Shows a movie
Microsoft Forms 2.0 Frame	Draws a frame on the page
Microsoft Forms 2.0 Image	Places an image on the page
Microsoft Forms 2.0 Label	Text labels
Microsoft Forms 2.0 TextBox	A multiline text entry control
Microsoft Forms 2.0 ComboBox	A drop-down list of options
Microsoft Forms 2.0 ListBox	A scrollable list of options
Microsoft Forms 2.0 CheckBox	A standard check box
Microsoft Forms 2.0 Option Button	Radio buttons that let the user choose one of several options

(continued)

Table 21-1 *(continued)*

ActiveX Control	What It Adds to Your Web Page
Microsoft Forms 2.0 Toggle Button	An On/Off button
Microsoft Forms 2.0 Command Button	A basic push button
Microsoft Forms 2.0 Tabstrip	A tab interface similar to those found in many Microsoft dialog boxes
Microsoft Forms 2.0 ScrollBar	Horizontal and vertical scroll bars
Microsoft Forms 2.0 Spin Button	A control that lets you spin a value up or down
The Microsoft ActiveX Image Control	Displays progressively rendered images
The Microsoft ActiveX Hot Spot Control	Creates clickable or pointable regions on the page
The Microsoft Web Browser Control	Lets you display documents such as Word documents, Excel worksheets, and so on
PopupMenu Object	Creates a pop-up menu on the page
Vrml Viewer Object	Displays a VRML world

ActiveX Control Pad also includes the new Microsoft HTML Layout Control —
an advanced but easy-to-use ActiveX control that gives you precise control over
the positioning of all elements on the Web pages. This type of control isn't
possible using HTML tags alone.

You can think of the HTML Layout Control as an object that contains a collection of ActiveX controls along with information on how each ActiveX control is
to be positioned on the page. The HTML document uses a single <OBJECT> tag
to include the HTML Layout Control object on the page. This object, in turn,
positions and displays all of the ActiveX Controls on the page, providing precise
layout control that isn't possible in HTML.

See the "Using the HTML Layout Control" section later in this chapter to find
out how to use layout controls.

Properties, methods, and events

Properties, methods, and events are the three keys to using ActiveX controls.
The following sections explain the purpose of each.

Properties

A *property* is an attribute of an object, such as its color, the text displayed on its
label (if the object has a label), and whether or not the object is visible. Every

ActiveX control has a number of properties that govern the behavior or appearance of the control.

For example, consider the lowly Label control, which enables you to display a bit of text on the page. The Label control has the following properties:

- ✔ **Caption property:** Specifies the text that appears by the label
- ✔ **Font property:** Specifies the font used to display the caption text
- ✔ **Visible property:** Specifies whether the control is visible on the page

You set the initial values for these properties from the ActiveX Control Pad when you design your Web page. You can even create VBScript code to change the property values while a viewer is displaying the page. In fact, this dynamic characteristic is probably the main reason you would use a Label control rather than place your text directly in HTML. With a Label control, simply by changing the Caption property, you can code a VBScript program so that the text displayed by the label changes on the fly.

For example, you may create a Label control that initially displays the message, "Don't click the button!" Then the page could also include a Command Button control with a VBScript module that runs when a Web surfer clicks the button. This program could change the Label control's caption to "I told you not to click the button!" whenever someone clicks the button.

Fortunately, you don't have to remember the names of all the properties that are available for each ActiveX control. The ActiveX Control Pad provides you with a list of all the properties for controls with which you are working.

Methods

Methods are functions that are built into ActiveX controls and that can be called from a VBScript program. As with properties, each ActiveX control has its own collection of methods.

For example, the ListBox control provides an AddItem method that enables the VBScript program to add a new item to the list box. The Web Browser control offers GoForward and GoBack methods, which correspond to the Internet Explorer Next and Previous buttons.

Events

All ActiveX controls have a collection of events that occur when a person viewing your Web site performs a certain action. For example, the Command Button control has a Click event that is generated when someone clicks the button. You can attach VBScript programs to events, causing the program to run whenever the event occurs.

Using the ActiveX Control Pad

To start the ActiveX Control Pad, click the Start button and choose Programs⇨ Microsoft ActiveX Control Pad⇨Microsoft ActiveX Control Pad. The ActiveX Control Pad comes to life, as shown in Figure 21-1.

When you first start the ActiveX Control Pad, a skeleton HTML document appears, with basic tags that provide a framework for a new Web page. You can work with this skeleton file to create a new HTML document, or you can choose File⇨Open to open an existing HTML file, which you can then modify with the ActiveX Control Pad.

Inserting an ActiveX control

To insert an ActiveX control into an HTML document, open the ActiveX Control Pad, open the HTML file you want to work with (or start fresh with a brand-new document) and follow these steps:

1. **Click the mouse pointer where you want to insert the ActiveX control.**

   Initially, you find the insertion point positioned between the ⟨BODY⟩ and ⟨/BODY⟩ tags.

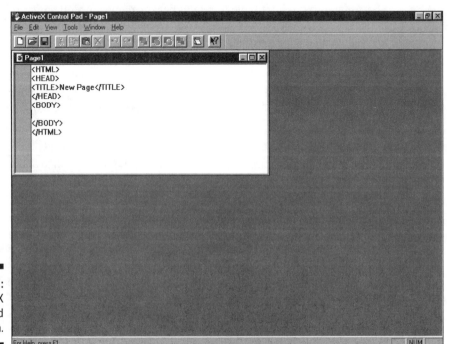

Figure 21-1:
The ActiveX
Control Pad
in action.

2. Choose Edit⇨Insert ActiveX Control.

The Insert ActiveX Control dialog box appears, as shown in Figure 21-2.

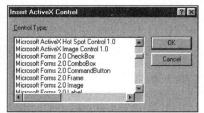

Figure 21-2:
The Insert
ActiveX
Control
dialog box.

3. Select the control you want to insert into your Web page.

The Insert ActiveX Control dialog box lists all the controls available on your computer.

4. Click OK.

The ActiveX Control Pad brings up two windows — an Edit window and a Properties dialog box — shown in Figure 21-3.

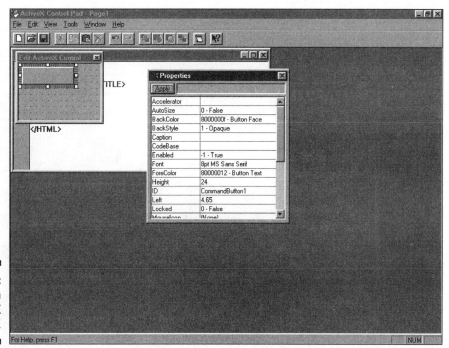

Figure 21-3:
Editing an
ActiveX
Control.

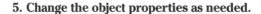
5. Change the object properties as needed.

For example, you can change the Caption property of the command button in Figure 21-3 to a meaningful name for the button, such as "Click Here." To change a property value, click the property name in the Properties dialog box, type a new value into the text box, and then click Apply.

For some properties, you can double-click the property name to bring up a dialog box where you can select an appropriate setting for the property.

6. To change the size of the control, drag the size handles in the Edit window.

You can modify the button size to best fit the layout of your Web page.

7. After you adjust the control size and modify the control properties, close the Edit window by clicking its close button.

The ActiveX Control Panel pauses for a moment and then adds an `<OBJECT>` tag to the HTML file to include the control in your document, as shown in Figure 21-4.

 Notice the little button that appears next to the `<OBJECT>` tag in the HTML file. You can click this button at any time to recall the Object Editor window so that you can modify the control's properties.

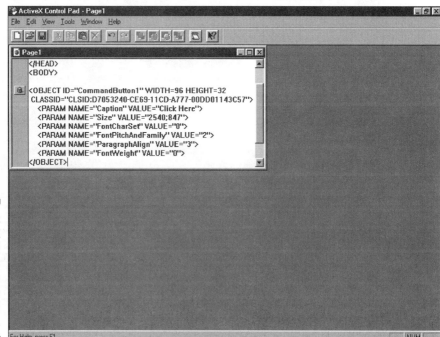

Figure 21-4:
The ActiveX Control Pad inserts an `<OBJECT>` tag for a command button.

Take a quick look at all the attributes listed in the ⟨OBJECT⟩ tag in Figure 21-4. One look at these attributes and you can understand why the ActiveX Control Pad is a *must* when working with ActiveX controls. Trust me: You don't want to bang out these ⟨OBJECT⟩ tag attributes yourself.

Checking out your ActiveX controls

After you add an ActiveX control to an HTML file, you can test the control to make sure that it looks and works the way you want in Internet Explorer. To test an ActiveX control, follow these steps:

1. **Choose File⇨Save to save the HTML file.**

   Choose a filename for your file, using the extension .htm. The filename in this example is active1.htm.

2. **Start Internet Explorer, if it isn't already running.**

3. **Open the HTML file you saved in Step 1.**

   You can type the complete path and filename for the file in the Address box, or you can use the File⇨Open command and browse for the file.

   Figure 21-5 shows how the command button appears in Internet Explorer.

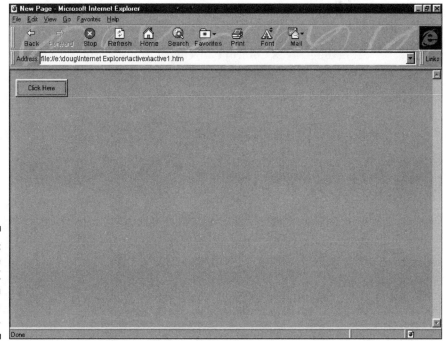

Figure 21-5:
A simple ActiveX control in place on a Web page.

4. Verify that the control is positioned properly and works as expected.

The command button in Figure 21-5 is pretty plain looking, and it doesn't do anything when you click it. Of course, creating a button that doesn't do anything is pretty pointless, but this example does demonstrate that you have successfully created a button and that the caption appears correctly. (To make the button do something, you must to create a VBScript program for its Click event. You can do this using the Script Wizard, which is described in the next section.)

You can now return to the ActiveX Control Pad to make modifications to the page. After you make more changes to the ActiveX control properties, you can return to Internet Explorer to verify your changes. When you return to Internet Explorer, make sure that you click the Refresh button so that any changes you make in the ActiveX Control Pad are reflected in Internet Explorer.

Using Script Wizard

A *script* is a small amount of VBScript code that runs whenever a particular event occurs. The ActiveX Control Pad lets you write VBScript code yourself, but if you're not a proficient Visual Basic programmer, you may prefer to use the Script Wizard. This Wizard can automatically create many of the scripts your Web pages require, asking you for only a few mouse clicks to guide it in its wizardly tasks.

To use the Script Wizard, follow this procedure:

1. In the ActiveX Control Pad, choose Tools⇨Script Wizard.

The Script Wizard appears, as shown in Figure 21-6.

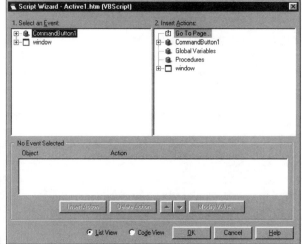

Figure 21-6:
The Script Wizard, ready for business.

2. Choose the event to which you want to attach a script.

All of the events to which you can attach scripts are listed in the Select an Event box at the top left of the Script Wizard window. Initially, this list shows only the controls that are present in the HTML file you are editing. In this case, two controls are listed: The command button (which you add to the document by following the steps in the preceding section) and a window (which is assumed to be present for all HTML pages).

When you click the little plus sign next to the control, a list of all the events that the control can receive appears, as shown in Figure 21-7. For example, you can see that CommandButton1 has events such as Click, DblClick, and MouseMove. Select the event to which you want to associate an action. For example, if you want to specify an action that occurs when someone viewing your Web site clicks the CommandButton1 button, select the Click event from the list.

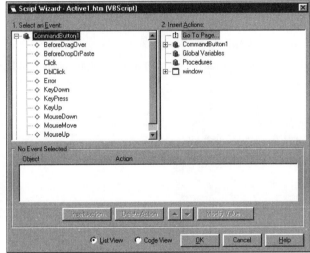

Figure 21-7:
The ActiveX Control Pad shows all the events for a control.

3. Choose the action you want to perform for the event.

The Insert Actions list box lists the possible actions you can take. In this example, I want the action to be: Modify the value of the Caption property for the command button.

To specify this action, you must first click the little plus sign next to the command button in the Insert Actions list box. When you do, a list of all the properties for the button appears, as shown in Figure 21-8. Here, you can see that the CommandButton1 control has properties such as BackColor, BackStyle, and Caption.

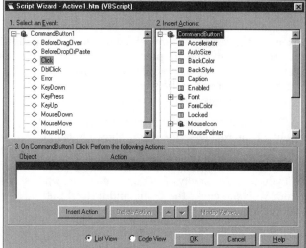

Figure 21-8:
The ActiveX
Control Pad
shows
all the
properties
for a control.

4. Double-click the Caption property.

This action displays a dialog box similar to the one shown in Figure 21-9.

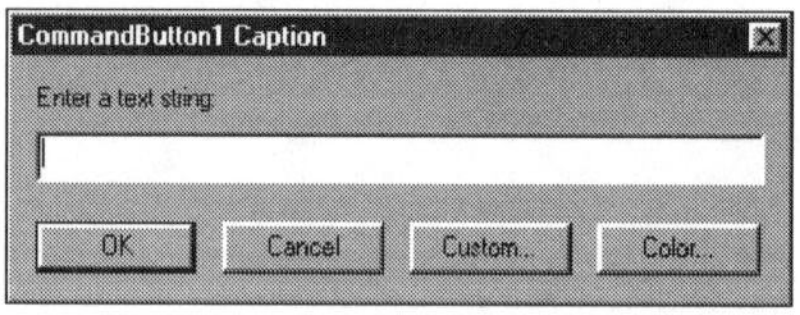

Figure 21-9:
This dialog
box appears
when the
action calls
for changing
the value of
a property.

5. Type a new caption in the Caption text box and then click OK.

In this example, I enter the caption, "Ouch!" When the Script Wizard
window reappears, the action appears near the bottom of the dialog box,
as shown in Figure 21-10.

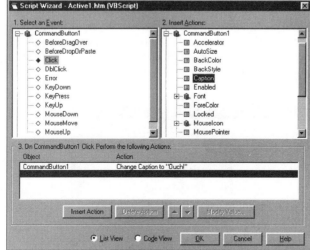

Figure 21-10:
Figure 21-10:
The Script
Wizard
shows what
action
occurs
when
someone
clicks the
command
button.

6. Add any other actions you want to include.

The Script Wizard can program more than one action for each event. For example, Figure 21-11 shows how the Script Wizard window appears after you add a second action for the command button Click event. Not only does the command button's Caption property change to "Ouch!" but the background color for the entire page changes to white. (#FFFFFF is the hex code for the color white, but you don't need to know that — the Script Wizard does the work for you.)

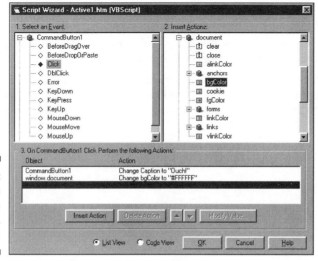

Figure 21-11:
Program
more than
one action,
if you want.

7. Switch to Code View — if you dare.

If you're a Visual Basic fan, you can switch the Script Wizard into Code View by clicking the Code View option button at the bottom of the Script Wizard window. This option displays the VBScript code that runs when the event procedure is triggered. See Figure 21-12.

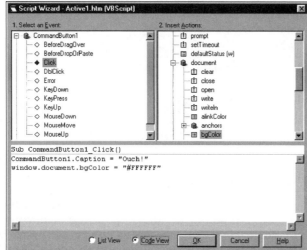

Figure 21-12:
The Script
Wizard in
Code View
mode.

8. Click OK to dismiss the Script Wizard.

The script you create is saved in your HTML file, as shown in Figure 21-13.

9. Save the HTML file and then return to Internet Explorer to test your script.

Don't forget to click the Refresh button to make sure that Internet Explorer loads the newly saved version of your HTML file.

If the script works correctly, when you click the command button, the text on the button should change from "Click Me" to "Ouch!" and the background of the page should change from gray to white, as shown in Figure 21-14.

VBScript

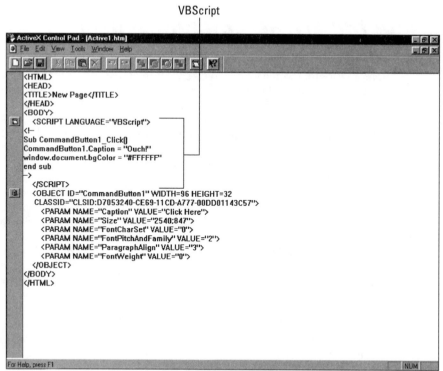

Figure 21-13:
VBScript
added to an
HTML file.

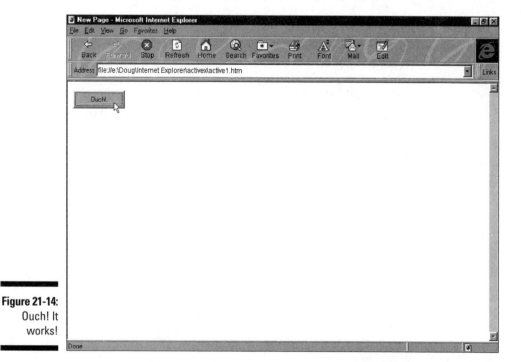

Figure 21-14:
Ouch! It
works!

Using the HTML Layout Control

The first things I went looking for when I started using ActiveX controls were the properties that would let me precisely control the position of the controls on the page. For example, I thoroughly expected to see properties named *x* and *y* or maybe *hor* and *vert* for each of the ActiveX controls. Alas, none of the controls have such properties. When you use an ActiveX control as described in the preceding sections, the position of the control on the page is determined by the HTML that surrounds the control. And, as you probably realize, HTML gives you only limited control over the position of elements on the page.

That's where the HTML Layout Control comes in. The HTML Layout Control enables you to design Web pages in the same way that you design forms in Visual Basic — by dragging and dropping controls onto a page design area, where you have exact control over the placement of each object on the page. Prior to Internet Explorer 3.0 and ActiveX, such precise control wasn't possible.

The HTML Layout Control automatically creates a separate layout file (with the filename extension of .alx) that contains all the layout information for your Web page. After you create an .alx layout file, you can insert the file into your HTML file as an object by choosing Edit⇨Insert HTML Layout. This command inserts an ⟨OBJECT⟩ tag, which includes a link to the .alx file so that browsers can access the layout information contained in the .alx file.

To create an HTML layout file, follow these steps:

 1. **In the ActiveX Control Pad, choose File⇨New HTML Layout (or click the New button and select HTML Layout from the dialog box that appears).**

   A Layout window and a Toolbox window appear, as shown in Figure 21-15. The toolbox provides handy access to the various types of controls you can draw in the Layout window.

2. **Select a control from the Toolbox and draw the control in the Layout window.**

   For example, to draw a label, select the Label control from the Toolbox and drag a rectangle in the Layout window to place the control in your layout. (Table 21-2 lists the controls that are available in the toolbox.)

   Figure 21-16 shows the ActiveX Control Pad after you draw a simple Label control onto the layout area.

3. **To change a control's properties, right-click the control in the Layout window and choose Properties.**

   The control's Properties dialog box appears, where you can change any of the control's properties according to your whims.

   You can change the caption for most controls by clicking the control to select it, and then clicking the caption. If an insertion point appears, you can edit the caption. If not, try again. You probably didn't click quite the right spot.

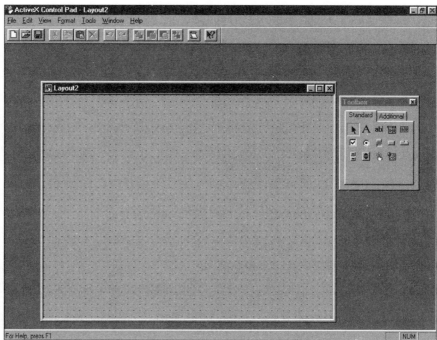

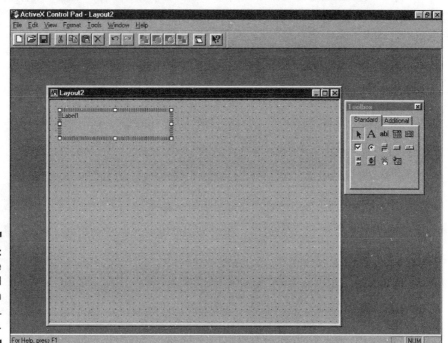

4. To move or resize a control, drag the control's border or resize handles.

Place the mouse pointer on one of the white squares on the corners or edges of the control outline and drag to resize the control. To move a control, grab it by one of the borders (between the corners) and drag it to its new location.

5. Add more controls, if you want.

The HTML Layout Control offers several interesting types of controls. For example, Figure 21-17 shows an HTML Layout that includes a TabSet control, which works like the tabbed dialog boxes found in many Microsoft applications.

To create the TabSet control shown in Figure 21-17, I dragged the control onto the Layout window and then modified several of the TabStrip controls properties. You can access many of the TabStrip controls by right-clicking the control in the Layout window to display a pop-up menu that lets you add new tabs or change the text displayed on the tabs.

6. Add scripts if you want.

To add a script, click the control to which you want to apply the script; then choose Tools⇨Script Wizard and create the script. For more information, refer to the "Using Script Wizard" section earlier in this chapter.

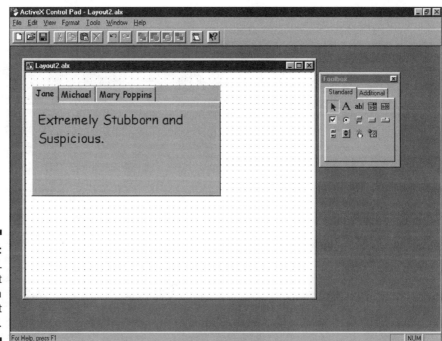

Figure 21-17:
An HTML
Layout that
features a
TabSet
control.

7. Choose File⟿Save to save the Web page layout as an .alx file.

8. Close the HTML Layout window by clicking its close button.

Table 21-2	Controls You Can Create from the HTML Layout Control Toolbox
Button	**Control**
A	Label
abl	Text box
	Combo box
	List box
	Check box
	Option button
	Toggle button
	Command button
	Tab strip
	Scrollbar
	Spin button
	Hot spot
	Image

After you create an HTML layout file, you can add the page layout to any HTML file. Follow these steps to insert the file into an HTML document:

1. **Open an existing HTML file or create a new HTML file by choosing File⟿New HTML.**

2. **Position the insertion point where you want to place the HTML Layout Control in your document.**

   Usually, you place the HTML Layout Control between an otherwise empty set of ⟨BODY⟩ and ⟨/BODY⟩ tags.

3. **Choose Edit⟿Insert HTML Layout.**

   A dialog box appears, offering a list of HTML Layout files (.alx files). Pick the layout you want to insert in your Web page and then click Open. This action inserts an ⟨OBJECT⟩ tag into the HTML file.

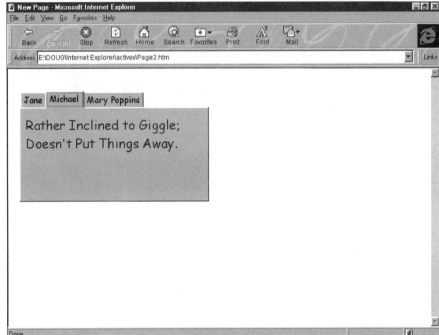

Figure 21-18:
A TabStrip
layout in
Internet
Explorer.

   **4. Save the HTML file and then pop over to Internet Explorer to test
   your work.**

   Figure 21-18 shows how the HTML layout in Figure 21-17 appears when
   viewed in Internet Explorer.

In case you're interested, the TabStrip page in Figures 21-17 and 21-18 shows a
description of the person listed on each of the three tabs. To create this type of
page layout, the Layout includes two controls:

   ✔ A TabStrip control
   ✔ A Label control

The Label control sits atop the TabStrip control. The following script is used for
the TabStrip control's Click event:

```
Sub TabStrip1_Click(Index)
Select Case TabStrip1.value
Case 0
    Label1.Caption = "Extremely Stubborn and Suspicious."
Case 1
    Label1.Caption = "Rather Inclined to Giggle; Doesn't Put
          Things Away."
```

```
Case 2
    Label1.Caption = "Practically Perfect in Every Way."
End Select
End Sub
```

This simple script changes the Caption for the Label control based on which tab is clicked.

Creating a Hot Spot

A *hot spot* is a portion of the page that reacts in some way when the person viewing your Web site moves the mouse over it. A hot spot may be a portion of a graphic, such as a picture of a door that opens when the mouse touches the doorknob. Or it may be another control, such as a button that causes a descriptive message to appear when the mouse hovers over the button. Or it may be an arbitrary region of the page that isn't a part of any other object on the page.

The easiest way to create a hot spot is to use the Hot Spot control, which is available from the HTML Layout Control toolbox. The Hot Spot control uses two events to create hot spots:

✔ **MouseEnter:** Occurs whenever the mouse enters the boundary of the control

✔ **MouseExit:** Occurs whenever the mouse leaves the boundary of the control

Typically, the MouseEnter event is tied to a VBScript module that changes the Visible property of some other control to *true,* and the MouseExit event is tied to a VBScript module that sets the Visible property of the other control to *false.* That way, the other control remains hidden from view until the mouse passes over the Hot Spot control, and the other control returns to obscurity when the mouse leaves the Hot Spot control.

For example, suppose you want a descriptive bit of text to appear next to a Command Button when the user drags the mouse over the button. Three controls are required to accomplish this:

✔ **A Command Button control:** Note that the Command Button control really has nothing to do with displaying or hiding the message; that feat is accomplished by a Hot Spot control.

✔ **A Label control:** You place this control adjacent to the Command Button control. The Caption property for the Label control should be the text you want displayed when a Web surfer moves the mouse over the command button. The Visible property for the Label control should be set to false so that the label is initially hidden from view.

✔ **A Hot Spot control:** You draw this control so that it's the same size and shape as the Command Button control and place it so that it completely overlaps the Command Button control. The Hot Spot control is actually the control that causes the Label control to be revealed when the mouse passes over the Command Button.

Creating the VBScript modules to display and hide the message when the mouse passes over the Hot Spot control is straightforward. Use the Script Wizard to create two procedures:

✔ The first procedure, for the Hot Spot control's MouseEnter event, sets the Visible property of the Label control to *true*.

✔ The second procedure, for the Hot Spot control's MouseExit event, sets the Visible property of the Label control to *false*.

Figure 21-19 shows how the Script Wizard appears after you create these procedures. Here, you can see that the script assigned to the MouseExit event for the Hot Spot control is set to hide the label control. If you switch to Code View, you see the following VBScript code for the MouseEnter and MouseExit events:

```
Sub HotSpot1_MouseEnter()
Label1.Visible = True
End Sub

Sub HotSpot1_MouseExit()
Label1.Visible = False
End Sub
```

Figure 21-20 shows how these controls appear when displayed by Internet Explorer. Here, you can see that the mouse pointer is over the command button, so the text message is displayed. If you move the mouse pointer away from the command button, the message disappears.

You don't have to use Hot Spot controls in conjunction with Command Button controls. For example, you can create a Hot Spot control that overlaps part of a graphic image so that your Web page responds in some way when the user moves the mouse over that part of the graphic. Or the Hot Spot can be completely independent of any other control.

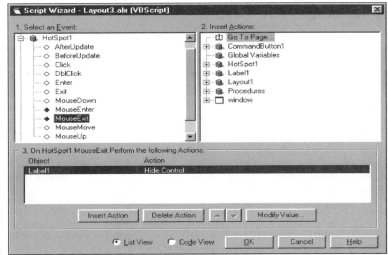

Figure 21-19:
Creating a
hot spot.

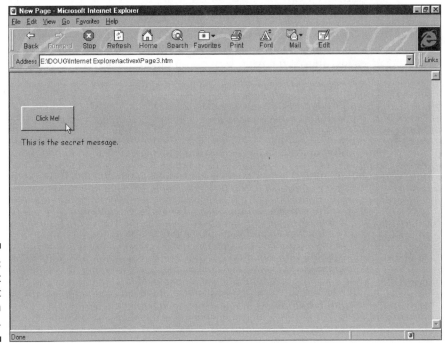

Figure 21-20:
The Hot
Spot
controls in
action.

Creating a Slide Show

An interesting ActiveX technique involves using the Timer object to create a slide show. A *slide show* is an HTML presentation that automatically moves from one page to another, without requiring any action on the part of the person viewing the Web site. The slide show uses an ActiveX Timer control to automatically invoke a VBScript program after a certain time interval elapses. This VBScript program then changes the Internet Explorer display to another page. Each page in the presentation has a Timer control with a script that causes the next page in the presentation to be displayed.

For example, suppose that you've created five HTML documents (chaucer1.htm, chaucer2.htm, and so on up to chaucer5.htm) that each present a portion of Chaucer's famous Canterbury Tales. For your slide show, you want the five pages to be displayed for 15 seconds each . . . just long enough for most viewers to read the entire thing (or fall asleep trying). To set up such a slide show, follow these steps:

1. **Insert a Timer control on the first page in the series.**

   To cause chaucer1.htm to automatically switch over to chaucer2.htm after a given amount of time elapses, all you have to do is use the ActiveX control pad to insert a Timer control on the page. The Timer control is invisible on the page, so it doesn't matter where you place it.

2. **Change the Timer control's Interval property to the amount of time you want the first page to remain on-screen.**

   The Timer control interval is measured in *milliseconds,* or thousandths of a second. To cause the Timer to "fire" after 15 seconds, you need to set the interval to 15000, as shown in Figure 21-21.

3. **Call up the Script Wizard to create a script for the Timer control's Timer event.**

4. **For the script's Action, select Go To Page.**

   A dialog box appears asking for a text string.

5. **Type the URL for the page you want displayed when the timer expires.**

   Figure 21-22 shows how the script appears in this example. If you switch to Code View, you find the following VBScript code:

```
Sub IeTimer1_Timer()
Window.location.href = "chaucer2.htm"
End Sub
```

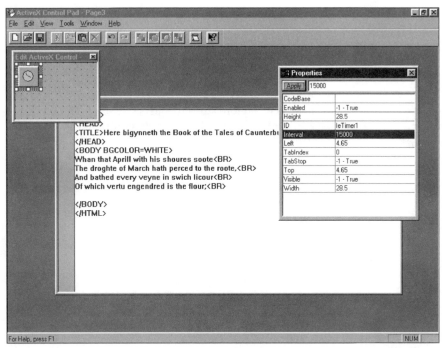

Figure 21-21:
Using a
Timer
control to
create a
slide show.

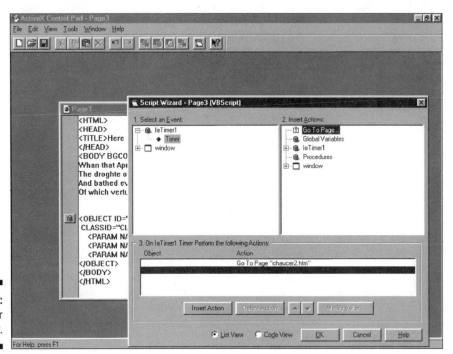

Figure 21-22:
A Timer
script.

6. **Repeat this process for each of the pages in your slide show.**

   To create the entire slide show for this example, you also need to add a Timer control to chaucer2.htm, with a script that goes to chaucer3.htm; chaucer3.htm and chaucer4.htm require similar Timer controls.

Omit the Timer control from the last Web page in the series if you want the slide show to stop when it reaches the last page. Or, if you want the slide show to loop back to the beginning, place a Timer control on the last page to lead viewers back to the first page.

Part VII
The Part of Tens

The 5th Wave — By Rich Tennant

"You know, I liked you a whole lot more on the Internet."

In this part . . .

1f you keep this book in the bathroom (where it rightfully belongs), the chapters in this part are the ones you'll read the most. Each of these chapters offers up ten (more or less) things that are worth knowing about various aspects of using Internet Explorer.

Without further ado, here they are, direct from the home office in Fresno, California. . . .

Chapter 22

Ten Hot New Features of Internet Explorer 3.0

● ●

In This Chapter

▶ ActiveX

▶ Style sheets

▶ Keyboard navigation

▶ Content Advisor

▶ Internet Mail and News

▶ Java support

▶ VRML

▶ Comic Chat

▶ NetMeeting

▶ It's Free

● ●

*M*icrosoft has made some pretty major improvements in its newest version of Internet Explorer. This chapter describes ten of the most important of these improvements. The folks at the Microsoft ad agency stay up late at night trying to come up with catchy slogans for these features, so look out.

ActiveX

ActiveX is a new technology that brings the object-oriented capabilities of the long-standing Microsoft OLE technology to the World Wide Web. In short, ActiveX enables Web developers to include functional objects as part of their Web pages. You can think of ActiveX as an Internet version of OLE.

According to Microsoft, ActiveX is the most revolutionary development to hit the computer industry since, well, the *last* revolutionary thing Microsoft unleashed on us. The computer industry must be very unsettled, because it seems to have a major revolution every few months.

In spite of all the hype, ActiveX really is a neat technology. ActiveX moves the World Wide Web from it's current state of being mostly a repository of crudely formatted and static pages to an exciting world of Web pages filled with sights and sounds and secret places to click. Figure 22-1 shows a Web page that sports ActiveX controls.

Truthfully, though, ActiveX is something that concerns Web developers. Those of us who merely surf the Web are impressed when we see cool pages created with ActiveX, but we don't have to know a thing about ActiveX to appreciate the new features. If you happen to be a Web-page author, grab your pocket protector and propeller hat and check out Chapter 21 for details.

Style Sheets

HTML is pretty dry when it comes to formatting capabilities. Heck, HTML can't even specify a font — even the old WordStar word processing program could do that! At last, the new *style sheets* feature of HTML gives Web-page authors nearly complete control over page layout. Style sheets enable you to customize the look of your Web pages with different fonts, letter sizes, line spacing, indentation, and other formatting features that have been standard fare in word processors for more than a decade. It's about time the Web catches up.

Style sheets are a feature of interest mostly to Web page authors. For us mortal users, we say, "Cool!" when we see a page that was created with style sheets, but we don't have to know a whit about style sheets to appreciate pages that rely on them.

If you happen to be a Web-page author (or a prospective one), you may be interested to know that style sheets enable you to customize the appearance of various HTML tags, such as <H1> and <P>. You can specify attributes for such things as the font, font size (in points!), color, background color, and so on. A new <STYLE> tag defines the styles that appear in an HTML document. Read Chapter 21 for more information.

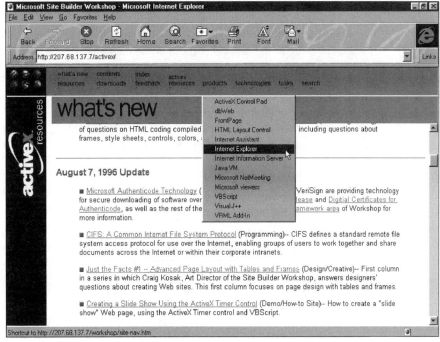

Figure 22-1:
This page
uses
ActiveX to
create a
splashy
appearance.

Keyboard Navigation

At last, here's something Web surfers can appreciate. All other Web browsers seem to think that the mouse is the only way to surf. Internet Explorer 3.0 is the first Web browser that recognizes that some people prefer to use the keyboard. In fact, some people are unable to use the mouse because of physical disabilities. As a result, anything that you can do with the mouse in Internet Explorer 3.0, you can also accomplish on the keyboard. In particular, you can use the Tab key to move among hyperlinks or form fields in an HTML document. With other browsers, you have to click on the links and form fields to activate them.

Content Advisor

Internet Explorer now lets parents prevent their kids from accessing Web sites that may contain offensive material. The new Internet Explorer Content Advisor feature (covered in detail in Chapter 9) enables Web publishers to rate their site according to the degree of sexual content, offensive language, nudity, and violence. Parents can set threshold levels for each of these ratings to effectively block Web pages that are inappropriate for their children. You can bypass the ratings control by entering a password, allowing adults to use Internet Explorer without restriction.

The Content Advisor feature isn't perfect — it doesn't stop all offensive content and sometimes mistakenly blocks browser access to inoffensive Web sites — but it's a major step in the right direction. The Internet is just too risky a place for kids to be roaming around without some controls.

Internet Mail and News

Internet newsgroups are discussion areas where Internet users post messages, called *articles,* about various topics. Thousands of different newsgroups exist, each with its own subject matter. Whether you're interested in astronomy or zoology, you can find one or two newsgroups that pique your interest.

Internet Explorer 3.0 comes with a brand new program from Microsoft, called Internet News. This program enables you to access Internet newsgroups, read articles posted by other users, and post your own articles. You can also quickly access your favorite newsgroups. Internet Explorer automatically launches Internet News whenever you enter the address of a newsgroup or click a hyperlink that represents a newsgroup.

Another Internet Explorer companion program is Internet Mail. This program is a simple but effective e-mail program that can send and receive e-mail messages over the Internet. Internet Mail is not as sophisticated as other e-mail programs, including Microsoft Exchange or Microsoft Mail. But if your only source of e-mail is the Internet, Internet Mail is a fast and efficient e-mail program.

Figures 22-2 and 22-3 show Internet Mail and Internet News.

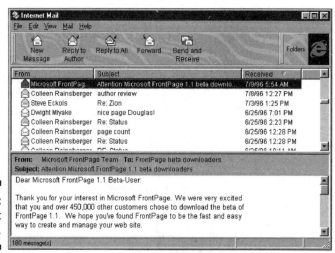

Figure 22-2:
Internet
Mail.

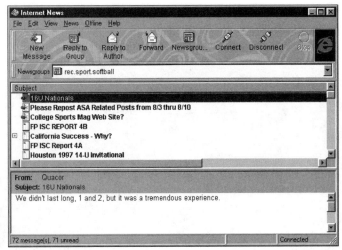

Figure 22-3:
Internet
News.

Java Support

So many people are talking about Java these days that Microsoft couldn't afford to not include built-in Java support with Internet Explorer 3.0. Java was originally developed by Sun Microsystems, and the Netscape Navigator browser recently came out with Java support.

Many Internet pundits believe that Microsoft is only reluctantly supporting Java; after all, Microsoft has its own, competing technology in the form of ActiveX and Visual Basic. That claim may be true, but Microsoft hasn't cut corners on its Java implementation for Internet Explorer 3.0: This browser delivers fast, reliable, and — best of all — free Java.

VRML

VRML is a relatively new part of the Web. It creates three-dimensional virtual worlds that you can explore (see Figure 22-4). If you've played DOOM, you know what I mean. In most Web browsers, VRML is a troublesome add-on or, worse, a separate program altogether. In Internet Explorer 3.0, VRML is built in, so you don't have to fuss with a separate program. You can find out more about VRML in Chapter 16.

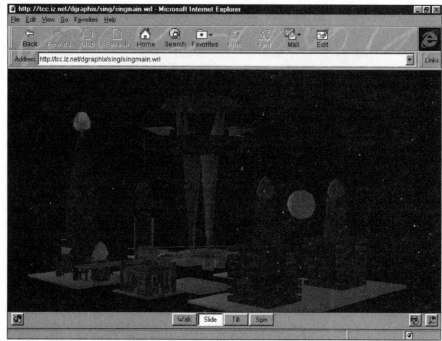

Figure 22-4:
VRML lets
you explore
surreal
worlds.

Comic Chat

Internet Relay Chat has been around for a while, enabling Internet users to converse with each other instantly. But even with topics ranging from racy to riveting, the text-only nature of IRC made chatting seem dry and boring.

The new Microsoft program for participating in online chats changes all that with its unique interface: It presents the chat as a running comic strip, in which chat participants are represented as cartoon characters. Figure 22-5 shows Comic Chat in action. Chapter 13 provides the nitty-gritty details.

NetMeeting

Although Comic Chat is cool and funny, for really powerful chatting, you need NetMeeting, instead. NetMeeting goes beyond IRC chatting to provide voice communications, whiteboard capabilities, file exchange, and application sharing.

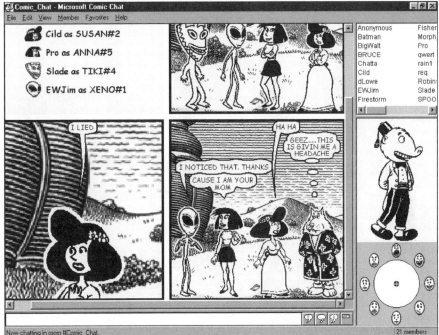

You can download NetMeeting as a part of Internet Explorer, but you must request the full installation when you download it. NetMeeting isn't included if you download the minimum or typical Internet Explorer installation. You can also download NetMeeting separately. For more information on NetMeeting, see Chapter 14.

It's Free

The very best new feature of Internet Explorer is that it's absolutely free. You can download Internet Explorer 3.0 from the Microsoft Web site (http://www.microsoft.com/ie) and use it with no fee of any kind. Microsoft does ask you to register Internet Explorer after you download it, but you don't have to pay a fee for registering or using the software.

Chapter 23

My Ten Favorite Web Sites

· ·

In This Chapter

▶ The Library of Congress

▶ Microsoft

▶ The House of Representatives

▶ The Smithsonian Institution

▶ The National Park Service

▶ NASA

▶ The Late Show with David Letterman

▶ Shakespearean Insult Server

▶ Games Domain

▶ Internet Anagram Server

· ·

*I*t is a sign of the times that in addition to their favorite TV shows, movies, and rock stars, people now have favorite Web sites. This chapter presents ten of mine. All ten of these Web sites are in my Favorites folder, and I visit them frequently. Some of these Web sites contain genuinely useful information, but others are of a more frivolous nature.

The Library of Congress

```
www.loc.gov
```

The Library of Congress home page, shown in Figure 23-1, is one of my favorite pages anywhere on the Web. Apparently, I'm not alone: About 45,000 pages are retrieved from this site *every day*.

In addition to allowing you to search through its vast catalogs of books, this home page also provides special exhibits of the library's fascinating collections. For example, the following special exhibits were available in June 1996:

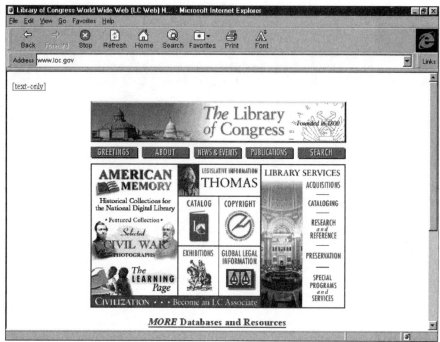

Figure 23-1:
The Library
of Congress
Web page.

- ✔ Dresden: Treasures from the Saxon State Library
- ✔ Women Come to the Front: Journalists, Photographers, and Broadcasters During WWII
- ✔ Creating French Culture: Treasures from the Bibliothèque Nationale de France
- ✔ Declaring Independence: Drafting the Documents
- ✔ Temple of Liberty: Building the Capitol for a New Nation
- ✔ The Gettysburg Address
- ✔ The Russian Church and Native Alaskan Cultures
- ✔ African-American Culture and History
- ✔ 1492: An Ongoing Voyage
- ✔ Scrolls from the Dead Sea
- ✔ Rome Reborn: The Vatican Library and Renaissance Culture
- ✔ Revelations from the Russian Archives

Plus, the Library of Congress is constructing a digital library called *American Memory,* that includes, among other items of interest, documents from the Continental Congress and Constitutional Convention, digitized images of Walt

Whitman's notebooks, thousands of photographs from the Civil War, and early motion pictures that you can download and play on your computer.

Microsoft

www.microsoft.com

Microsoft has one of the most active pages on the World Wide Web. The page serves as a portal to all kinds of information and support provided free by Microsoft. The opening page for the Microsoft Web site is shown in Figure 23-2.

Microsoft figured that you'd want to visit its Web site so often that it built a link to the Microsoft home page right into Internet Explorer 3.0. All you have to do is click Quick Links to reveal the Quick Links toolbar; then click the Microsoft icon.

The Microsoft Web site offers many different features, including product information, schedules of upcoming events, and press releases. But when you have a problem, you can find the most useful information in the support section, shown in Figure 23-3. (To access the Support Online page, click the Support icon on the Microsoft home page.)

Figure 23-2:
The
Microsoft
Web page.

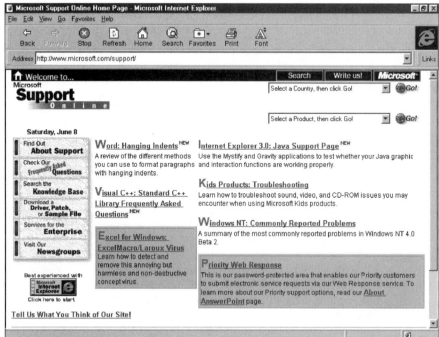

Figure 23-3:
The
Microsoft
Support
Online page.

Several support services are available from this Web page:

✔ For information about a specific product, select the product you're interested in from the drop-down list at the top of the page and then click Go! Product-specific Web pages are available for most Microsoft products.

✔ The Knowledge Base is a searchable database of answers to thousands of technical questions about Microsoft software. The Knowledge Base is usually the best place to begin your quest for help, because someone has probably already solved whatever problem you are experiencing.

✔ The download area contains updated program files and drivers. If you purchase a new printer but can't find a driver for it, check here.

✔ Microsoft maintains its own news server with newsgroups for each of its products. To access these newsgroups, click the Visit Our Newsgroups tab. In the newsgroups, you can post a specific question and then check back the following day to see what responses you have received.

Of course, Microsoft also maintains a Web site devoted entirely to Internet Explorer (see Figure 23-4), which you can find at the following address:

www.microsoft.com/ie

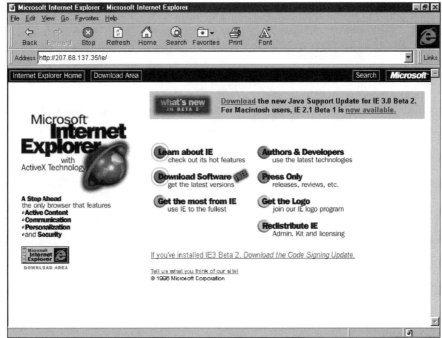

Figure 23-4:
The Internet
Explorer
page.

From the Internet Explorer home page, you can download the latest version of Internet Explorer and its add-on components, view a showcase of sample pages that demonstrate the coolest new features of Internet Explorer 3.0, and find out about the latest Internet Explorer features.

The U.S. House of Representatives

www.house.gov

All the major branches of government have Web pages, but my favorite is the Web page for the House of Representatives, shown in Figure 23-5.

Here are some of the services that are available from the House of Representatives Web page:

- ✔ The complete text of all bills introduced during the current Congress (If you read this stuff, you'll be doing more than many of the representatives who actually vote on it!)

- ✔ Information about the status of current bills, amendments, voting records, committees, and so on

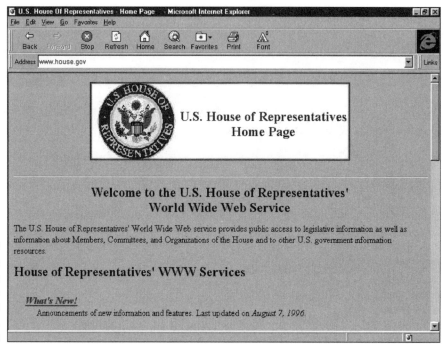

Figure 23-5:
The House
of Repre-
sentatives
Web page.

> ✔ The names, addresses, and phone numbers of all legislators
>
> ✔ Information about visiting Capitol Hill
>
> ✔ A schedule of legislative activity

The Smithsonian Institution

```
www.si.edu
```

Take a tour of the nation's premier museum by checking out the Smithsonian Institution's Web site. From the home page, you can visit any of the Smithsonian's 18 museums, including the National Air and Space Museum, the National Museum of American History, the National Museum of American Art, and the National Zoo. You can also visit Smithsonian research institutions, and you can make use of a travel planner that helps you plan a trip to the nation's capital. The opening page of the Smithsonian Web site is shown in Figure 23-6.

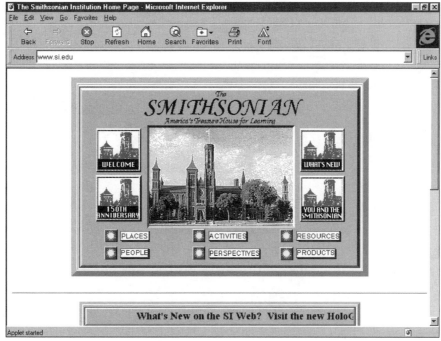

Figure 23-6:
The
Smithsonian
Web site.

A visit to any of the museums leads you to digitized images of the museum's most priceless treasures. For example, you can find images of the Apollo 11 command module, which is displayed in the entrance gallery of the National Air and Space Museum along with other milestone aircraft, including the Wright Brothers' original flyer and The Spirit of St. Louis.

The National Park Service

www.nps.gov

The National Park Service maintains an excellent Web site, called ParkNet, which offers information about hundreds of national parks, monuments, and historical sites. Figure 23-7 shows the NPS home page.

You can find the following information at the National Park Service Web site:

  ✔ Information about national parks and monuments, indexed by park name or searchable via regional map

  ✔ Camping and park reservation information

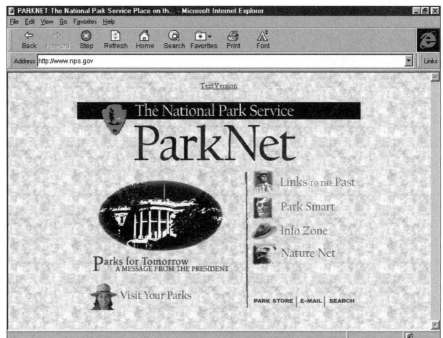

Figure 23-7:
The National
Park Service
on the Web.

  ✔ Suggestions for visiting the national parks

  ✔ Historical information about the national parks

  ✔ Educational resources

NASA

```
www.nasa.gov
```

I'm a space nut, so the NASA site is one of my favorite places to visit on the
Internet. Figure 23-8 shows the NASA home page.

The NASA Web site includes the following interesting features:

  ✔ A Gallery of pictures, sounds, and videos from NASA

  ✔ Detailed flight information for all the NASA manned flights, dating back to
    the Mercury program

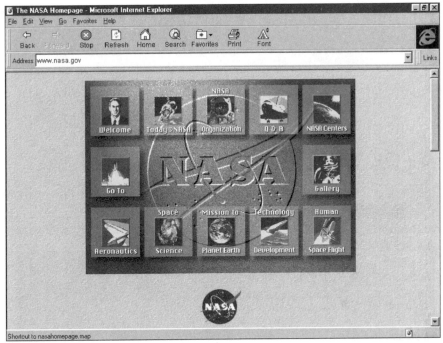

Figure 23-8:
The NASA
Web page.

✓ Information about the Space Station project

✓ Links to other NASA centers, such as Jet Propulsion Laboratory in Pasadena, California; Dryden Flight Research Facility at Edwards Air Force Base, California; and the Johnson Space Center in Houston, Texas

The Late Show with David Letterman

```
www.cbs.com/lateshow
```

Couldn't stay up late enough last night to watch the *Late Show with David Letterman*? Check out this page (shown in Figure 23-9) to get the current Top 10 list or access an archive of past Top 10 lists. You can also find information about guests and news about the show.

Not to be outdone, Jay Leno also has a Web site for *The Tonight Show,* located at www.nbctonightshow.com. In addition to guest lineups, the *Tonight Show* page also includes quips from Jay's recent monologues, plus excerpts from his regular Monday night Headlines feature.

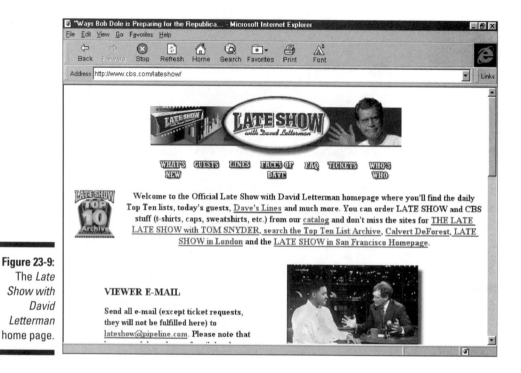

Figure 23-9:
The *Late Show with David Letterman* home page.

Shakespearean Insult Server

www.nova.edu/Inter-Links/cgi-bin/bard.pl

- ✔ Thou fawning rump-fed puttock
- ✔ Thou quailing fen-sucked pignut
- ✔ Thou beslubbering idle-headed harpy
- ✔ Thou reeky fool-born hedge-pig

If these insults, culled from the work of the immortal Insult Master himself, tickle thy fancy, then check out the Shakespearean Insult Server, shown in Figure 23-10. This Web page spews out a new Shakespearean insult each time you view the page. To get a new insult without leaving the page, click the Refresh button.

Note that you can drag the mouse over the insult to select it, press Ctrl+C to copy it to the clipboard, switch to a word processing document (or better yet, the Microsoft Exchange mail editor), and press Ctrl+V to paste the insult into your text.

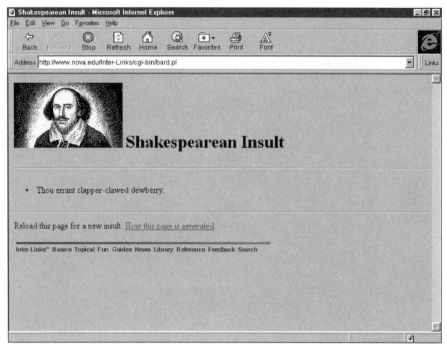

Figure 23-10:
The Shake-
spearean
Insult page.

Games Domain

www.gamesdomain.com

All work and no play make for boring Internet exploring. Fortunately, the World Wide Web is full of fun, frivolous, and sometimes freaky places to visit. Games Domain, illustrated in Figure 23-11, is one of the most complete gaming Web sites you can find. Although the Games Domain doesn't maintain its own library of downloadable games, it does include a directory with more than 3,000 links to games you can download from the Internet. That should be enough to keep you playing for a while!

In addition to links to downloadable games, Games Domain also includes HTML format FAQs (Frequently Asked Questions files) for more than 100 games, plus links to hundreds of other game-related Web sites.

If you find yourself stuck in a game, you can also check out one of the *walkthroughs,* which provide complete solutions for more than 200 computer games. Of course, reading one of these walkthroughs spoils the game for you, so read them only if you are *really* stuck.

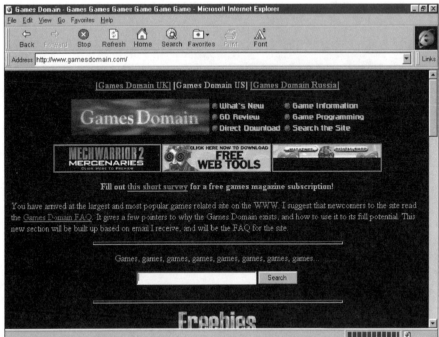

Internet Anagram Server

```
www.wordsmith.org/awad-cgibin/anagram
```

An *anagram* is a word or phrase that is made up of the same letters as another word or phrase. For example, the letters in my name, "Doug Lowe," can also be used to spell "Wood Glue" or "We Go Loud!"

The Internet hosts several Web sites that generate anagrams for you based on any word or phrase. The best of these Web sites is the Internet Anagram Server, illustrated in Figure 23-12. All you have to do to use the Internet Anagram Server is type a word or phrase into the text box and then press Enter. After a few moments, a long list of anagrams for the word or phrase appears. (I'm not kidding — in many cases, thousands of possible anagrams are displayed. Most of the anagrams produced don't make sense; the trick is searching through the list to find something clever and poignant.)

In addition to creating anagrams, the Internet Anagram Server also includes general information about anagrams and a link to the Usenet anagram discussion group — `alt.anagrams`.

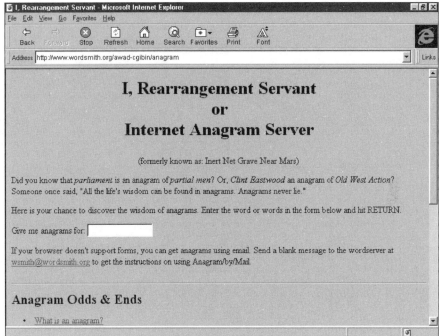

Figure 23-12:
The Internet
Anagram
Server.

Chapter 24

Ten Things That Sometimes Go Wrong

● ●

In This Chapter

▶ Not having Internet Explorer

▶ Not being able to get a modem connection

▶ Forgetting your password

▶ Getting strange messages about unexpected errors

▶ Being unable to find Internet Explorer

▶ Losing a file you know you downloaded

▶ Getting cut off from the Internet in the middle of a big download

▶ Forgetting where to find your favorite Web page

● ●

Actually, probably more like 10,000 things *can* go wrong, but this chapter describes some of the things that go wrong most often.

I Don't Have Internet Explorer!

No problem. Internet Explorer is available from many sources, and it's free. If you have any type of access to the Internet, you can find Internet Explorer at the Microsoft Web site, located at the following address:

```
http://www.microsoft.com
```

If you don't have any access to the Internet, you can obtain Internet Explorer as a part of the Microsoft Internet Kit for Windows 95. The Internet Kit includes not only Internet Explorer and Microsoft Internet Mail and News, but also extends the Windows 95 Explorer interface in a way that integrates Internet Explorer with your computer's desktop.

I Can't Connect to the Internet!

You double-click the Internet Explorer icon, the Connect To dialog box appears, and you type in your name and password, but you can't get any further. For some reason, you are unable to connect to the Internet. Arghhhhh!

Many, many things could be wrong. Here are a few general troubleshooting procedures that should help you solve the problem, or at least narrow it down:

✔ Make sure that the modem is securely connected to the telephone wall jack and the correct jack on the back of the modem. Phone cables sometimes jar loose. They go bad sometimes, too, so replacing the cable may solve the problem. If you're not sure which jack is the correct one, consult the manual that came with the modem.

✔ Make sure that the modem is not in use by another program, such as a fax program or the Windows 95 Hyperterminal program.

✔ Make sure that your teenager isn't talking on a phone that shares the same phone line as the modem. (This very thing has happened to me several times.)

✔ Try calling your Internet access number on a regular phone to see if it answers. If you get a busy signal or it just rings on and on and on, something may be wrong with the local access number. Try again later, and call your Internet provider's customer service if the problem persists.

✔ Double check the phone number in the Connect To dialog box. If your Internet provider supplies an alternate phone number, try that one instead.

If you just installed the modem or if the modem never has worked right, you should make sure that the modem is configured to use the proper Communications Port within your computer. To change the port setting, follow these steps:

1. **Click the Start button and choose Settings⇨Control Panel.**

2. **Double-click the Modems icon.**

3. **Click the Properties button.**

4. **Change the Port setting for the modem.**

5. **Click OK twice.**

6. **Try dialing in again.**

Sometimes, removing and reinstalling the modem within Windows 95 solves the problem. If all else fails, try this:

1. **Click the Start button and choose Settings⇨Control Panel.**

2. **Double-click the Modems icon.**

3. **Click the modem to select it and then click the R̲emove button.**

4. **Click Add.**

5. **Follow the Install a New Modem wizard to reinstall the modem.**

I Forgot My Password!

Didn't I tell you to write it down and keep it in a safe place? Sigh. If you really did forget your password, and you didn't write it down anywhere, you have to call your Internet provider for assistance. If you can convince the person on the other end of the line that you really are who you say you are, he or she will reset your password for you.

Now, so you don't find yourself in this mess again, make sure that the S̲ave Password option on the Connect To dialog box is selected so that you don't have to always type your password. Then write down your password and store it in a secure location. Here's a list of several not-so-secure places to hide your password:

- ✔ In a desk drawer, in a file folder labeled *Not My Internet Password*
- ✔ On a magnet stuck to the refrigerator (No one, including you, will ever be able to pick it out from all the other junk stuck up there.)
- ✔ On the inside cover of this book, in Pig Latin so that no one will be able to understand it
- ✔ Carved on the back of a park bench
- ✔ On the wall in a public restroom
- ✔ Tattooed on your left buttock, backward so that you can read it in a mirror

I Got an Unexpected Error Message!

Sometimes, when you try to follow a link to a cool Web page, or you type a URL yourself and press Enter, instead of getting the page you expected, you get a message that looks something like this:

```
Cannot open the Internet site http://www.whatever.com
             An unexpected error has occurred.
```

The *unexpected error* means that, for one reason or another, your browser couldn't find the page you tried to access. Several possible explanations may account for this error:

✔ The page you are trying to display may no longer exist. The person who created the page may have removed it.

✔ The page may have been moved to a new address. Sometimes you get a message telling you about the new address, sometimes not.

✔ The Web site that hosts the page may be having technical trouble. Try again later.

✔ The page may be just too darn popular, causing the server to be busy. Try again later.

The Internet Explorer Window Disappeared!

You know that you are signed in to the Internet, but you can't seem to find Internet Explorer anywhere. The window has mysteriously vanished!

Here are a few things to check before giving up in despair:

✔ Find the taskbar, that Windows 95 thingy that usually lurks down at the bottom of your screen. The taskbar has a button for every window that's open. If you find the Internet Explorer button in the taskbar, clicking it should bring the window to the front. (You may have to move your mouse all the way to the bottom edge of the screen to make the taskbar appear. Also, if you moved your taskbar, it may be on the top, left, or right edge of the screen rather than the bottom.)

✔ If no Internet Explorer window appears in the taskbar, you may have closed Internet Explorer but remained connected to the Internet. To make Internet Explorer come alive again, just double-click on the desktop Internet Explorer icon or click Start and choose the Internet Explorer Programs menu. Because you are already connected to the Internet, you don't have to go through the Connect To dialog box again.

✔ You may have been disconnected from the Internet for one reason or another. Normally when that happens, a dialog box appears, informing you that you have been disconnected and offering to reconnect. If no dialog box appears, you can reconnect by clicking Start and choosing Programs⇨ Accessories⇨Dial-Up Networking, and then double-clicking the icon for your Internet connection.

You can tell whether you're connected to the Internet by looking for the little modem icon in the corner of the taskbar, next to the clock; it sort of looks like two beady, red eyes blinking out at you. If the icon is present, you are connected. If the icon is missing, you're not.

MSN Is My Internet Provider, but I Can't Get Internet Explorer to Work!

You are able to sign on to The Microsoft Network just fine and find your way around the various MSN services, and you can even access Internet Newsgroups. But whenever you try to display an Internet World Wide Web page, the Internet Explorer chokes on you. All you get is a message about the address being incorrect or the service being unavailable.

Several possible scenarios could be causing this problem:

- ✔ Make sure that you're connected to The Microsoft Network using a phone number that supports both MSN service and Internet service. To check, choose the Tools⇨Connection Settings command and then look for the Service Type. If it says MSN Only, click the Access Numbers button and change the Service Type drop-down list field to Internet and The Microsoft Network. Then disconnect from MSN and try again.

- ✔ Make sure that you're running the most current version of MSN. Go to Member Assistance to see whether you can download an upgrade.

- ✔ The Internet address you are trying to access may be temporarily unavailable. For example, that guy who has the Web server that's attached to a video camera aimed at his Lava Lamp may have accidentally turned his computer off. If you think that's the case, try again tomorrow.

I Can't Find a File I Downloaded!

Don't worry. The file is probably around; you're just not looking in the right place. Internet Explorer offers a Save As dialog box that you must complete before downloading a file, so presumably you know where the file has been saved. However, you can all too easily click OK without really looking at this dialog box when it appears .

Fortunately, all you have to do is choose File⇨Save As File to recall the Save As dialog box, which by default opens the same folder the dialog box was opened to last. Just check the Save In field at the top of the dialog box to find out the folder where you saved your file.

If you can't remember the name of the file you downloaded, here's a trick that may help you find it:

1. **Open a My Computer window for the folder in which you saved the file.**

   Click My Computer and then navigate your way through your drives and folders until you come to the one where you saved the file.

2. **Click the View Details button.**

   If you can't find this button, choose View⇨Details and make sure that your toolbar is visible.

3. **Choose View⇨Arrange Icons⇨By Date.**

   The list of files is sorted into date sequence, with the newest files appearing at the top of the list.

4. **Look at the files at the top of the list.**

   With luck, one of these files rings a bell.

I Was Disconnected in the Middle of a Two-Hour Download!

Wow. Tough break. Unfortunately, the Internet doesn't have any way to restart a big download, picking up where you left off. The only solution is to download the entire file again.

Don't blame me; I'm just the messenger.

I Can't Find That Cool Web Page I Saw Yesterday!

I've faced this problem myself. The Web is such a large place that you can easily stumble into a page you really like and then not be able to find it again later.

If you can't seem to retrace your steps, you may still have a record of where you were. Choose Go⇨Open History Folder to display the URLs for all the pages you recently visited. With some luck, you can find the page in the history folder. If you do, double-click it, and you're on your way.

To avoid the frustration of misplacing the Web sites you love, always do one of the following the moment you find a page that you may want to visit again:

> ✔ Click the Favorites button and choose <u>A</u>dd to Favorites to add the page to your favorites list. This way, you can always find the page again by choosing the F<u>a</u>vorites command. If you later decide that the page isn't so great after all, you can always delete it from Favorites.
>
> ✔ Choose <u>F</u>ile⇨Cr<u>e</u>ate Shortcut to place a shortcut to the page on your desktop. You can then double-click the shortcut icon at any time to return to the page.

I've Started a Nuclear War!

If you're minding your own business, enjoying a nice game of Global Thermonuclear War at `www.wargames.com`, and you suddenly hear air-raid sirens and see mushroom clouds on the horizon, don't panic. See if you can interest the computer in a nice game of chess instead.

Just kidding. Nothing you do can start a nuclear war from the Internet. Experienced computer hackers have been trying to start nuclear wars on the Internet for years, and no one has succeeded, at least not yet.

Chapter 25

Ten Safety Tips for Kids on the Net

In This Chapter

▶ Safety tips for kids and their parents

▶ Ways to help keep the Internet a safe place for everyone

*T*he Internet is an inherently risky place for kids (and adults, too). Along with pictures of Neil Armstrong on the moon, your kids can just as easily find pictures you probably don't want them to see. And although chatting online can be fun and enlightening, it can also be unhealthy and possibly even dangerous.

This chapter lists ten important safety tips that parents should drill into their kids' heads before they allow them to go online.

I really don't want to be an alarmist here. Overall, the Internet is a pretty wholesome place. Don't be afraid to let your kids venture out online, but don't let them go it alone, either. Make sure that they understand the ground rules.

Don't Believe That People Really Are Who They Say They Are

When you sign up with an Internet service provider, you can type anything you want for your user ID. And no one makes you tell the truth in e-mail, newsgroups, or chats. Just because someone claims to be a 16-year-old female is not reason enough to believe it. That person can be a 12-year-old boy, a 19-year-old girl, or a 35-year-old pervert.

Never Give Out Your Address, Phone Number, Real Last Name, or Credit Card Number

If you're not sure why Rule #2 exists, see Rule #1.

Never Pretend to Be Someone You're Not

The flip side of not believing who someone says he or she is, is that other people may believe that you are who you say you are. If you are 13 years old and claim to be 17, you're inviting trouble.

We all like to gloss over our weaknesses. When I'm online, I don't generally draw attention to the fact that a substantial portion of my hair is gone, and I'm a bit pudgy around the waistline (well, OK, I'm a *lot* pudgy around the waistline). But I don't represent myself as a super athlete or a rock star, either. Just be yourself.

Save Inappropriate Postings to a File So That You Can Show Them to an Adult

If someone sends you inappropriate e-mail, not just something that makes you feel angry or upset, but something that seems downright inappropriate, choose File⇔Save As to save the message as a file. Then show it to an adult.

If Someone Says Something Inappropriate to You in a Chat, Save the Chat Log

If someone is vulgar or offensive in an online chat, save the chat log to a file. Then show it to an adult.

Watch Your Language

The Internet isn't censored. In fact, it can be a pretty rough place. Crude language abounds, especially on Usenet. But that doesn't mean you have to contribute to the endless flow of colorful metaphors. Watch your language while chatting online or posting messages.

Don't Obsess

The Internet can be fun, but there's more to life than going online. The best friendships are the ones where you actually spend time in the presence of other people. If you find yourself spending hour upon hour online, maybe you should cut back a bit.

Report Inappropriate Behavior to an Adult

If something seems really amiss in your Internet experience — for example, if you think someone is harassing you beyond what should be normal, or if someone asks you questions that make you uncomfortable — tell an adult.

You can also complain by sending mail to the administrator of the perpetrator's service provider. If the perp is clever, you may not be able to figure out his or her true e-mail address. But you often can. If you receive harassing mail from `idiot@jerk.com`, try sending a complaint to `postmaster@jerk.com`.

If You Feel Uncomfortable, Leave

Don't stick around in a chat session if you feel uncomfortable. Just leave.

Similarly, don't bother to reply to inappropriate e-mail messages or newsgroup articles.

Parents: Be Involved with Your Kids' Online Activities

Don't let your kids run loose on the Internet! Get involved with what they are doing. You don't have to monitor them every moment they are online. Just be interested in what they are doing, what friends they have made over the network, what they like, and what they don't like. Ask them to show you around their favorite Internet pages.

Chapter 26

Ten Nifty Features You May Otherwise Miss

● ●

In This Chapter

▶ Downloading and browsing at the same time

▶ Saving a page you haven't yet opened

▶ Saving the background image as a graphics file

▶ Browsing in separate windows

▶ Using the keyboard to navigate

▶ Changing the font size to make text more legible

▶ Copying text or graphics to a document

▶ Visiting virtual worlds

▶ Sending mail to multiple users

▶ Cross-posting to several newsgroups

● ●

*T*his chapter lists ten obscure but useful Internet Explorer features that you might otherwise overlook. Some of these features are covered elsewhere in this book; others are covered only in this chapter. Oh, and the last two pertain to Internet Mail and Internet News, two components of Internet Explorer that you may or may not have chosen to include when you downloaded Internet Explorer. If this chapter leaves you hankering for some of these additional features, you can go back to the Internet Explorer download page (www.microsoft.com/ie/download) to add these components at any time.

Don't Wait for Downloads

Although downloading long files *can* take a long time, you don't have to idly twiddle your thumbs while waiting for a lengthy download. All you have to do is click anywhere in the Internet Explorer screen to return Internet Explorer to life, and you are free to explore other parts of the Internet while the download proceeds in the background.

You can even download another file while a file is already downloading. Keep in mind, however, that Internet Explorer and any files you are downloading are all competing for time on your modem. Thus, continuing to explore the Internet while downloading a file makes the download take longer. But at least you won't be wasting time.

Saving a Page without Actually Opening It

Internet Explorer is capable of saving a page without actually opening the page. All you have to do is find a link to the page you want to save. Then, instead of clicking the link to open the page, right-click the link to call up a shortcut menu. From the shortcut menu, choose Save Target As to download the page and save it on your hard disk. You can view the page at your convenience at a later time.

Saving the Background

Find a page with a stunning background that you want to use for yourself? You can save the background image as a bitmap file by right-clicking anywhere on the background to call up the shortcut menu and then choosing Save Background As. A dialog box appears, asking you where you want to save the background image.

Displaying a Page in a New Window

You can browse the Internet in more than one window if you wish. This option allows you to keep several pages open at the same time. To start browsing in a new window, right-click a link to call up the shortcut menu and then choose Open in New Window.

Using the Keyboard

Exploring the Internet is a mouse-intensive job, but what if you have trouble using your mouse, either because of a physical disability or because you just aren't good at it? Fortunately, Internet Explorer lets you navigate pages using the keyboard as well as the mouse.

Try using the following keys:

- ✔ **Tab:** Moves from one field or link to the next. Keep pressing Tab until you get to the field you want to click. This approach even works for image maps.
- ✔ **Shift+Tab:** Moves through fields and links backwards
- ✔ **Enter:** Simulates a mouse click
- ✔ **Shift+Enter:** Opens a link in a new window
- ✔ **Arrow keys:** Scroll the window

Changing Font Sizes

If the text on a page is too big or too small, you can change its size by choosing View⇨Fonts. Using this command changes the relative size of all the fonts on the page.

Copying Stuff to a Document

If you find some text or a graphic that you want to use in one of your documents, you can copy it to your document via the clipboard. Just follow these steps:

1. **Select the text or graphic you want to copy.**

2. **Press Ctrl+C.**

3. **Switch to your document.**

4. **Position the insertion point where you want the text or graphic inserted.**

5. **Press Ctrl+V.**

Customizing Your Quick Links

The Links toolbar lets you get to five of the choicest Web sites with a single mouse click. Unfortunately, many Web surfers don't realize that they don't have to be content with the five Web sites Microsoft deems as worthy of inclusion on the Links toolbar. You can change any of the five Quick Links so that it points to any Web site you wish. Here's how:

1. **Navigate to the site you want to make a Quick Link.**

2. **Choose View⇨Options and click the Navigation tab.**

3. **Choose one of the Quick Links from the Page drop-down list.**

4. **Type a title for the Quick Link.**

5. **Click the Use Current button.**

   Voilà!

Sending Mail to Multiple Recipients

When you send an e-mail message using Microsoft Mail, you can send the message to more than one recipient at a time. All you have to do is type two or more e-mail addresses in the To: field, separating each address with a semi-colon.

Keep in mind that each recipient knows that you sent the mail to the others, because the entire To: list shows up in the message header.

Cross-Posting

Sometimes, a newsgroup article is of interest to more than one newsgroup. In such cases, you may want to *cross-post* the article to several newsgroups. To do so, just type the name of each newsgroup you want the article posted to, separated by semicolons. For example, to post a message to `rec.backcountry` and `rec.outdoors.camping`, type the following in the To: field when composing your article:

```
rec.backcountry;rec.outdoors.camping
```

That does it!

Glossary

ActiveX

The new Microsoft Web-based object technology, which enables intelligent objects to be embedded in Web documents to create interactive pages. See *object linking and embedding*.

ActiveX control

An ActiveX object that can be embedded in a Web page. Most ActiveX controls are user-interface gadgets such as list boxes and command buttons, but some provide behind-the-scenes functions, such as timers.

address book

A file that stores the Internet e-mail addresses of the people with whom you correspond regularly.

afk

Away from keyboard, an abbreviation commonly used when chatting. See *IRC*.

America Online

A popular online information service that also provides Internet access. America Online is often referred to as AOL. To send e-mail to an AOL user, address the message to the user's America Online name followed by the domain name (@aol.com). For example, if the user's AOL name is Barney, send an e-mail message to Barney@aol.com.

anonymous FTP

An FTP site that allows access to anyone, without requiring an account.

AOL

See *America Online.*

applet

A program written in the Java language and embedded in an HTML document. An applet runs automatically whenever someone views the Web page that contains the applet.

article

A message posted to a Usenet newsgroup.

ASCII

The standard character set for most computers. Internet newsgroups are *ASCII-only,* meaning that they can support only text-based messages.

attach

Sending a file along with an e-mail message or newsgroup article. Internet Explorer automatically encodes and decodes attachments.

attachment

A file attached to an e-mail message or a newsgroup article.

AVI

The Microsoft standard for video files that can be viewed in Windows. AVI is one of the most popular video formats on the Web, but other formats such as QuickTime and MPEG are also widely used.

bandwidth

The amount of information that can flow through a network connection. Bandwidth is to computer networks what pipe diameter is to plumbing: The bigger the pipe, the more water can flow.

baud

See *bits per second*. (Actually, a technical difference does exist between *baud* and *bits per second*, but only people with pocket protectors and taped glasses care.)

binary file

A non-ASCII file, such as a computer program, a picture, a sound, or a video.

BITNET

A large network connecting colleges and universities in North America and Europe through the Internet. BITNET mailing lists are presented as Usenet newsgroups under the bit hierarchy.

bits per second (bps)

A measure of how fast your modem can transmit or receive information between your computer and a remote computer, such as your Internet service provider. You won't be happy browsing the Internet using anything less than a 14,400 bps modem (commonly referred to as a *14.4 modem*). Note that the term *Kbps* is often used to designate thousands of bits per second. Thus, 28,800 bps and 28.8 Kbps are equivalent.

brb

Be right back, an abbreviation commonly used when chatting. See *IRC.*

browser

A program, such as Internet Explorer, that you can use to access and view the World Wide Web. Internet Explorer is, at its core, a browser.

cache

An area of your computer's hard disk used to store data recently downloaded from the network so the data can be redisplayed quickly.

cappuccino

An Italian coffee drink that blends espresso, steamed milk, foam, and (if you're lucky) a dash of cinnamon. Not to be confused with *Java.*

Certificates

An online form of identification that gives one computer assurance that the other computer is whom it claims to be. Certificates are a relatively new phenomenon on the Internet. When you first install Internet Explorer, you have the option of obtaining a certificate that identifes you to other computers. You may as well accept the certificate — after all, it's free!

CGI

Common Gateway Interface. A method of programming Web sites, mostly used to handle online forms. CGI utilizes script programs that run on the server computer, as opposed to Java or VBScript programs, which run on client computers. Because client-side programming is more efficient, CGI is losing popularity.

chat

See *IRC.*

Chaucer

A dead English dude who didn't spell very well.

Coke machine

A coin-operated device that dispenses Coke and other Coca-Cola products. The latest rage in the computer science departments of many universities is to hook the Coke machine up to a Web server so that Web surfers all across the globe can find out how much Coke and Diet Coke remains in the machine. Go figure.

compressed file

A file that has been processed by a special *compression program* that reduces the amount of disk space required to store the file. If you download the file to your computer, you must decompress the file before you can use it using a program such as WinZip or PKUNZIP.

CompuServe

A popular online service that also provides Internet access. To send Internet mail to a CompuServe member, address the mail to the user's CompuServe user ID (two groups of numbers separated by a comma) followed by @compuserve.com. However, use a period instead of a comma in the user ID. For example, if the user's ID is 55555,1234, send mail to 55555.1234@compuserve.com. You have to use the period because Internet e-mail standards don't allow for commas in e-mail addresses.

connect time

The amount of time you are connected to the Internet or your online service. Some Internet service providers limit your monthly connect time or charge you by the hour.

cookie

A file that a Web server stores on your computer. The most common use for cookies is to customize the way a Web page appears when you view it. For example, customizable Web pages such as www.msn.com use cookies to store your viewing preferences so that the next time you visit that Web page, only the elements that you request are displayed.

cyberspace

An avant-garde term used to refer to the Internet.

decode

The process of reconstructing a binary file that was encoded using the uuencode scheme, used in e-mail and newsgroups. Internet Mail and Internet News can automatically decode encoded files.

decompression

The process of restoring compressed files to their original state. Decompression is usually accomplished with a program such as WinZip and PKUNZIP. (You can download the shareware version of PKUNZIP at www.pkware.com.)

decryption

See *Tales from Decrypt*. Just kidding. Decryption is the process of unscrambling a message that has been encrypted (scrambled up so that only the intended recipient can read it). See *encryption*.

DNS

Domain Name Server. The system that allows us to use almost intelligible names such as www.microsoft.com rather than completely incomprehensible addresses such as 283.939.12.74.

domain

The last portion of an Internet address (also known as the *top-level domain*), which indicates whether the address belongs to a company (`com`), an educational institution (`edu`), a government agency (`gov`), a military organization (`mil`), or another organization (`org`).

domain name

The address of an Internet site, which generally includes the organization domain name followed by the top-level domain, as in `www.idgbooks.com`.

download

Copying a file from another computer to your computer — via a modem.

e-mail

Electronic mail, an Internet service that enables you to send and receive messages to and from other Internet users.

emoticon

Another word for a *smiley* — an expressive face you can create with nothing more than a few keystrokes and some imagination :-)

encode

A method of converting a *binary file* to ASCII text, which can be sent by Internet e-mail or posted to an Internet newsgroup. When displayed, encoded information looks like a stream of random characters. But when you run the encoded message through a decoder program, the original binary file is reconstructed. Internet Mail and Internet News automatically encode and decode messages, so you don't have to worry about using a separate program for this purpose.

encryption

Scrambling a message so that no one can read it, except of course the intended recipient, who must *decrypt* the message before reading it.

ETLA

Extended three letter acronym. A four-letter acronym.

Explorer

A Windows 95 program that lets you view the contents of folders alongside a hierarchical representation of the computer's folders. Essentially, Explorer is the Windows 95 version of the old Program Manager and File Manager programs found in Windows 3.1.

FAQ

A *frequently asked questions* file. Contains answers to the most commonly asked questions. Always check to see if a FAQ file exists for a forum or Usenet newsgroup before asking basic questions. (If you post a question on an Internet newsgroup and the answer is in the FAQ, you'll get flamed for sure.)

Favorites

A collection of Web page addresses that you visit frequently. Internet Explorer lets you store your favorite Web addresses in a special folder so that you can recall them quickly.

File Transfer Protocol (FTP)

A system that allows the transfer of program and data files over the Internet.

finger

An Internet program that lets you obtain information about another Internet user.

flame

A painfully brutal response to a dumb posting on a BBS or Internet newsgroup. (On some newsgroups, just having `aol.com` in your Internet address is cause enough to get flamed.)

freeware

Software that you can download and use without paying a fee.

FTP

See *File Transfer Protocol*.

FTP site

An Internet server that has a library of files available for downloading with FTP.

gateway

A computer that enables other computers on a local area network (LAN) to access the Internet.

GIF

Graphic Interchange Format. A popular format for picture files. The GIF format uses an efficient compression technique that results in less data loss and higher quality graphics than other formats such as PCX.

home page

The introductory page at a Web site; sometimes refers to the entire Web site. Not to be confused with *start page*.

host computer

A computer to which you can connect via the Internet.

HTML

Hypertext Markup Language. A system of special tags used to create pages for the World Wide Web.

HTTP

Hypertext Transfer Protocol. The protocol used to transmit HTML documents over the Internet.

hyperlink

A bit of text or a graphic in a Web page that you can click to retrieve another Web page. The new Web page may be on the same Web server as the original page, or it may be on an entirely different Web server halfway around the globe.

hypermedia

A variation of hypertext in which hyperlinks can be graphics, sounds, or videos, as well as text. The World Wide Web is based on hypermedia, but the term *hypertext* is often loosely used instead.

hypertext

A system in which documents are linked to one another by text links. When the user clicks on a text link, the document referred to by the link is displayed. See *hypermedia*.

IBM

A big computer company.

Internet

A vast world-wide collection of networked computers, the largest computer network in the world.

Internet address

A complete address used to send e-mail to someone over the Internet. Your Internet address consists of a user ID plus the host name of your Internet service provider. For example, if your user ID is `JClampet` and your service provider's host name is `beverly.hills.com`, your Internet address is `JClampet@beverly.hills.com`.

Internet Explorer

The Microsoft program for browsing the World Wide Web and other Internet resources such as FTP and Gopher.

Internet Relay Chat

See *IRC*.

Internet service provider

Also known as *ISP*. A company that provides access to the Internet.

IP

Internet Protocol. The data transmission protocol that enables networks to exchange messages; serves as the foundation for communications over the Internet.

IRC

Internet Relay Chat. A system that enables you to carry on live conversations (known as *chats*) with other Internet users.

ISDN

A digital telephone line that can transmit data at 128 Kbps. ISDNs still cost a bit too much for the average home user. Watch, though; the price will come down.

ISP

See *Internet service provider*.

Java

An object-oriented programming language designed to be used on the World Wide Web, created by Sun Microsystems. Java is one way to add sound, animation, and interactivity to Web pages. Although Internet Explorer supports Java, Microsoft prefers you use VBScript instead.

JavaScript

A version of Java used with Netscape Navigator that enables Web-page authors to embed Java programs in HTML documents. *JScript* is the Internet Explorer version of JavaScript.

JPEG

Joint Photographic Experts Group. A popular format for picture files. JPEG uses a compression technique that greatly reduces a graphic's file size, but also results in some loss of resolution. For photographic images, this loss is usually not noticeable. Because of its small file sizes, JPEG is a popular graphics format for the Internet.

JScript

The Microsoft implementation of JavaScript for use with Internet Explorer 3.0.

KB

An abbreviation for *kilobyte* (roughly 1,024 bytes).

Kbps

A measure of a modem's speed in thousands of bits per second. The two most common modem speeds are 14.4 Kbps and 28.8 Kbps.

LAN

See *local area network*.

link

See *hyperlink*.

LISTSERV

A server program used for mailing lists, which are basically e-mail versions of newsgroups. See *mailing list*.

local area network

Also referred to as a *LAN.* Two or more computers that are connected to one another to form a network. A LAN enables the computers to share resources such as disk drives and printers. A LAN is usually located within a relatively small area such as a building or on a campus.

LOL

Laughing out loud. A common abbreviation used to express mirth or joy when chatting on IRC, in e-mail messages, or in newsgroup articles.

lurk

To read articles in a newsgroup without contributing your own postings. Lurking is one of the few approved forms of eaves-dropping. Lurking for a while in a newsgroup before posting your own articles is the polite thing to do.

mailing list

An e-mail version of a newsgroup. Any messages sent to the mailing list server are automatically sent to each person who has subscribed to the list.

MB

Megabyte. Roughly a million bytes.

Microsoft

The largest software company in the world. Among other things, Microsoft is the maker of MS-DOS, Windows 95, and the Microsoft Office suite, which includes Word, Excel, PowerPoint, and Access. Oh, and I almost forgot — Internet Explorer, too.

Microsoft Exchange

A Windows 95 program that handles e-mail and fax communications. Microsoft Internet Mail is easier to use than Exchange. But you should use Internet Mail only if your only source of e-mail is through the Internet.

MIME

Multipurpose Internet mail extensions. One of the standard methods for attaching binary files to e-mail messages and newsgroup articles. See *uuencode.*

modem

A device that enables your computer to connect with other computers over a phone line. Most modems are *internal* — they are housed within the computer's cabinet. *External* modems are contained in their own boxes and must be connected to the back of the computer via a serial cable.

moderated newsgroup

A newsgroup whose postings are controlled by a moderator, which helps to ensure that articles in the newsgroup follow the guide-lines established by the moderator.

Mosaic

The original Web browser, available free of charge. Internet Explorer, which is also available free of charge, is much better. So why bother with Mosaic?

MPEG

Motion Picture Experts Group. A standard for compressing video images based on the popular JPEG standard used for still images. Internet Explorer 3.0 includes built-in support for MPEG videos.

MSN

The Microsoft Network, a commercial online service. The MSN home page happens to be The Internet Explorer default start page. Hmmm. Imagine that.

Netscape

The company that makes the popular *Netscape Navigator* browser software for the Internet. Internet Explorer and Navigator are currently duking it out for the title of "Most Popular Web Browser." Although Navigator currently has the lead, Internet Explorer is gaining fast.

newsgroup

An Internet bulletin board area where you can post messages, called *articles,* about a particular topic and read articles posted by other Internet users. Thousands of different newsgroups are out there, covering just about every conceivable subject.

news server

A host computer that stores newsgroup articles. You must connect to a news server to access newsgroups; your Internet service provider probably has its own news server to which you can connect. Microsoft uses its own news servers for its product support newsgroups.

object linking and embedding

Commonly known as *OLE.* A funky feature of Windows that enables you to embed documents (or portions of documents) from other programs into a document. For example, you can embed an Excel spreadsheet in a Word document. When you double-click the spreadsheet object, Excel takes over to let you edit the spreadsheet.

OIC

Oh, I see. A commonly-used abbreviation in chats or e-mail messages.

OLE

See *object linking and embedding.*

online

Connecting your computer to a network, to an online service provider, or to the Internet.

PKZIP

A popular shareware program used to compress files or to expand compressed files. You can get your copy at `www.pkware.com`.

PMJI

Pardon me for jumping in. A commonly-used abbreviation in newsgroup articles.

posting

Adding an article to a newsgroup.

PPP

Point to Point Protocol. The protocol that enables you to access Internet services with Internet Explorer.

protocol

A set of conventions that govern communications between computers in a network.

public domain

Computer software or other information that is available free of charge. See *shareware.*

QuickTime

A video format popularized by Apple for its Macintosh computers. Internet Explorer provides built-in support for QuickTime movies, so you don't need separate software to view Quicktime files.

ROFL

Rolling on the floor laughing. A common abbreviation used in chats, newsgroup articles, and e-mail messages. You may see variations such as ROFLPP and ROFLMAO. Figure those out yourself — this is a family book.

script

A type of program that you can embed in an HTML document. Internet Explorer 3.0 allows scripts that are written in one of two languages: VBScript or JScript.

server

A computer that provides services to other computers on the Internet or on a local area network. Specific types of Internet servers include news servers, mail servers, FTP servers, and Web servers.

service provider

See *Internet service provider.*

shareware

A software program that you can download and try — free of charge. The program is not free, however. If you like the program and continue to use it, you are obligated to send in a modest registration fee. See *public domain.*

shortcut

An icon that can represent a link to a location on the Internet. You can place shortcuts just about anywhere, including on your desktop, in a Windows 95 folder, or even in a document.

signature

A fancy block of text that some users routinely place at the end of their e-mail messages and newsgroup articles.

SLIP

Serial Line Internet Protocol. A method for accessing the Web that has been largely replaced by PPP connections.

smiley

A smiley face or other *emoticon* created from keyboard characters and used to convey emotions in otherwise emotionless e-mail messages or newsgroup postings. Some examples include:

:-)	Feelin' happy
:-D	Super-duper happy
8^)	Smiling Orphan Annie (Leapin' lizards!)
;-)	Conspiratorial wink
:-o	You surprise me
:-(	So sad
:-|	Apathetic

start page

The first page displayed when you fire up Internet Explorer. The start page serves as your jumping-off point onto the World Wide Web. One popular start page is www.msn.com. You can change your start page by choosing Tools⇨Options.

taskbar

A Windows 95 feature that displays icons for all open windows, a clock, and the Start button, which you use to run programs. Normally, the taskbar appears at the bottom of the screen, but it can be repositioned at any edge of the screen you prefer. If the taskbar is not visible, try moving the mouse to the very bottom of the screen, or to the left, right, or top edge of the screen.

TCP/IP

Transmission Control Protocol/Internet Protocol. The basic set of conventions that the Internet uses to enable different types of computers to communicate with one another.

Telnet

A protocol that allows you to log in to a remote computer as if you were actually a terminal attached to that remote computer.

TIFF

Tagged Image File Format. A format for picture files. TIFF files are large compared with other formats such as JPEG and GIF, but preserve all of the original image's quality. Because of their large size, TIFF files aren't all that popular on the Internet.

thread

An exchange of articles in a newsgroup. Specifically, an original article, all of its replies, all of the replies to replies, and so on.

TLA

Three letter acronym. Ever notice how just about all computer terms can be reduced to a three letter acronym? It all started with IBM. Now you've got URL, AOL, CGI, and who knows what else. I guess I shouldn't complain; this book is being published by IDG.

Uniform Resource Locator

Also knows as a *URL.* A method of specifying the address of any resource available on the Internet, used when browsing the Internet. For example, the URL of IDG Books World-wide, for example, is www.idgbooks.com.

UNIX

A computer operating system that is popular among Internet users. The Internet was developed by UNIX users, which is why much of the Internet has a UNIX look and feel — especially when you leave the World Wide Web and venture into older parts of the Internet, such as FTP sites.

upload

Copying a file from your computer to the Internet.

URL

See *Uniform Resource Locator.*

Usenet

A network of Internet newsgroups that contains many of the most popular newsgroups. Internet Explorer 3.0 includes Microsoft Internet News, which you can use to access Usenet newsgroups.

uuencode

A method of attaching binary files, such as programs or documents, to mail messages and newsgroup articles. The other method is called MIME.

VBScript

A version of Visual Basic that enables you to create programs that can be embedded in HTML documents.

Vidcam

A video camera attached to a Web server so that you can view the camera's image over the Net. This setup is kind of a crazy thing to do, but seems to be the rage. See *Coke machine.*

virus

An evil computer program that slips into your computer undetected, tries to spread itself to other computers, and may eventually do something bad like trash your hard disk. Because Internet Explorer doesn't include built-in virus detection, I suggest that you consider using one of the many virus-protection programs available if you're worried about catching an electronic virus.

Visual J++

The Microsoft Java compiler, which programmers can use to create ActiveX controls in their Web pages. Visual J++ provides a sophisticated visual development environment that's similar to the popular Visual C++ environment.

Web

See *World Wide Web.*

Web browser

A program that can find pages on the World Wide Web and display them on your home computer. Internet Explorer is an example of a Web browser.

Web page

An HTML document available for display on the Word Wide Web. The document may contain links to other documents located on the same server or on other Web servers.

Web server

A server computer that stores HTML documents so that they can be accessed on the World Wide Web.

Web Voyager

A Web directory that can be reached at `webspace.com/pub/wvoyager/ wvtext.htm`.

wide area network

Commonly called *WAN.* A computer network that spans a large area, such as an entire campus, or perhaps a network that links branches of a company in several cities.

Wincode

A program used to encode and decode binary files transmitted over Internet newsgroups, using the uuencode encoding technique.

WinSock

Short for *Win*dows *Sock*ets. The standard by which Windows programs are able to communicate with TCP/IP and the Internet. Fortunately, you don't have to know anything about WinSock to use it. In fact, you don't even have to know you're using it at all.

Windows 95

The newest version of the Microsoft Windows operating system. Windows 95 is the main operating system for Internet Explorer, although versions of Internet Explorer exist for Windows NT, Windows 3.1, and Macintosh computers.

WinZip

A Windows version of the popular PKZIP compression program.

World Wide Web

Abbreviated WWW, and also referred to simply as *the Web.* This relatively new part of the Internet displays information using fancy graphics. The Web is based on *links,* which enable Web surfers to travel quickly from one Web server to another.

WWW Virtual Library, The

A large Web directory that you can reach at `www.w3.org/hypertext/DataSources/bySubject/Overview.html`.

zipped file

A file that has been compressed using the PKZIP or WinZip programs.

Index

• G •

● *K* ●

• *P* •

• *Q* •